STUFFED!

STUFFED!

by Glenn Eichler & Nick Bertozzi

First Second

New York & London

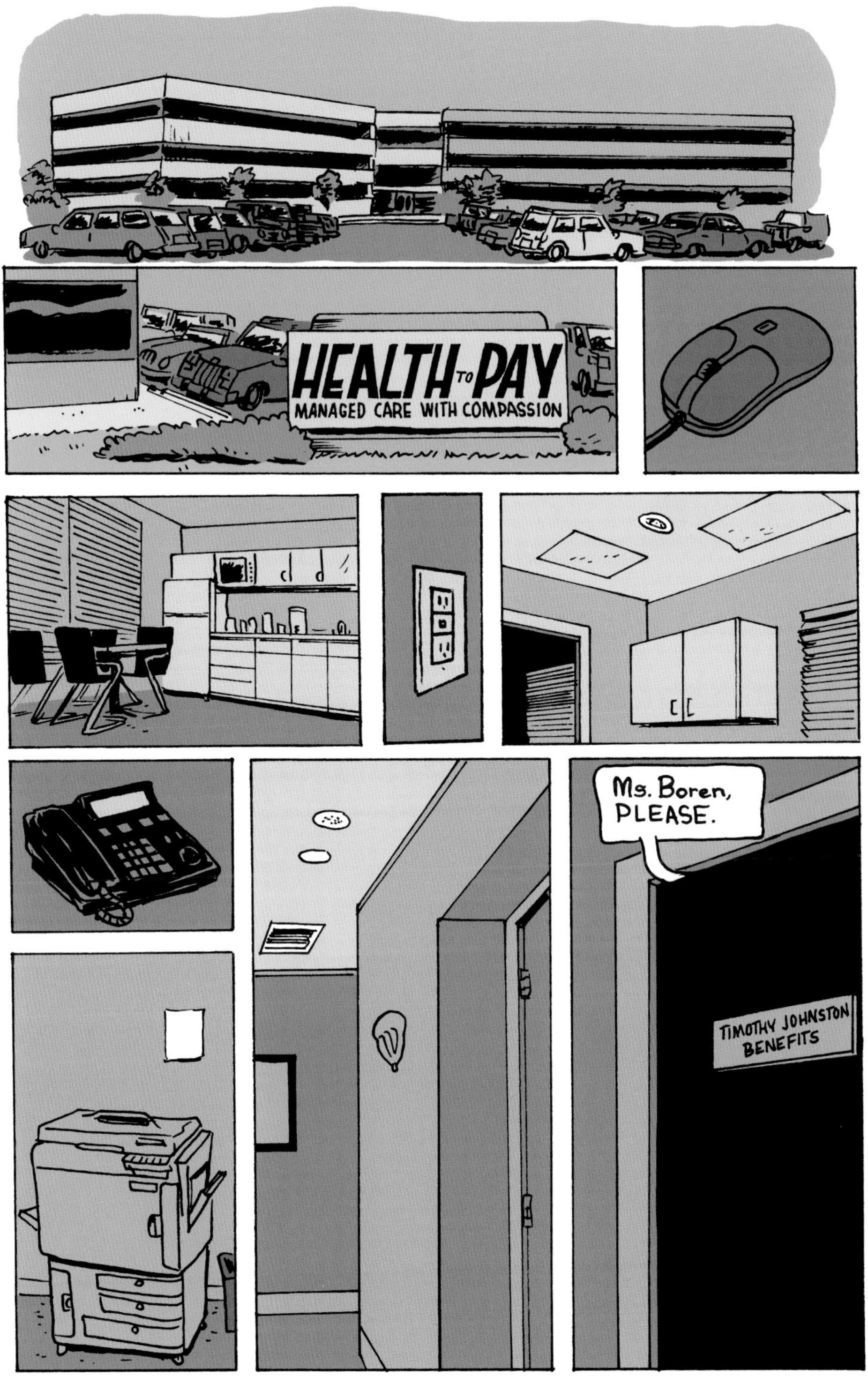
HEALTH TO PAY
MANAGED CARE WITH COMPASSION
Ms. Boren, PLEASE.
TIMOTHY JOHNSTON
BENEFITS

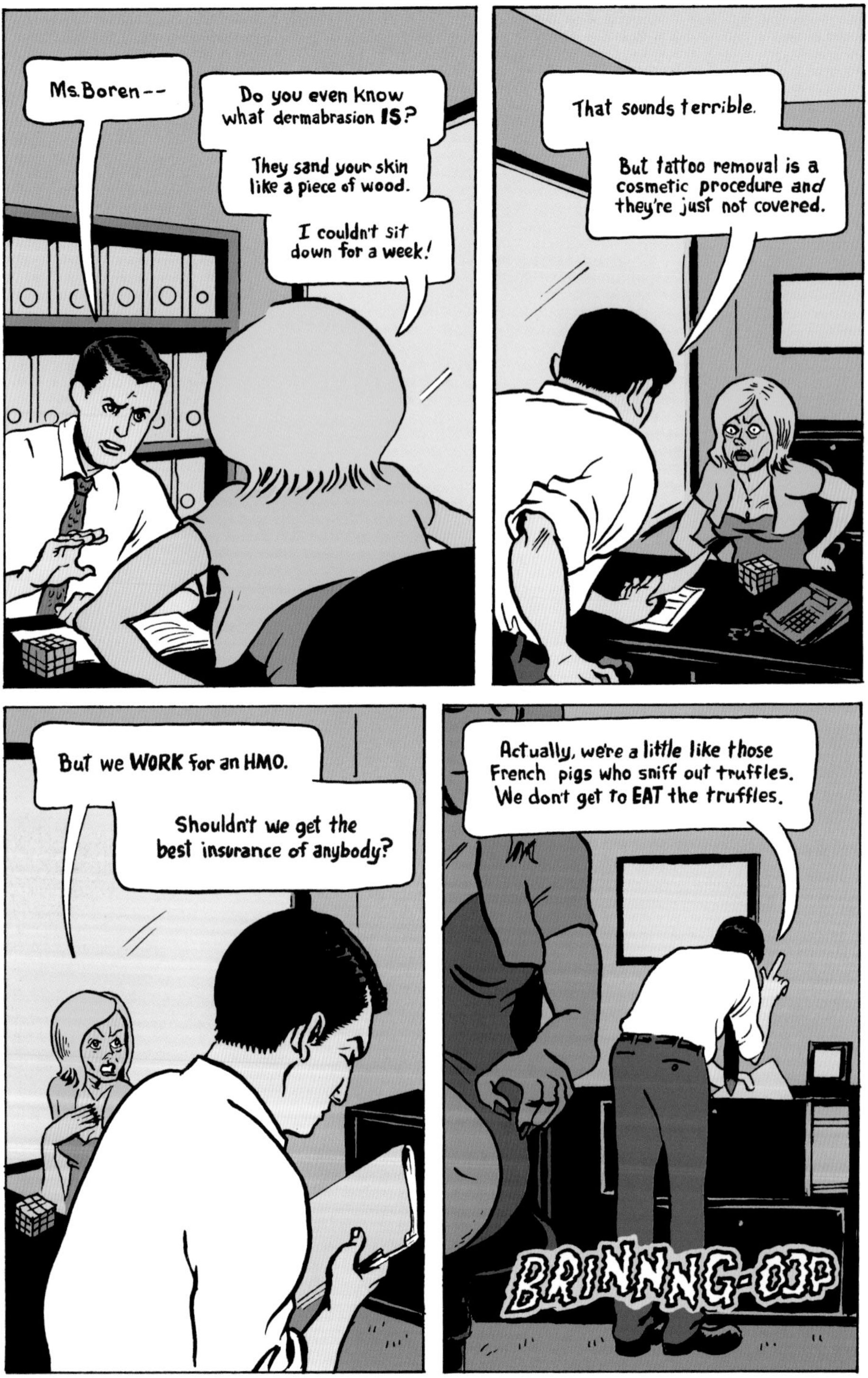
Ms. Boren--
Do you even know what dermabrasion IS?
They sand your skin like a piece of wood.
I couldn't sit down for a week!
That sounds terrible.
But tattoo removal is a cosmetic procedure and they're just not covered.
But we WORK for an HMO.
Shouldn't we get the best insurance of anybody?
Actually, we're a little like those French pigs who sniff out truffles. We don't get to EAT the truffles.
BRINNNG-OOP

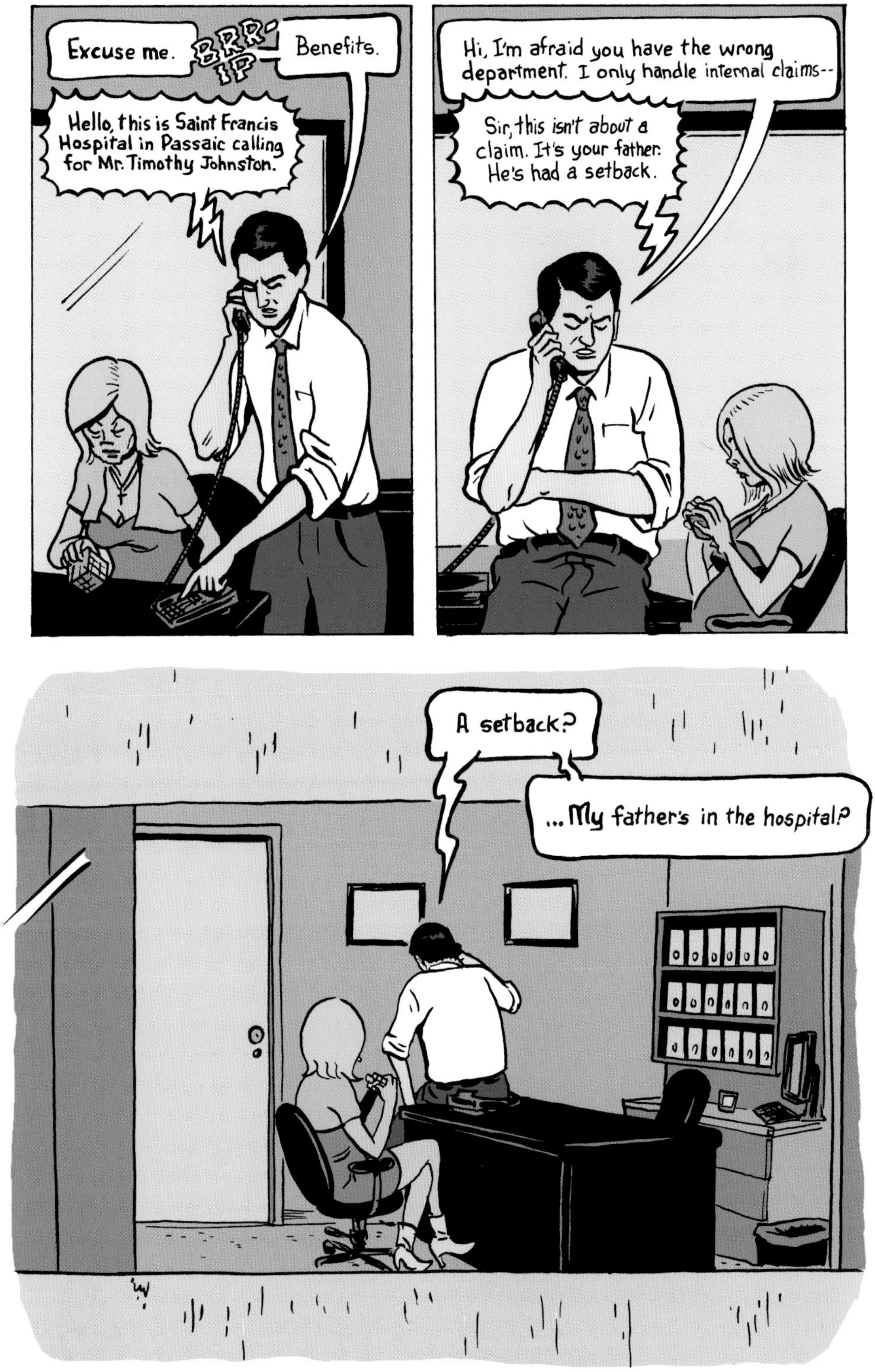
Excuse me.
BRR-IP
Benefits.
Hello, this is Saint Francis Hospital in Passaic calling for Mr. Timothy Johnston.
Hi, I'm afraid you have the wrong department. I only handle internal claims--
Sir, this isn't about a claim. It's your father. He's had a setback.
A setback?
...My father's in the hospital?

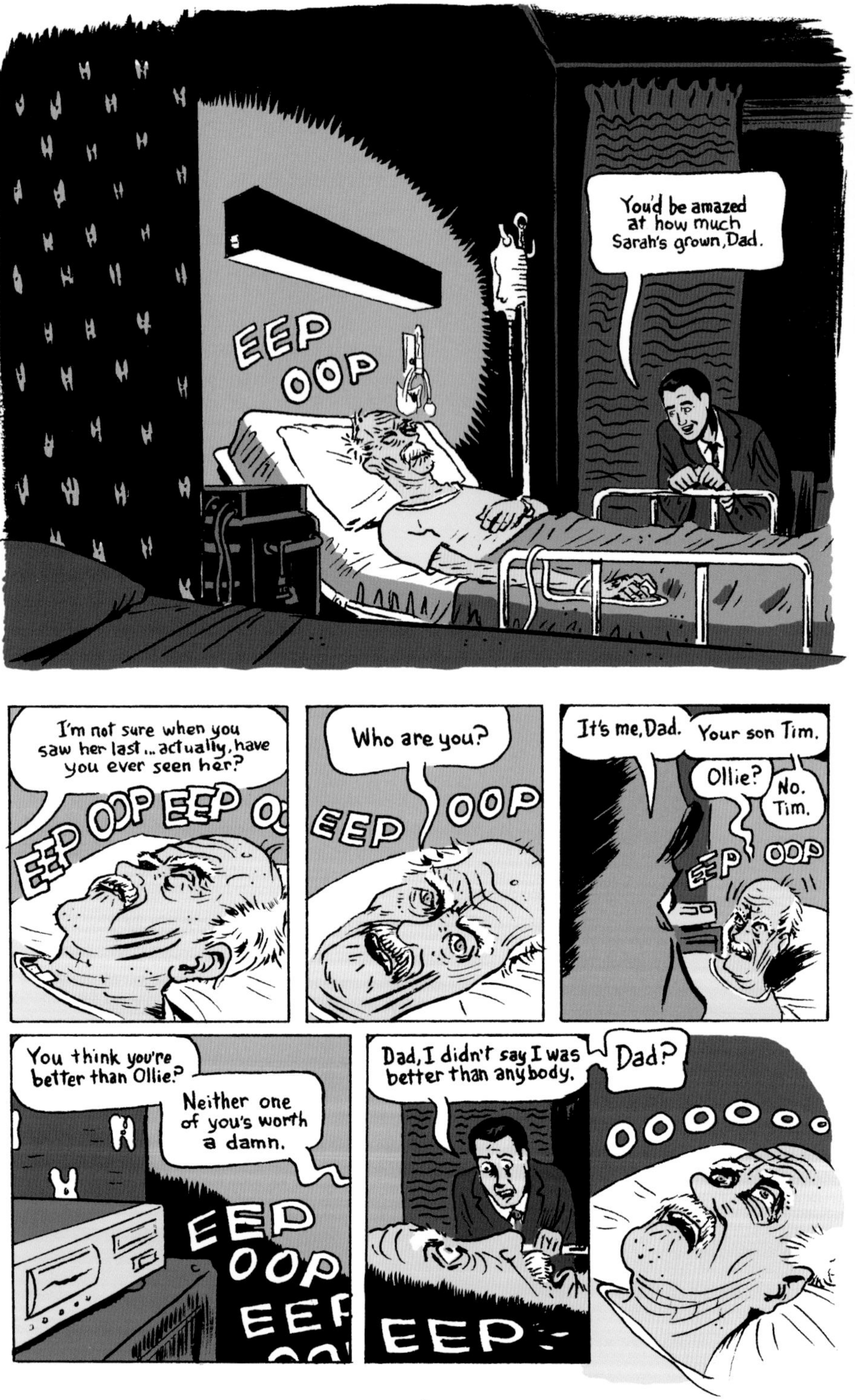
You'd be amazed at how much Sarah's grown, Dad.
EEP
OOP
I'm not sure when you saw her last... actually, have you ever seen her?
EEP OOP EEP
Who are you?
EEP
OOP
It's me, Dad.
Your son Tim.
Ollie?
No. Tim.
EEP
OOP
You think you're better than Ollie?
Neither one of you's worth a damn.
EEP
OOP
Dad, I didn't say I was better than anybody.
Dad?
EEP
OOOOOO

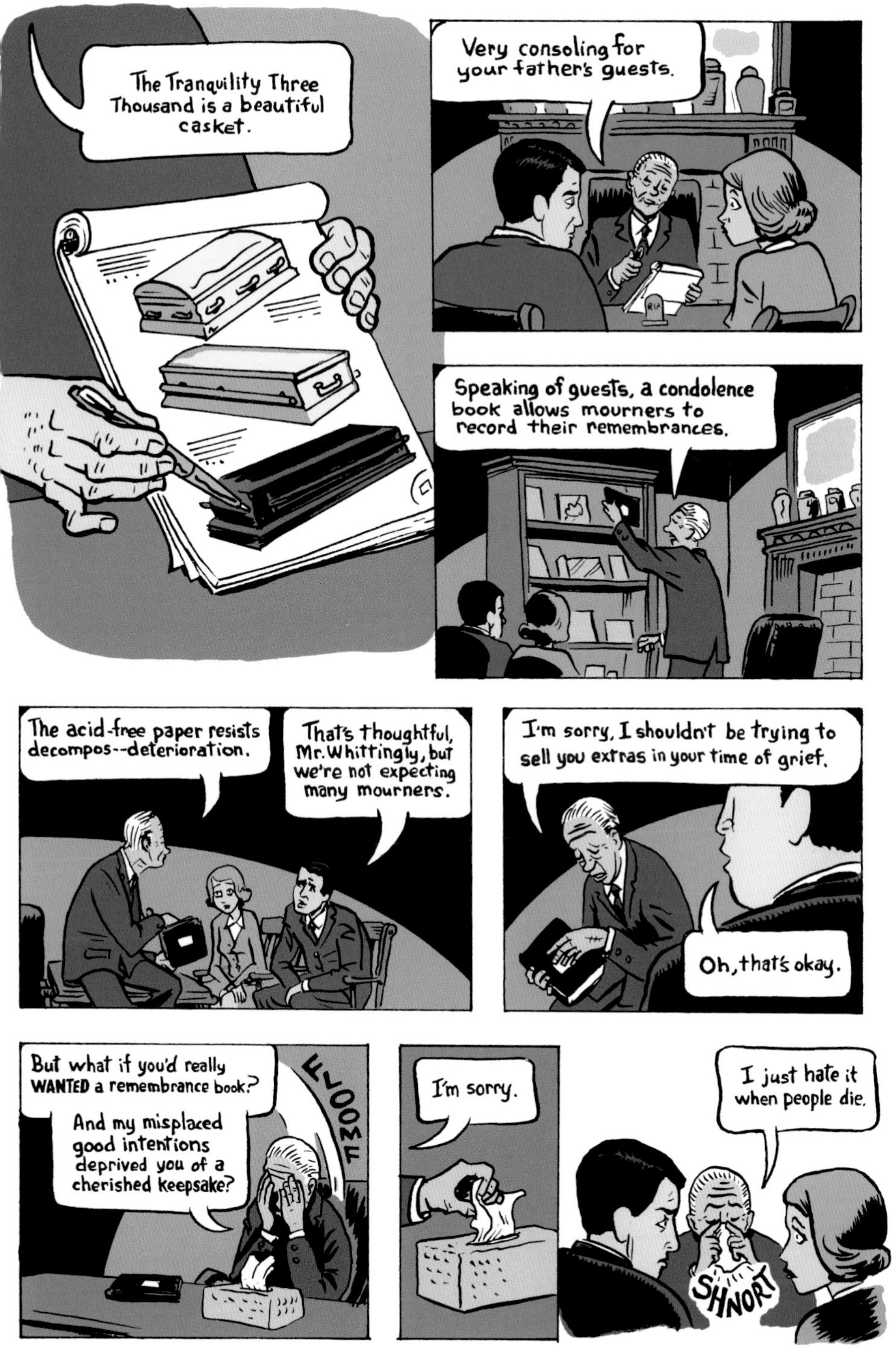
The Tranquility Three Thousand is a beautiful casket.
Very consoling for your father's guests.
Speaking of guests, a condolence book allows mourners to record their remembrances.
The acid-free paper resists decompos--deterioration.
That's thoughtful, Mr. Whittingly, but we're not expecting many mourners.
I'm sorry, I shouldn't be trying to sell you extras in your time of grief.
Oh, that's okay.
But what if you'd really WANTED a remembrance book?
And my misplaced good intentions deprived you of a cherished keepsake?
FLOOMF
I'm sorry.
I just hate it when people die.
SHNORT

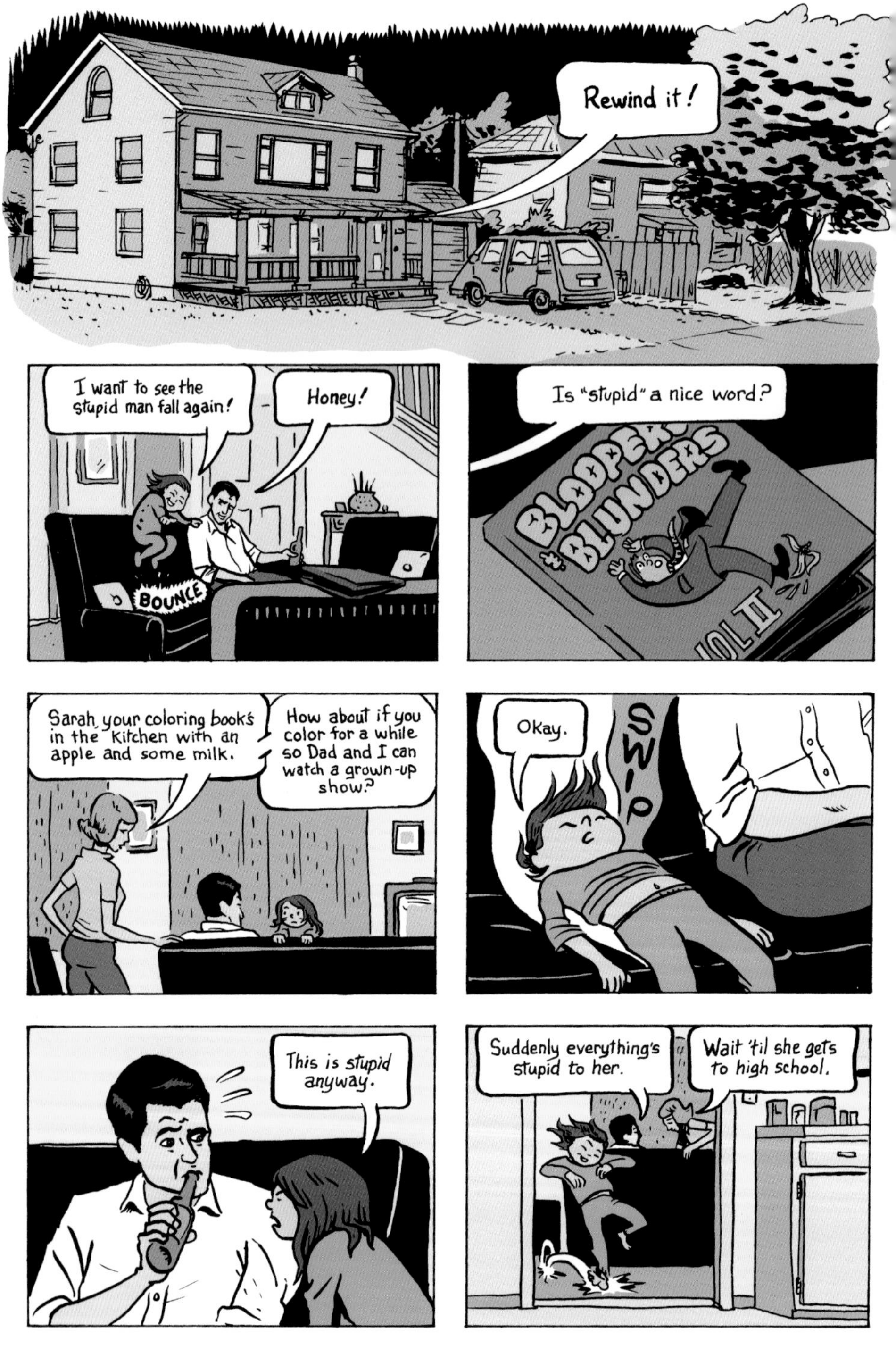
Rewind it!
I want to see the stupid man fall again!
BOUNCE
Honey!
Is "stupid" a nice word?
BLOOPERS & BLUNDERS
VOL II
Sarah, your coloring book's in the kitchen with an apple and some milk.
How about if you color for a while so Dad and I can watch a grown-up show?
Okay.
SWIP
This is stupid anyway.
Suddenly everything's stupid to her.
Wait 'til she gets to high school.

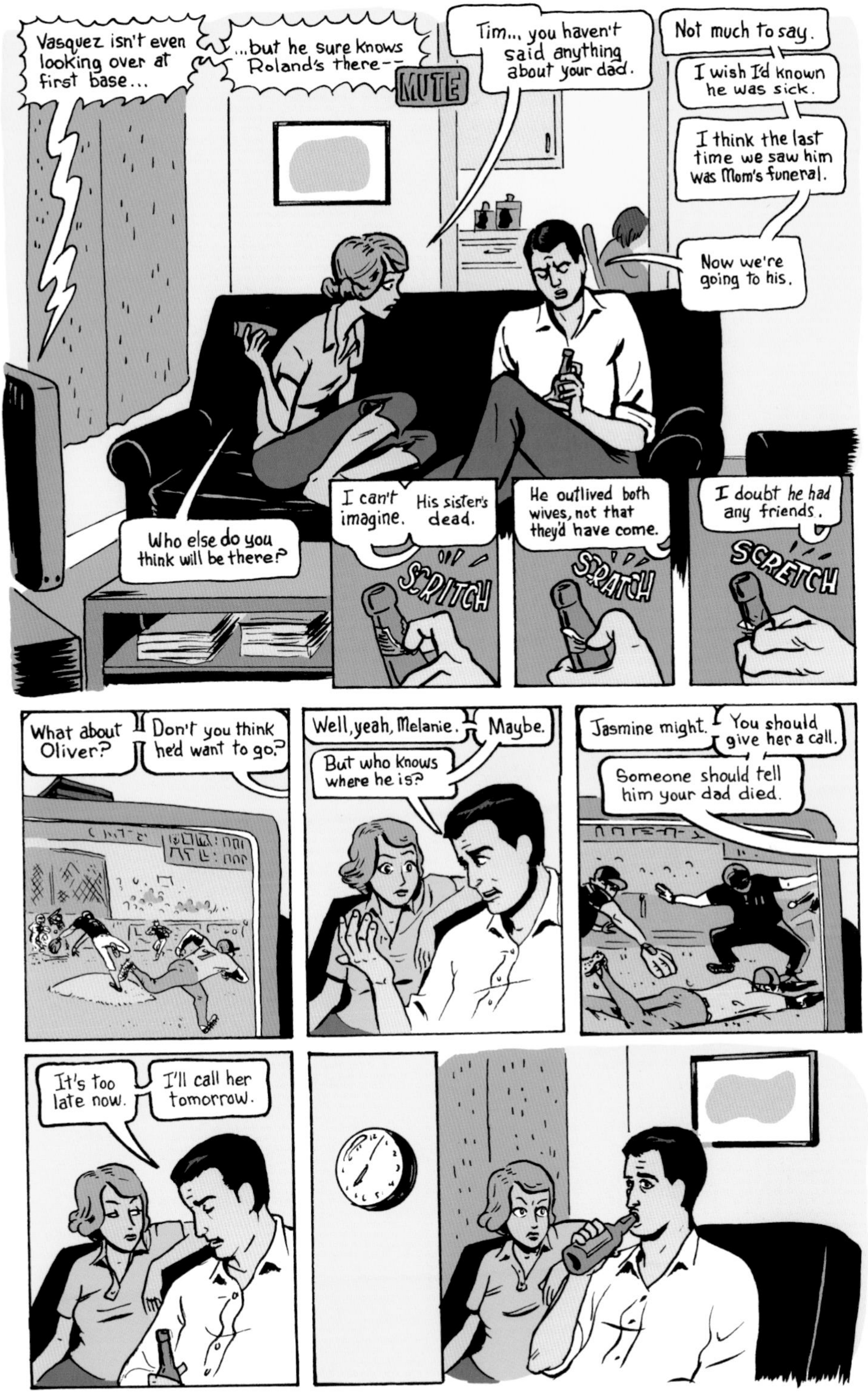
Vasquez isn't even looking over at first base...
...but he sure knows Roland's there--
MUTE
Tim... you haven't said anything about your dad.
Not much to say.
I wish I'd known he was sick.
I think the last time we saw him was Mom's funeral.
Now we're going to his.
Who else do you think will be there?
I can't imagine.
His sister's dead.
SCRITCH
He outlived both wives, not that they'd have come.
SCRATCH
I doubt he had any friends.
SCRETCH
What about Oliver?
Don't you think he'd want to go?
Well, yeah, Melanie.
But who knows where he is?
Maybe.
Jasmine might.
You should give her a call.
Someone should tell him your dad died.
It's too late now.
I'll call her tomorrow.

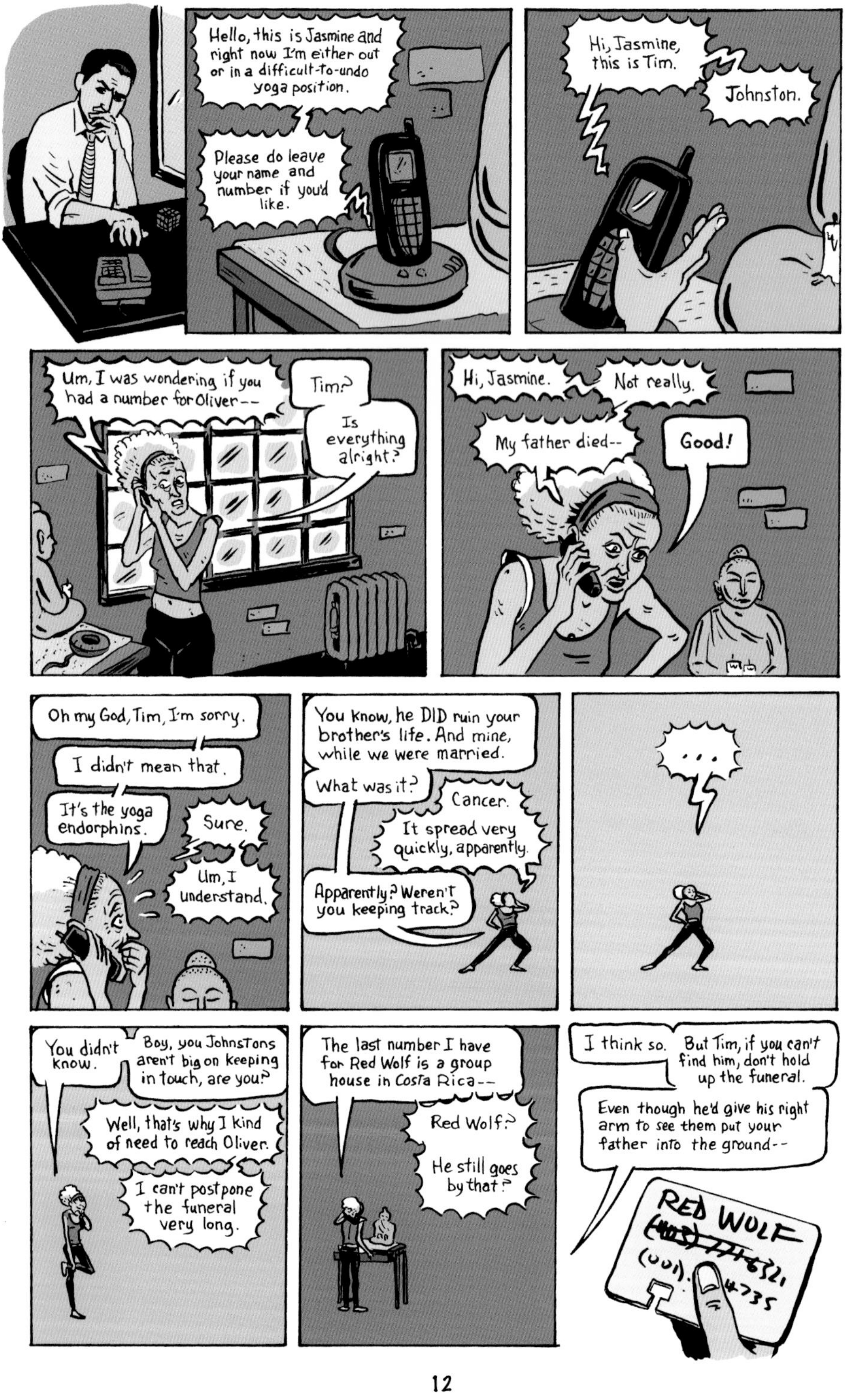

Hello, this is Jasmine and right now I'm either out or in a difficult-to-undo yoga position.
Please do leave your name and number if you'd like.
Hi, Jasmine, this is Tim.
Johnston.
Um, I was wondering if you had a number for Oliver--
Tim?
Is everything alright?
Hi, Jasmine.
Not really.
My father died--
Good!
Oh my God, Tim, I'm sorry.
I didn't mean that.
It's the yoga endorphins.
Sure.
Um, I understand.
You know, he DID ruin your brother's life. And mine, while we were married.
What was it?
Cancer.
It spread very quickly, apparently.
Apparently? Weren't you keeping track?
...
You didn't know.
Boy, you Johnstons aren't big on keeping in touch, are you?
Well, that's why I kind of need to reach Oliver.
I can't postpone the funeral very long.
The last number I have for Red Wolf is a group house in Costa Rica--
Red Wolf?
He still goes by that?
I think so.
But Tim, if you can't find him, don't hold up the funeral.
Even though he'd give his right arm to see them put your father into the ground--
RED WOLF

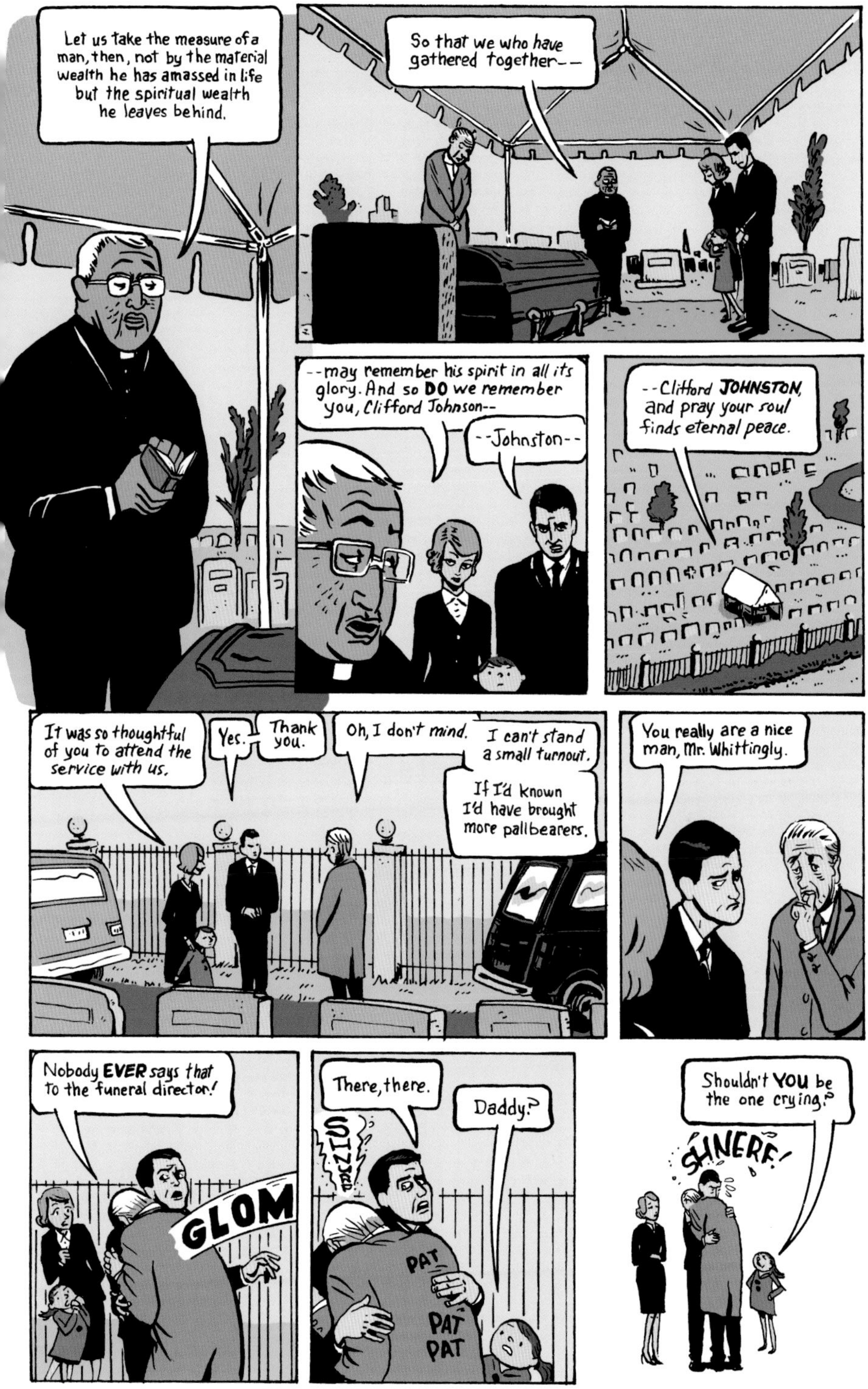
Let us take the measure of a man, then, not by the material wealth he has amassed in life but the spiritual wealth he leaves behind.
So that we who have gathered together--
--may remember his spirit in all its glory. And so DO we remember you, Clifford Johnson--
--Johnston--
--Clifford JOHNSTON, and pray your soul finds eternal peace.
It was so thoughtful of you to attend the service with us.
Yes.
Thank you.
Oh, I don't mind.
I can't stand a small turnout.
If I'd known I'd have brought more pallbearers.
You really are a nice man, Mr. Whittingly.
Nobody EVER says that to the funeral director!
GLOM
There, there.
Daddy?
PAT
PAT
PAT
Shouldn't YOU be the one crying?
SHNERF!

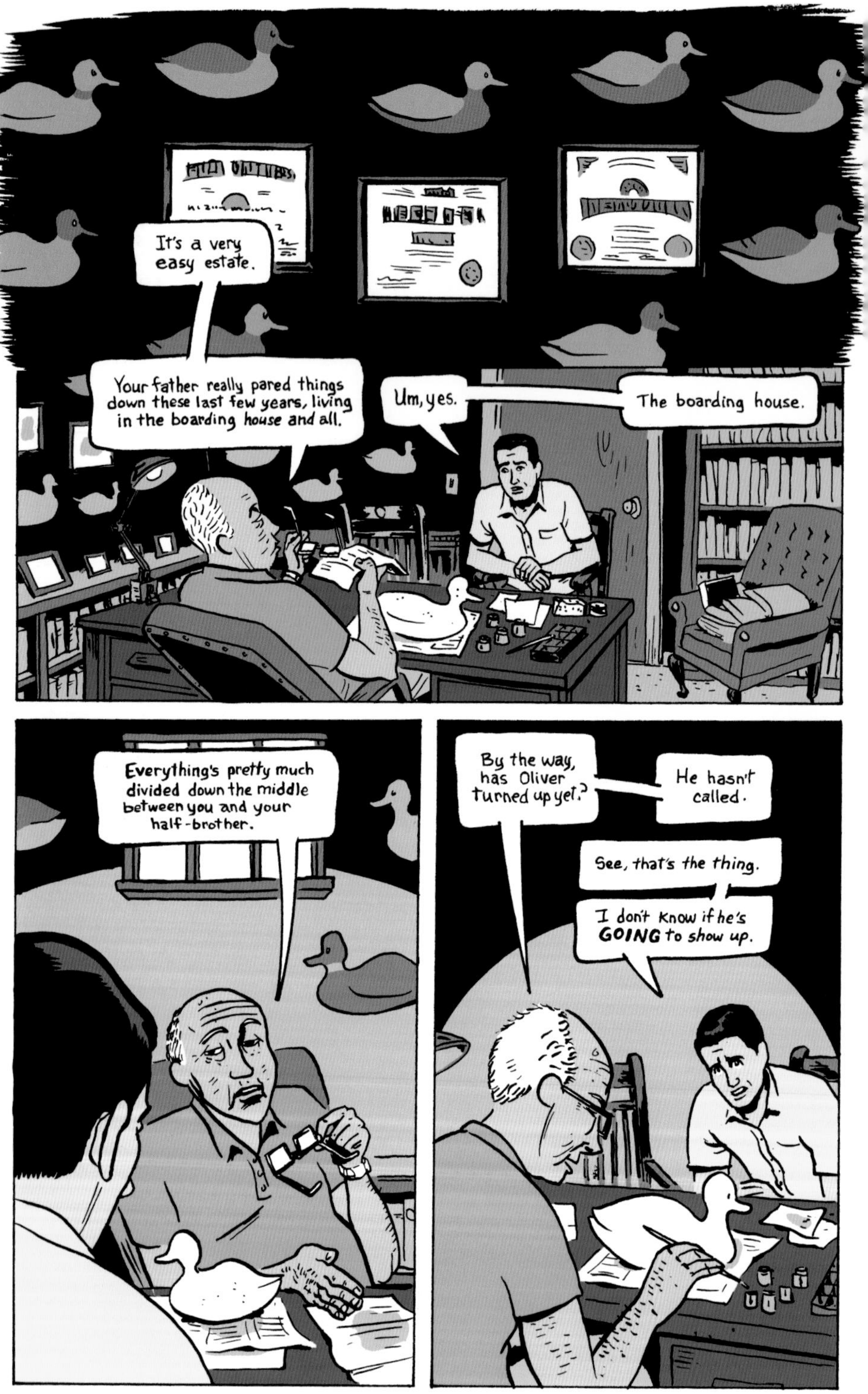
It's a very easy estate.
Your father really pared things down these last few years, living in the boarding house and all.
Um, yes.
The boarding house.
Everything's pretty much divided down the middle between you and your half-brother.
By the way, has Oliver turned up yet?
He hasn't called.
See, that's the thing.
I don't know if he's GOING to show up.

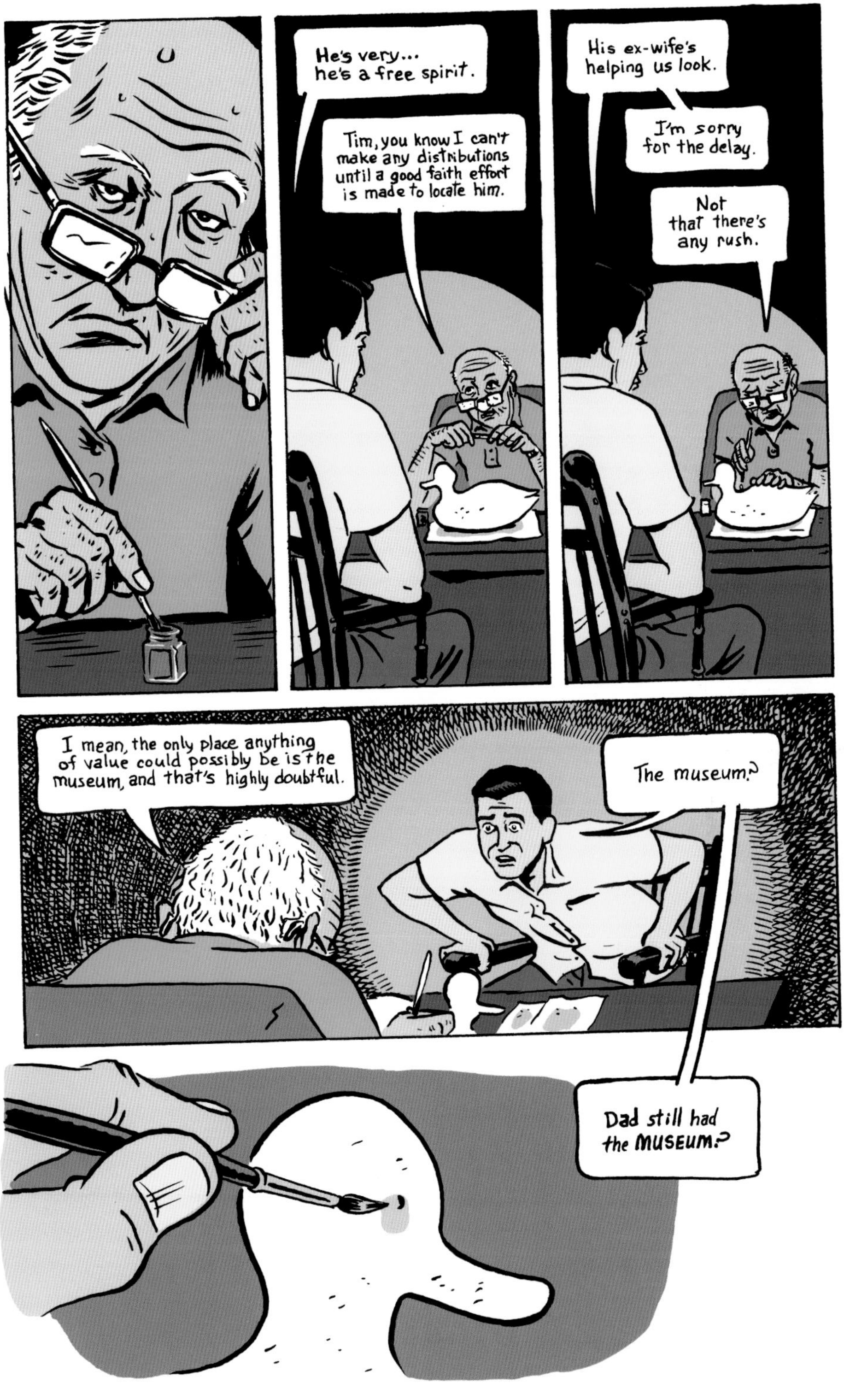
He's very...
he's a free spirit.
Tim, you know I can't make any distributions until a good faith effort is made to locate him.
His ex-wife's helping us look.
I'm sorry for the delay.
Not that there's any rush.
I mean, the only place anything of value could possibly be is the museum, and that's highly doubtful.
The museum?
Dad still had the MUSEUM?

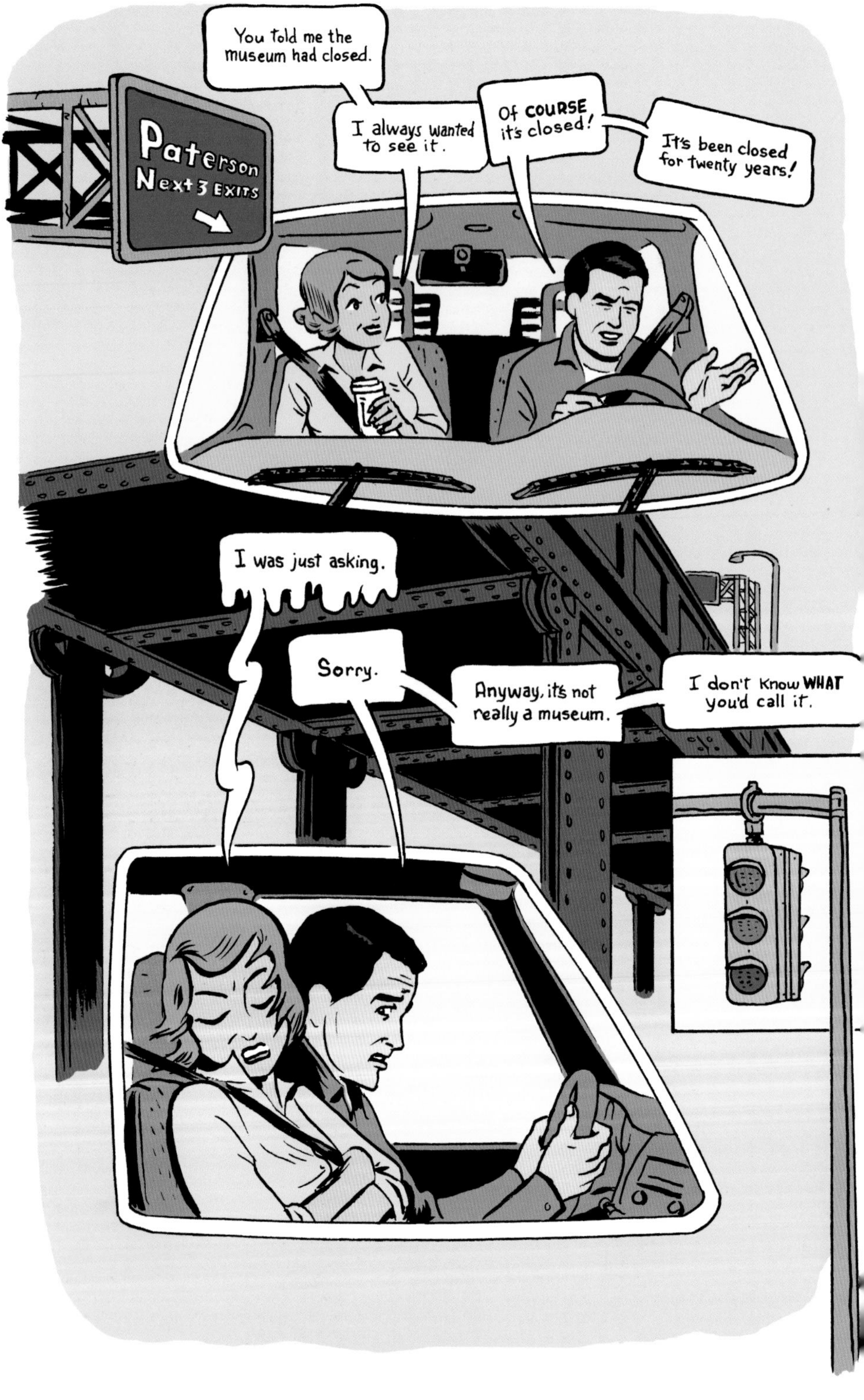
Paterson
Next 3 EXITS
You told me the museum had closed.
I always wanted to see it.
Of COURSE it's closed!
It's been closed for twenty years!
I was just asking.
Sorry.
Anyway, it's not really a museum.
I don't know WHAT you'd call it.

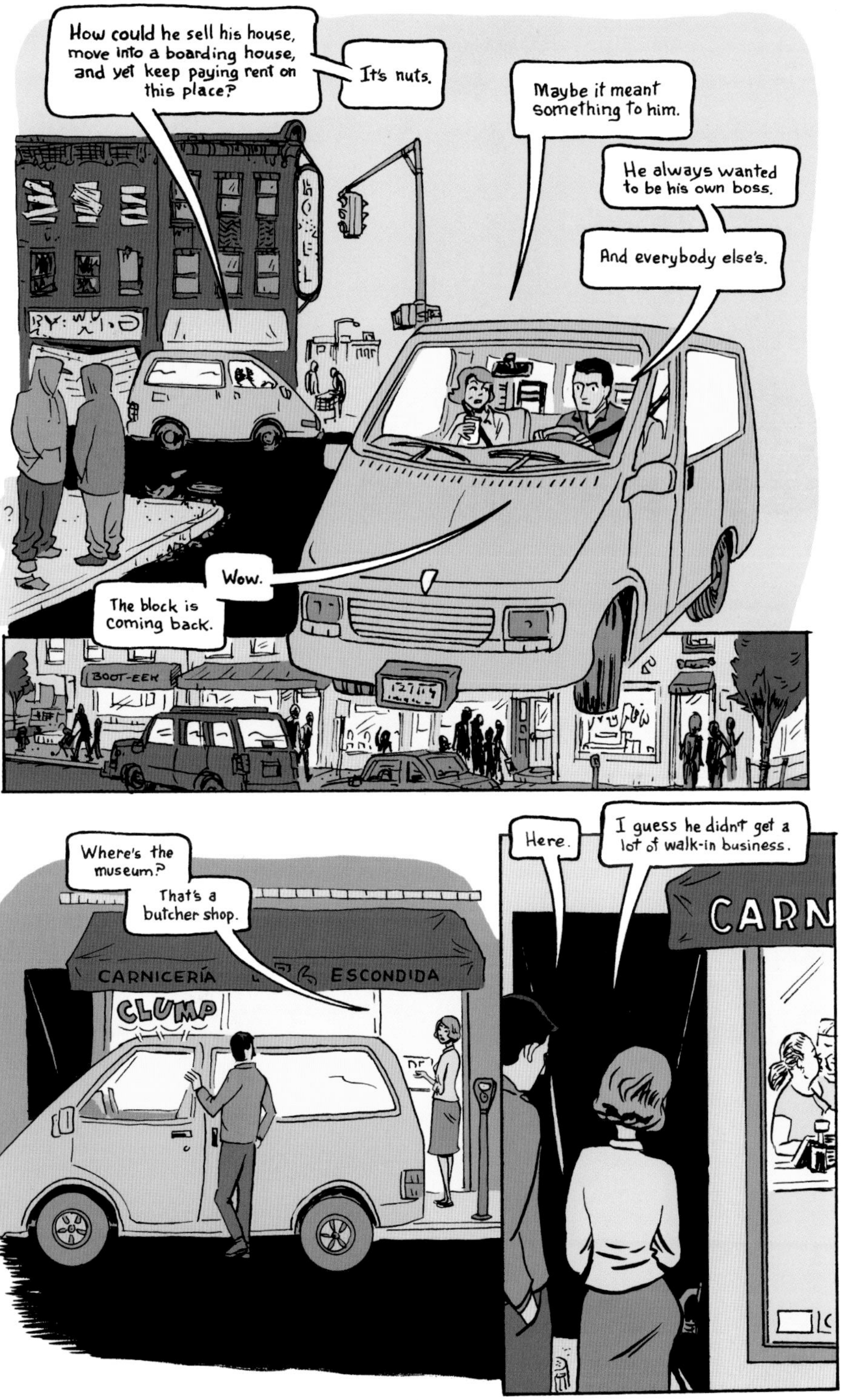
How could he sell his house, move into a boarding house, and yet keep paying rent on this place?
It's nuts.
Maybe it meant something to him.
He always wanted to be his own boss.
And everybody else's.
Wow.
The block is coming back.
BOOT-EEK
Where's the museum?
That's a butcher shop.
CARNICERÍA ESCONDIDA
CLUMP
Here.
I guess he didn't get a lot of walk-in business.
CARN

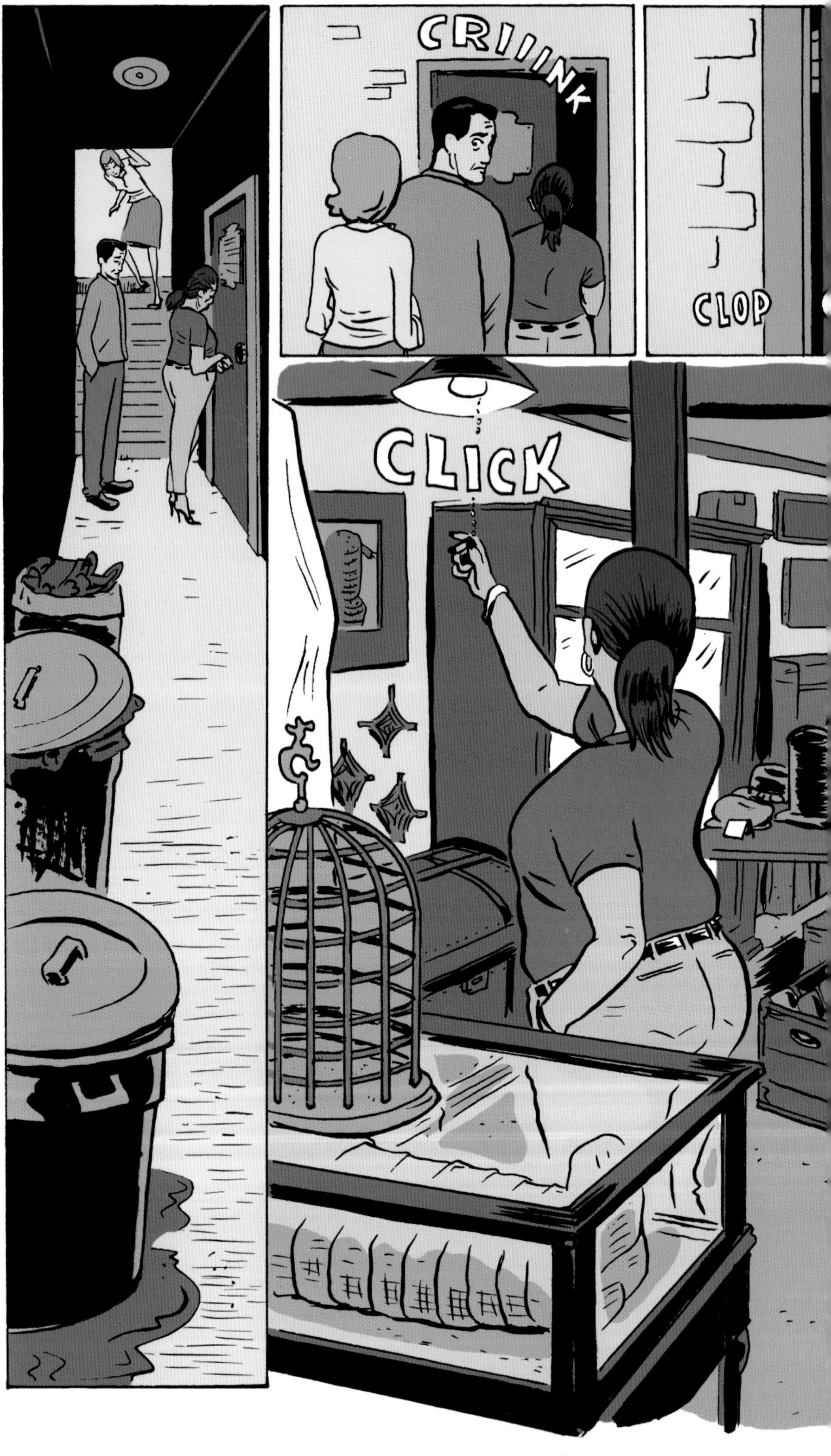
CRIIINK
CLOP
CLICK

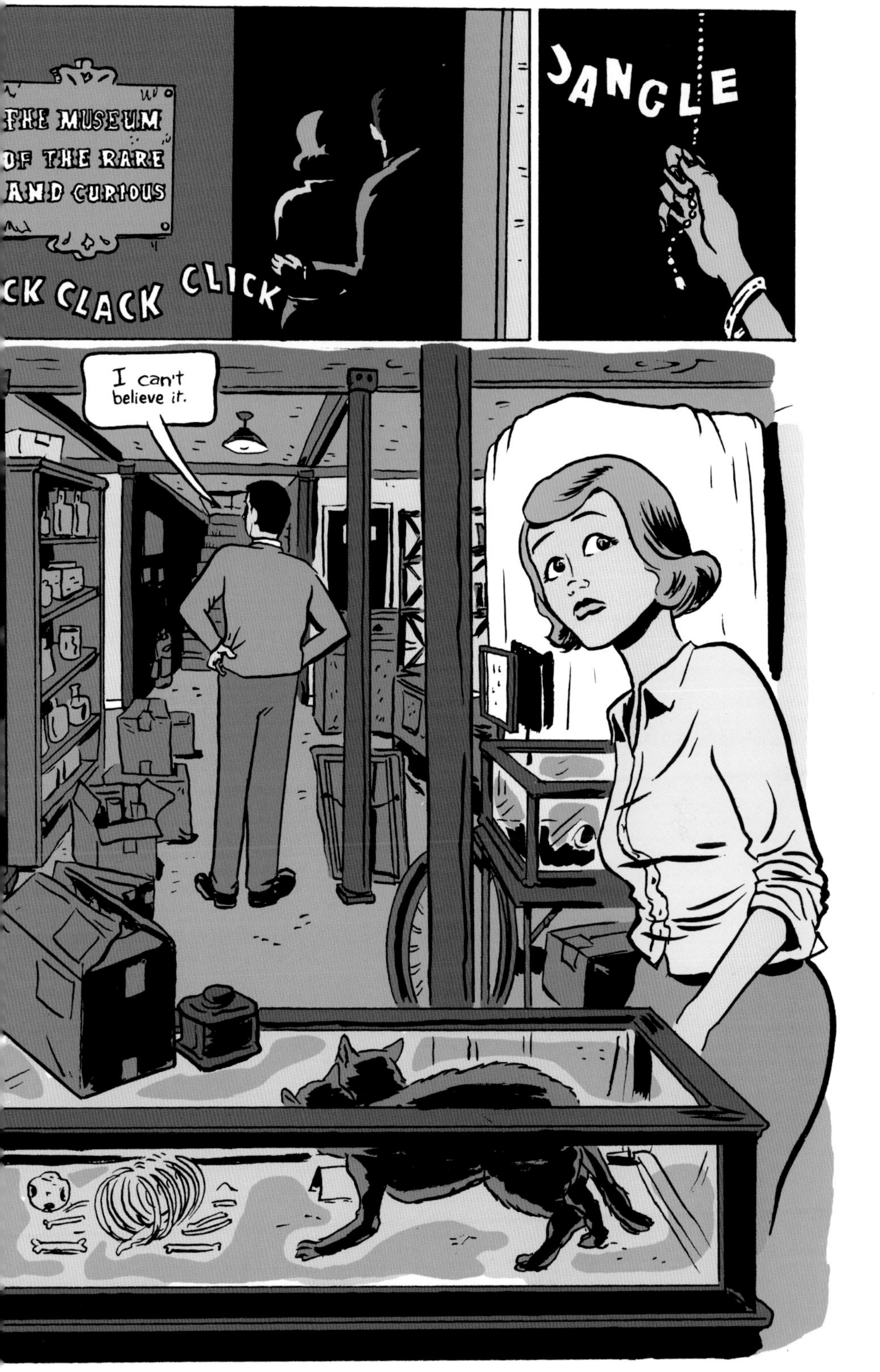
THE MUSEUM OF THE RARE AND CURIOUS
CK CLACK CLICK
JANGLE
I can't believe it.

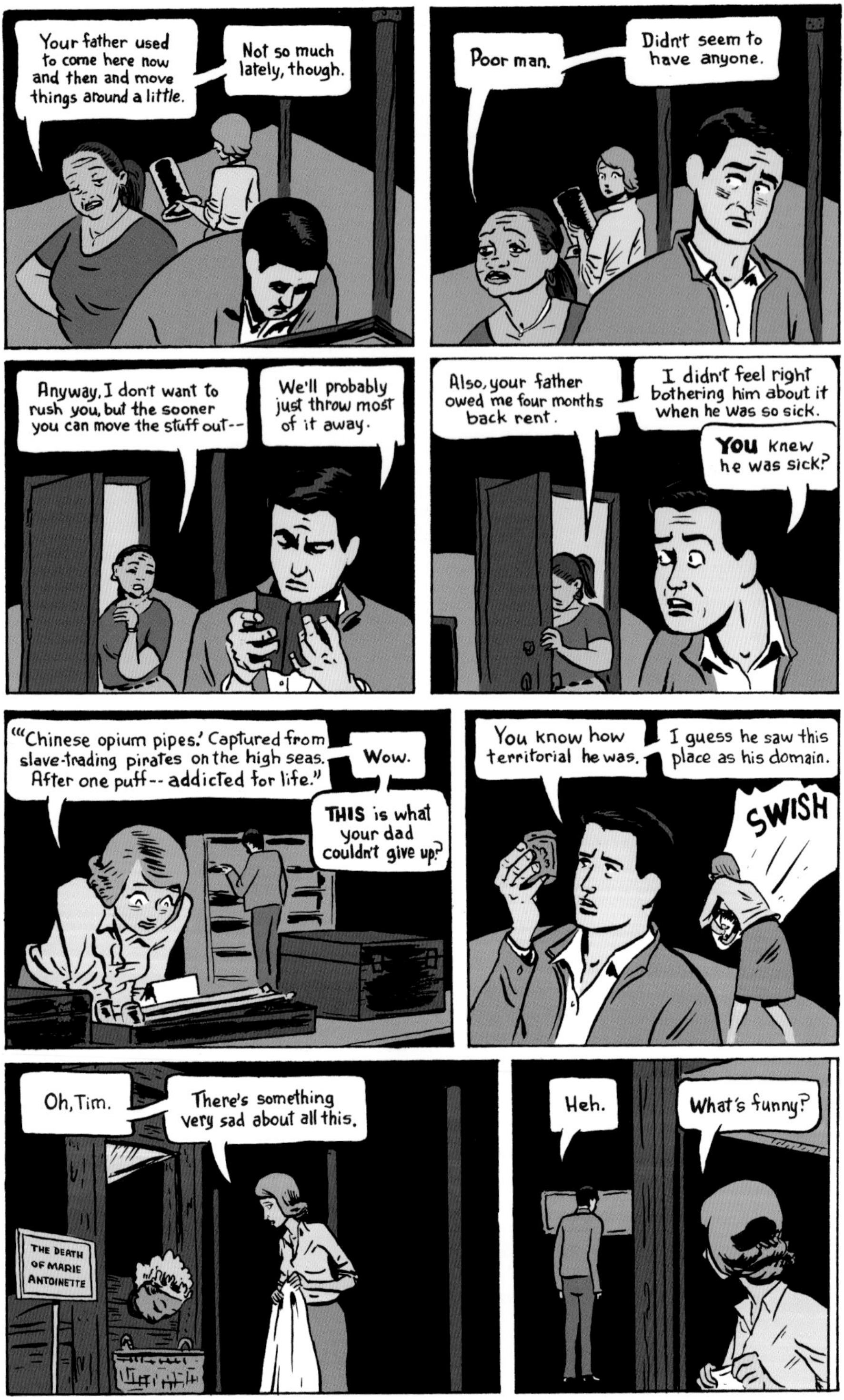
Your father used to come here now and then and move things around a little.
Not so much lately, though.
Poor man.
Didn't seem to have anyone.
Anyway, I don't want to rush you, but the sooner you can move the stuff out--
We'll probably just throw most of it away.
Also, your father owed me four months back rent.
I didn't feel right bothering him about it when he was so sick.
YOU knew he was sick?
"'Chinese opium pipes.' Captured from slave-trading pirates on the high seas. After one puff-- addicted for life."
Wow.
THIS is what your dad couldn't give up?
You know how territorial he was.
I guess he saw this place as his domain.
SWISH
Oh, Tim.
There's something very sad about all this.
THE DEATH OF MARIE ANTOINETTE
Heh.
What's funny?

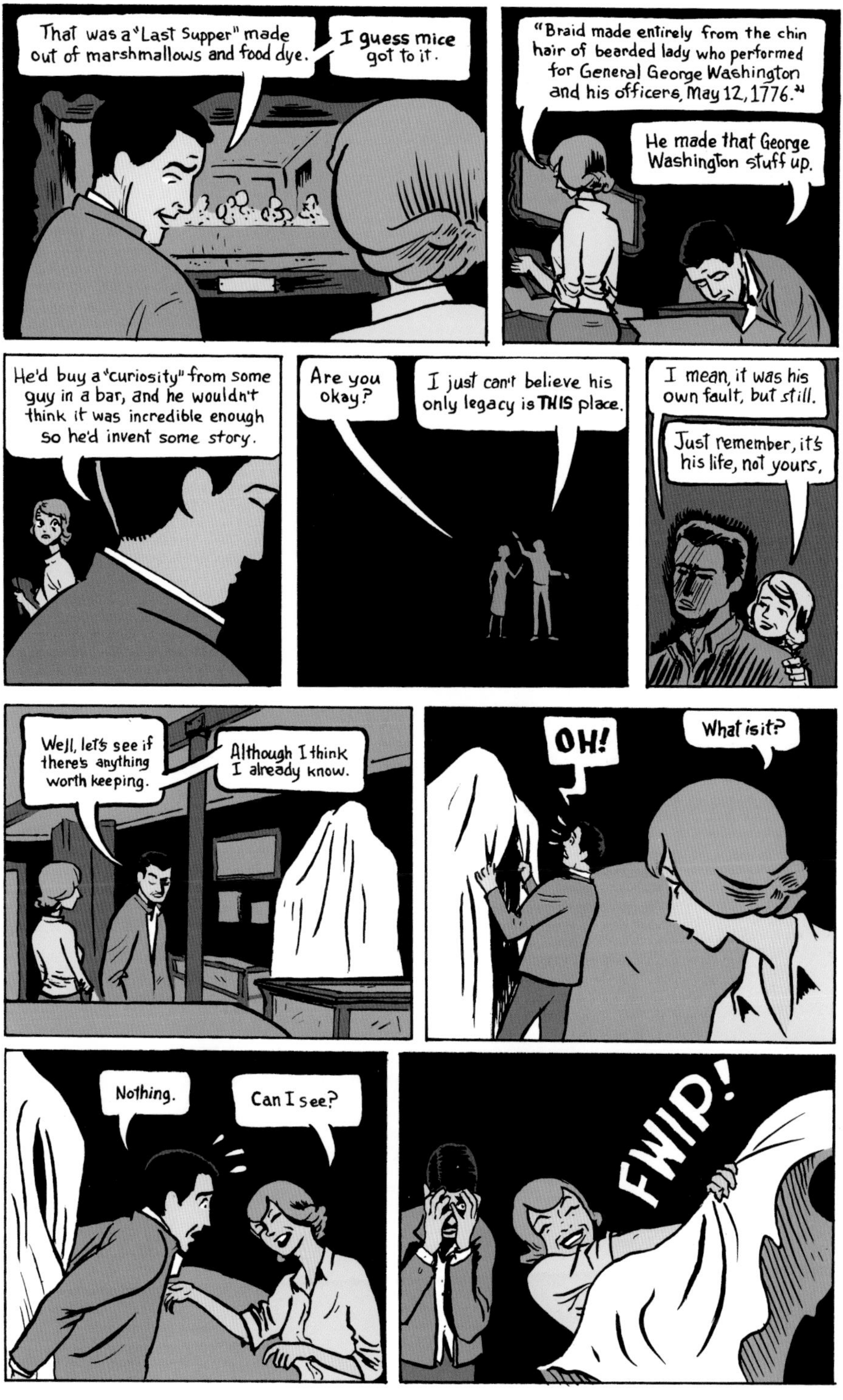
That was a "Last Supper" made out of marshmallows and food dye.
I guess mice got to it.
"Braid made entirely from the chin hair of bearded lady who performed for General George Washington and his officers, May 12, 1776."
He made that George Washington stuff up.
He'd buy a "curiosity" from some guy in a bar, and he wouldn't think it was incredible enough so he'd invent some story.
Are you okay?
I just can't believe his only legacy is THIS place.
I mean, it was his own fault, but still.
Just remember, it's his life, not yours.
Well, let's see if there's anything worth keeping.
Although I think I already know.
OH!
What is it?
Nothing.
Can I see?
FWIP!

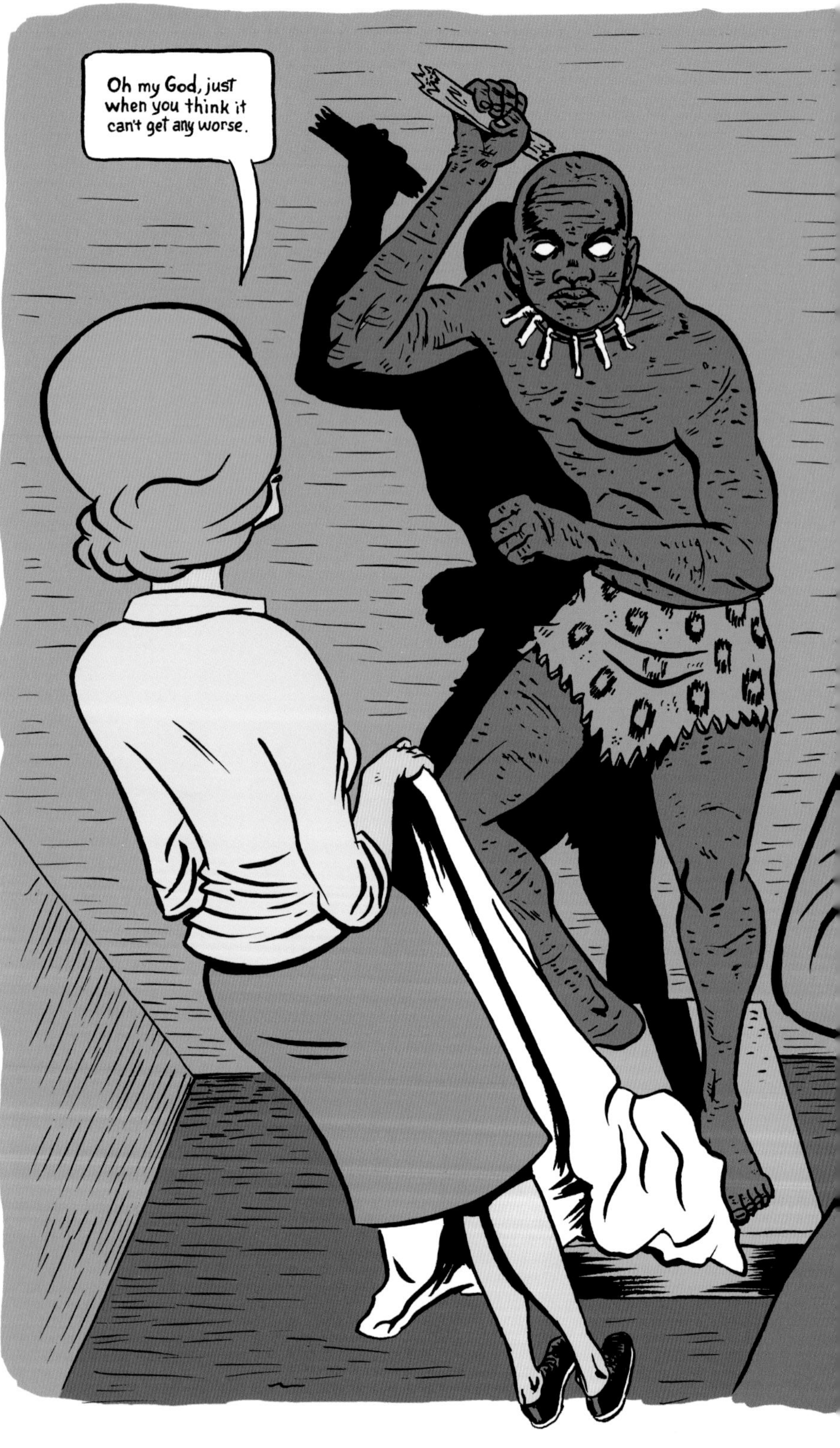
Oh my God, just when you think it can't get any worse.

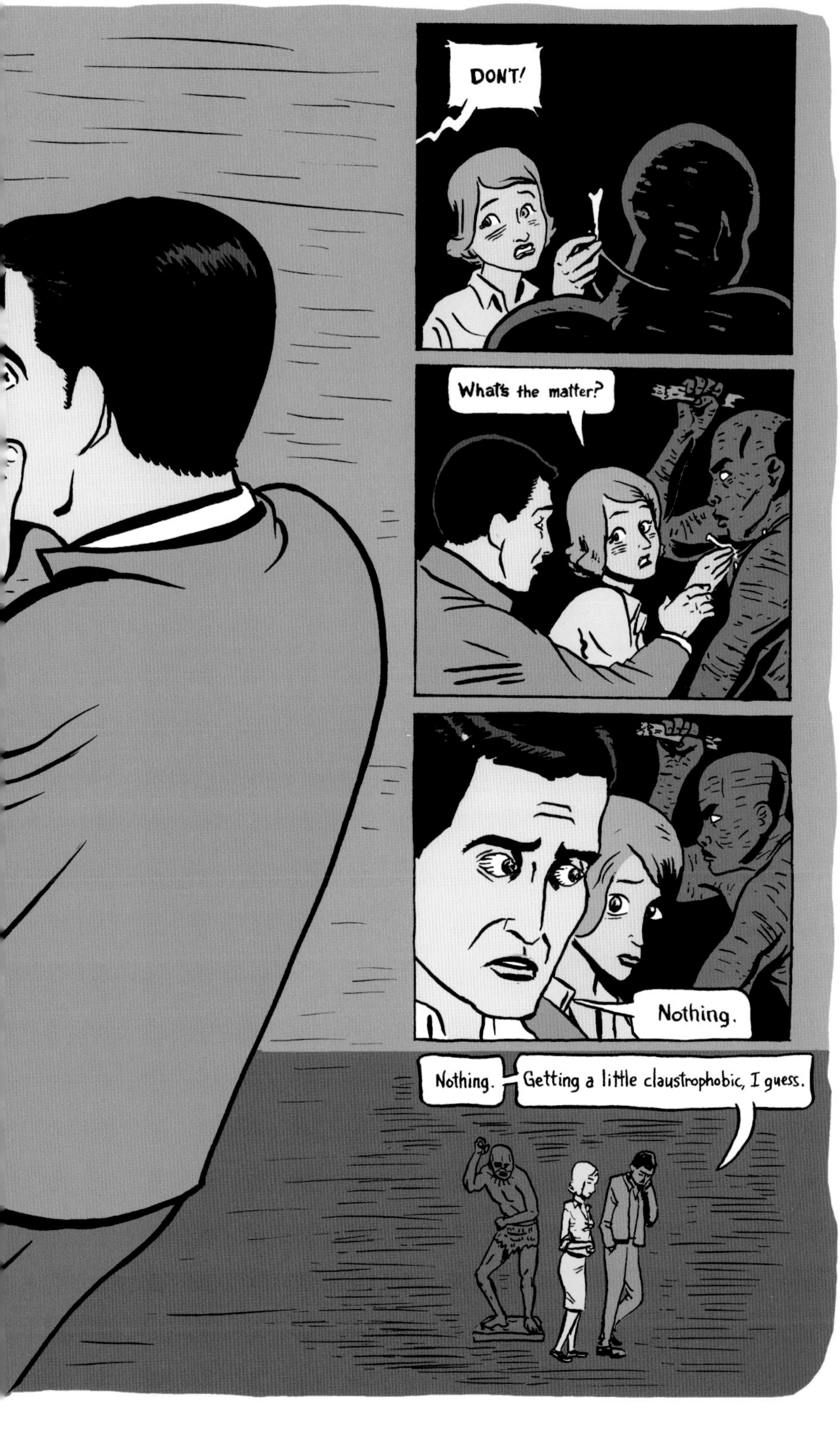
DON'T!
What's the matter?
Nothing.
Nothing.
Getting a little claustrophobic, I guess.

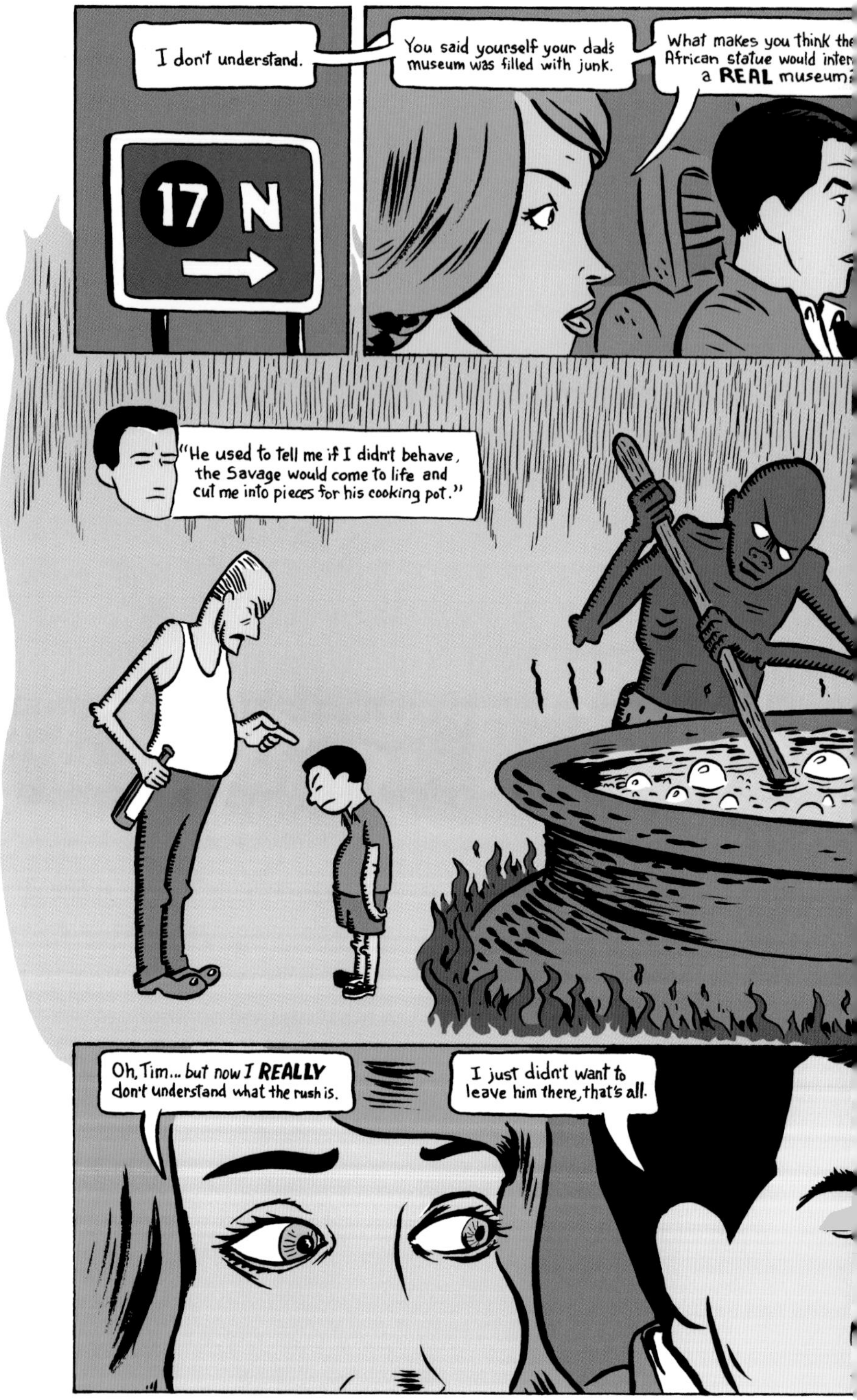

I don't understand.
You said yourself your dad's museum was filled with junk.
What makes you think th African statue would inter a REAL museum
"He used to tell me if I didn't behave, the Savage would come to life and cut me into pieces for his cooking pot."
Oh, Tim... but now I REALLY don't understand what the rush is.
I just didn't want to leave him there, that's all.

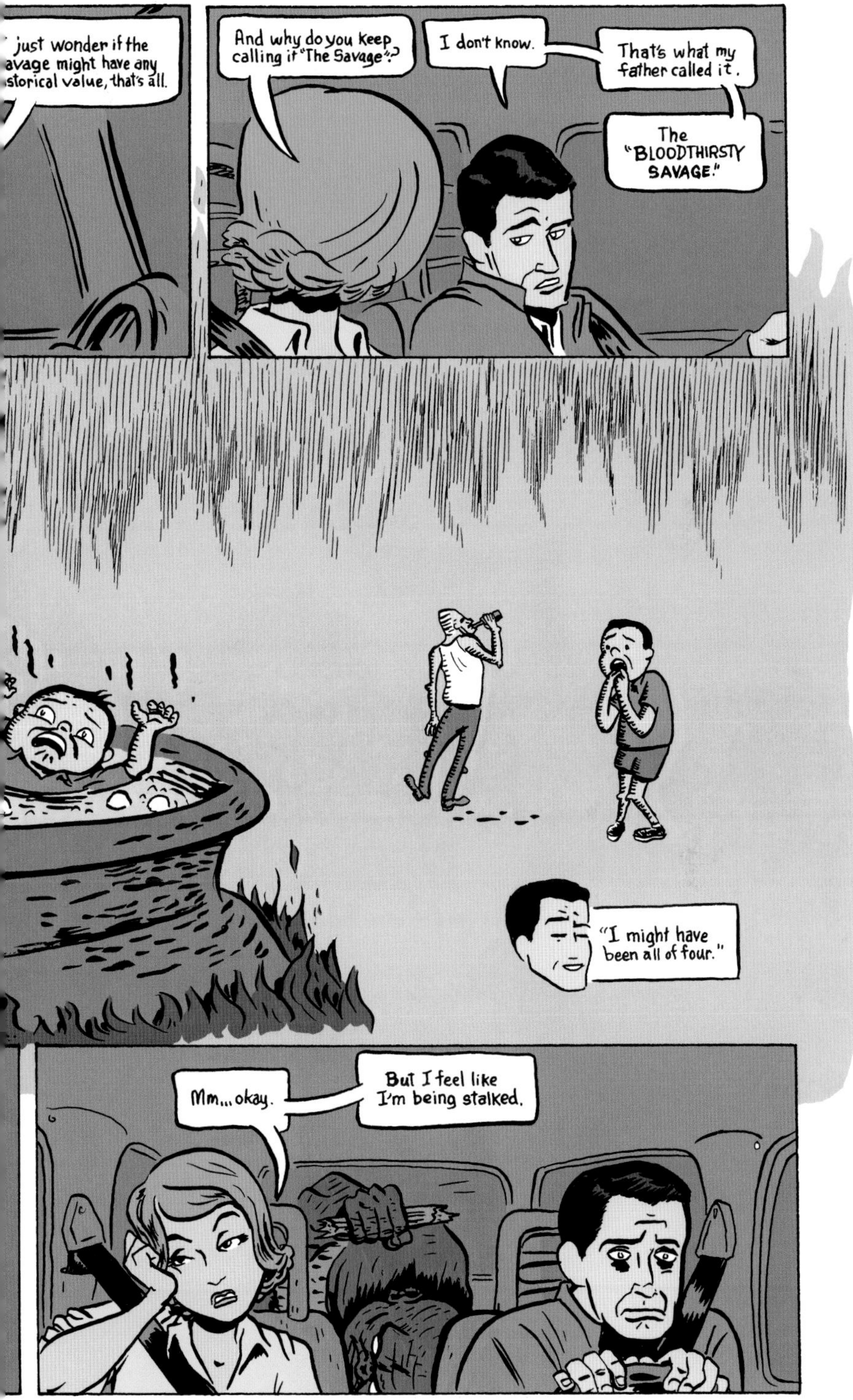
just wonder if the
avage might have any
storical value, that's all.
And why do you keep calling it "The Savage"?
I don't know.
That's what my father called it.
The "BLOODTHIRSTY SAVAGE."
"I might have been all of four."
Mm... okay.
But I feel like I'm being stalked.

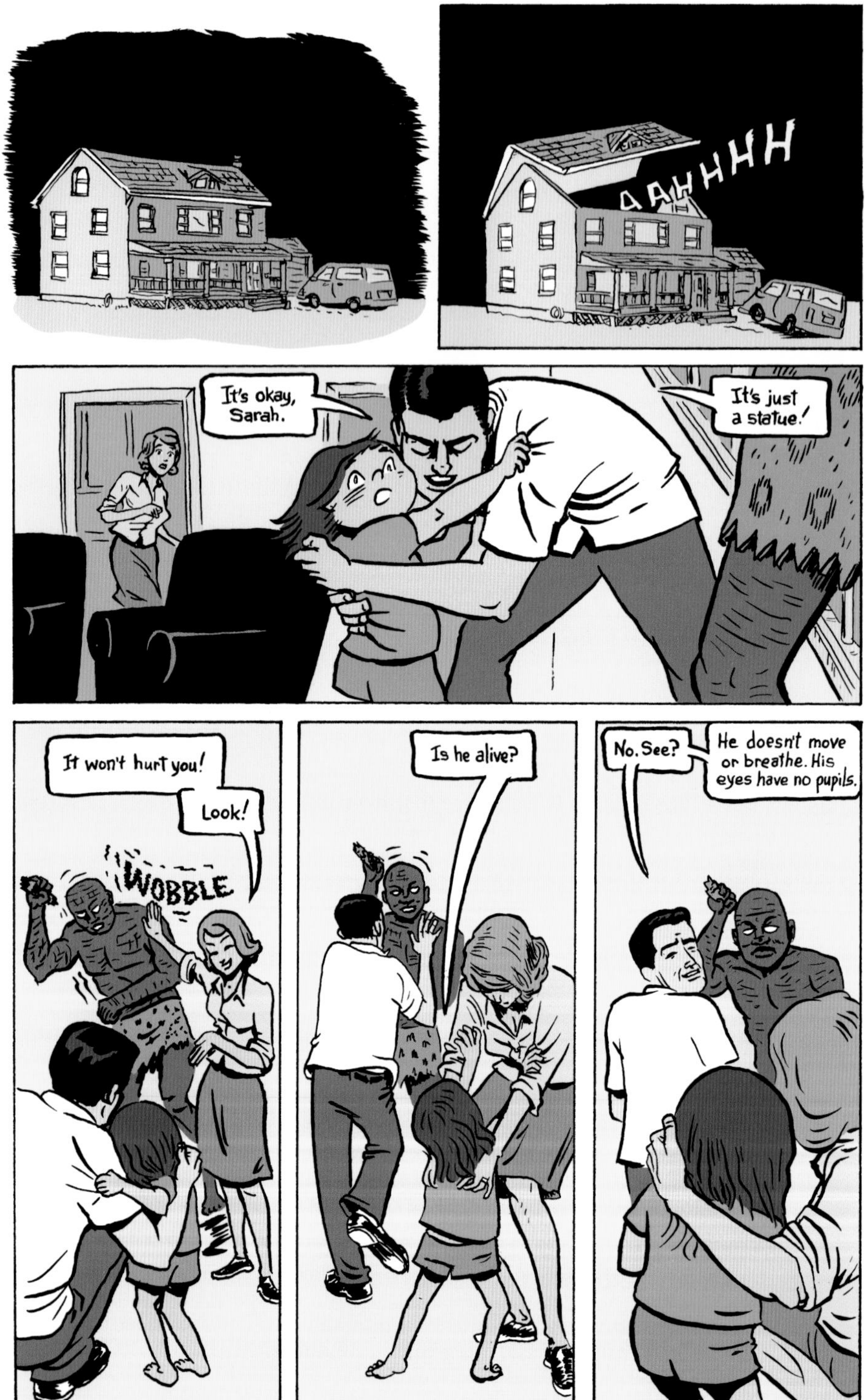
AAHHHHH
It's okay, Sarah.
It's just a statue!
It won't hurt you!
Look!
WOBBLE
Is he alive?
No. See?
He doesn't move or breathe. His eyes have no pupils.

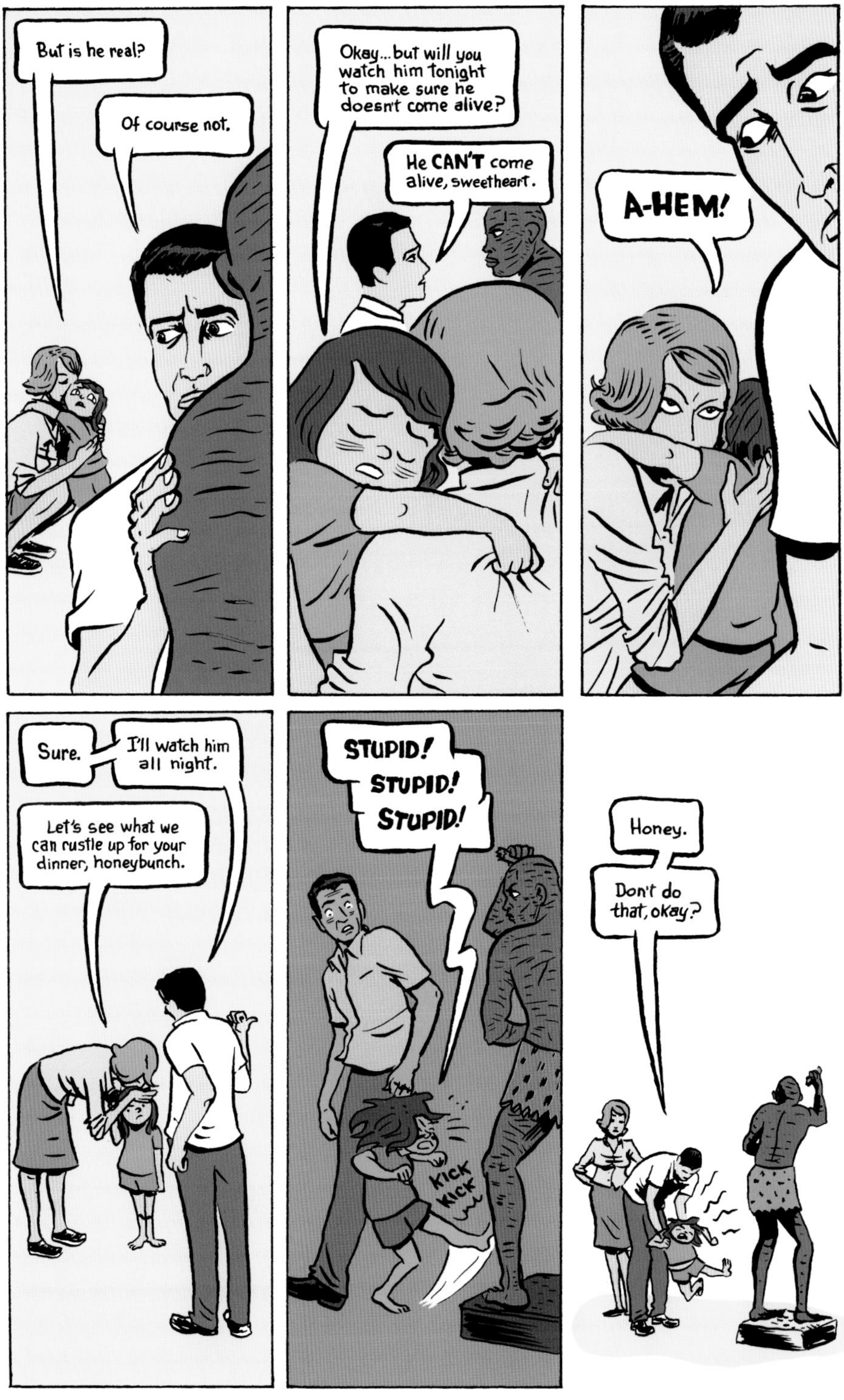
But is he real?
Of course not.
Okay... but will you watch him tonight to make sure he doesn't come alive?
He CAN'T come alive, sweetheart.
A-HEM!
Sure.
I'll watch him all night.
Let's see what we can rustle up for your dinner, honeybunch.
STUPID! STUPID! STUPID!
KICK KICK
Honey.
Don't do that, okay?

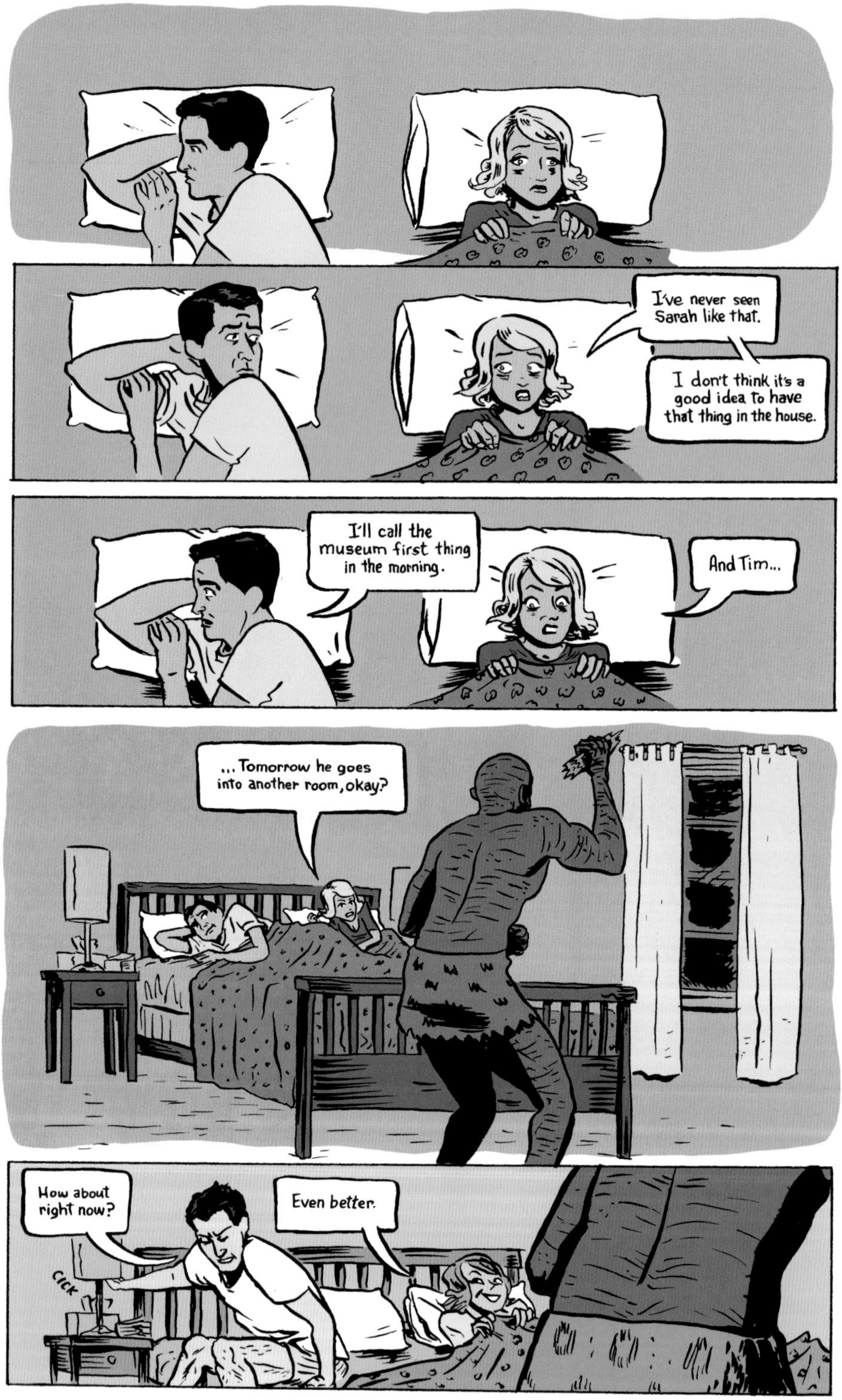
I've never seen Sarah like that.
I don't think it's a good idea to have that thing in the house.
I'll call the museum first thing in the morning.
And Tim...
...Tomorrow he goes into another room, okay?
How about right now?
Even better.

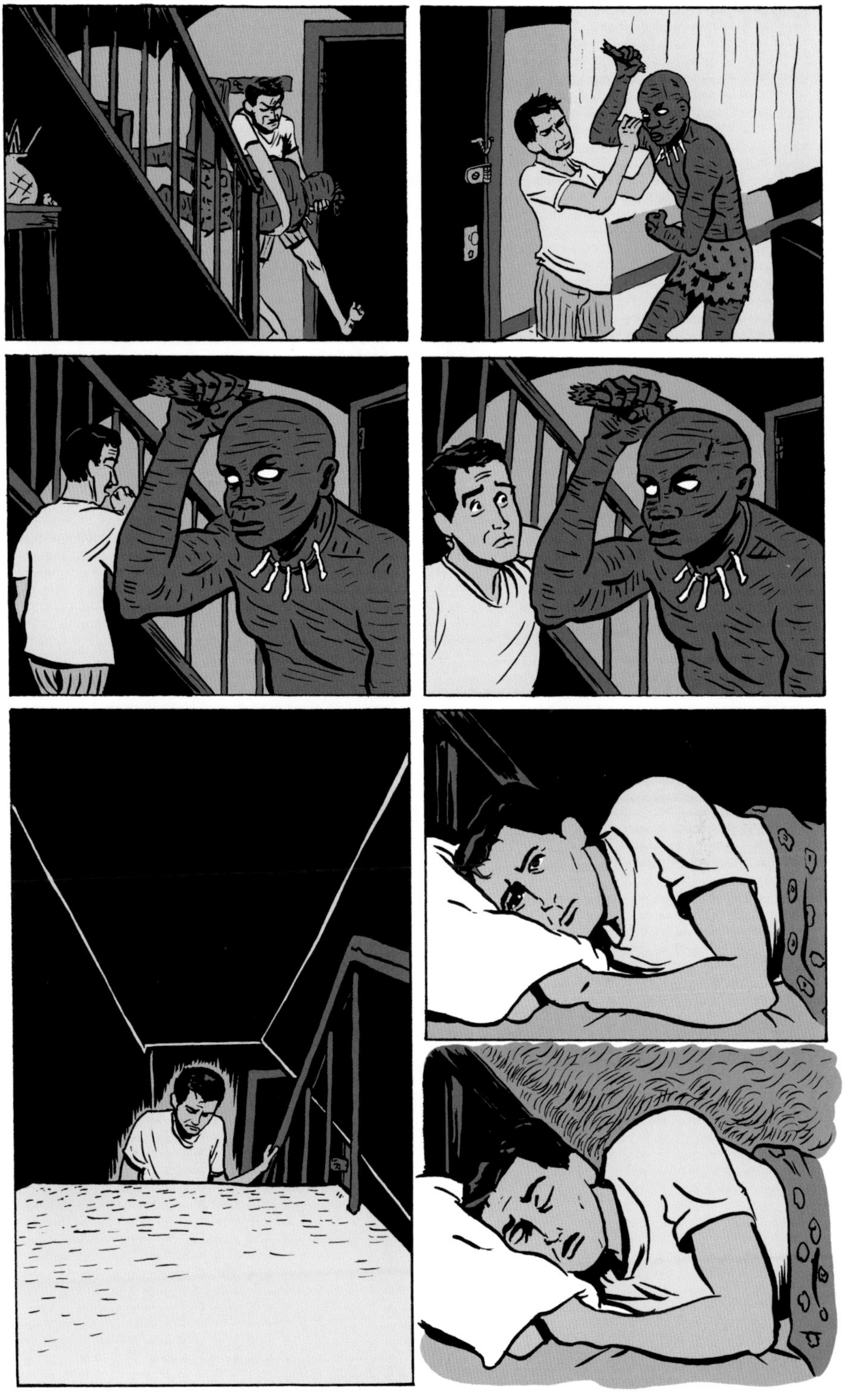

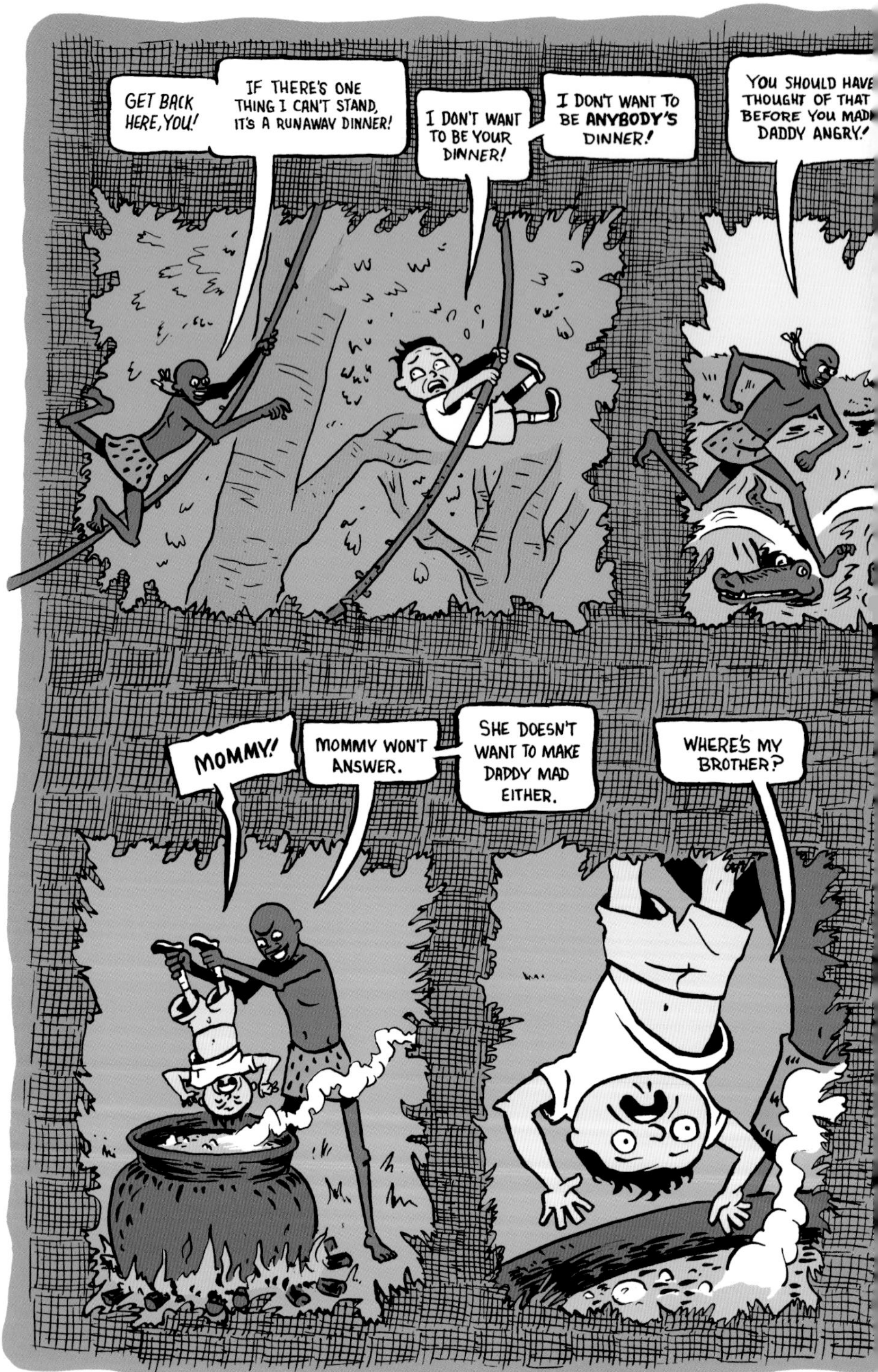
GET BACK HERE, YOU!
IF THERE'S ONE THING I CAN'T STAND, IT'S A RUNAWAY DINNER!
I DON'T WANT TO BE YOUR DINNER!
I DON'T WANT TO BE ANYBODY'S DINNER!
YOU SHOULD HAVE THOUGHT OF THAT BEFORE YOU MADE DADDY ANGRY!
MOMMY!
MOMMY WON'T ANSWER.
SHE DOESN'T WANT TO MAKE DADDY MAD EITHER.
WHERE'S MY BROTHER?

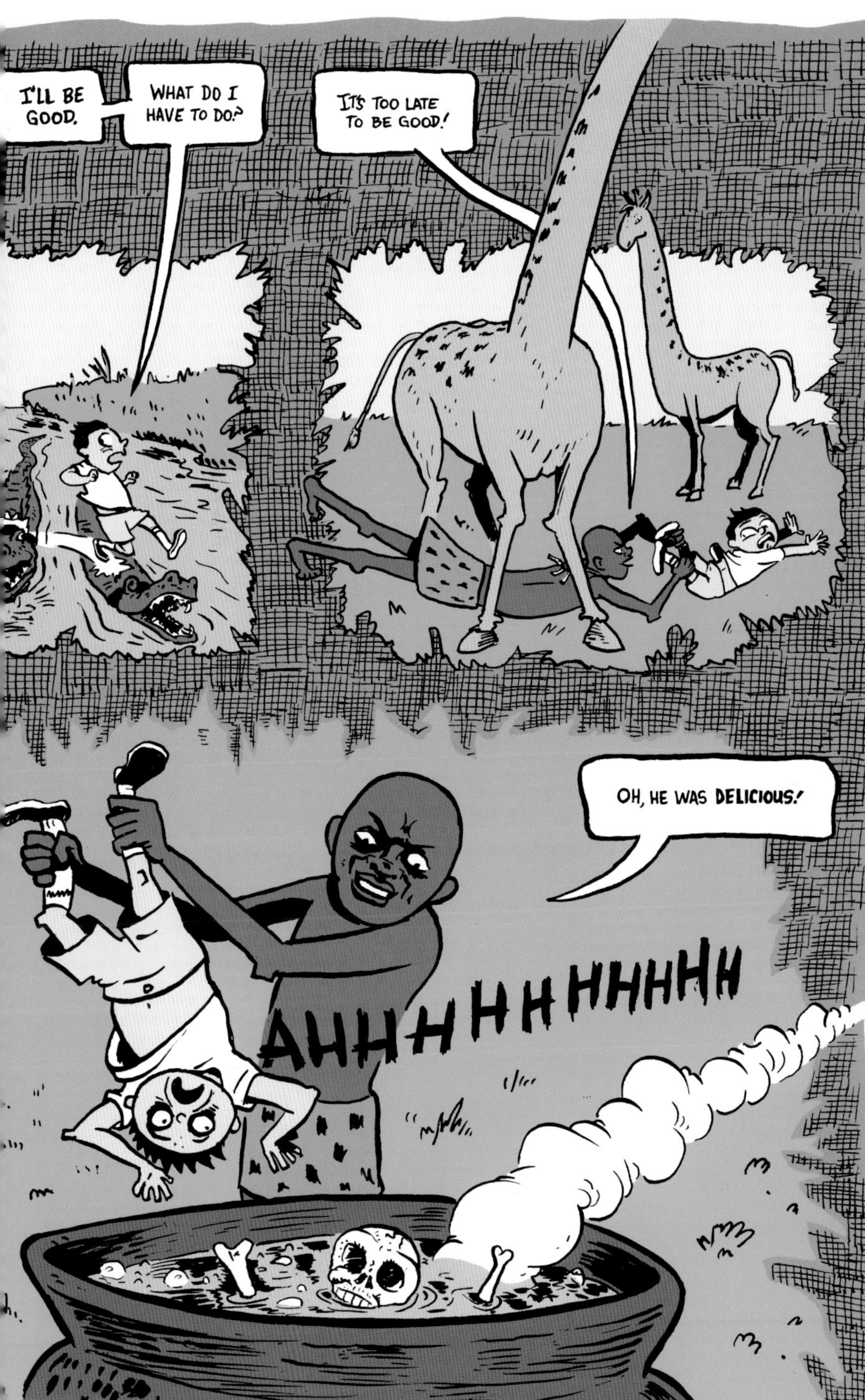
I'LL BE GOOD.
WHAT DO I HAVE TO DO?
IT'S TOO LATE TO BE GOOD!
OH, HE WAS DELICIOUS!
AHHHHHHHHHHHH

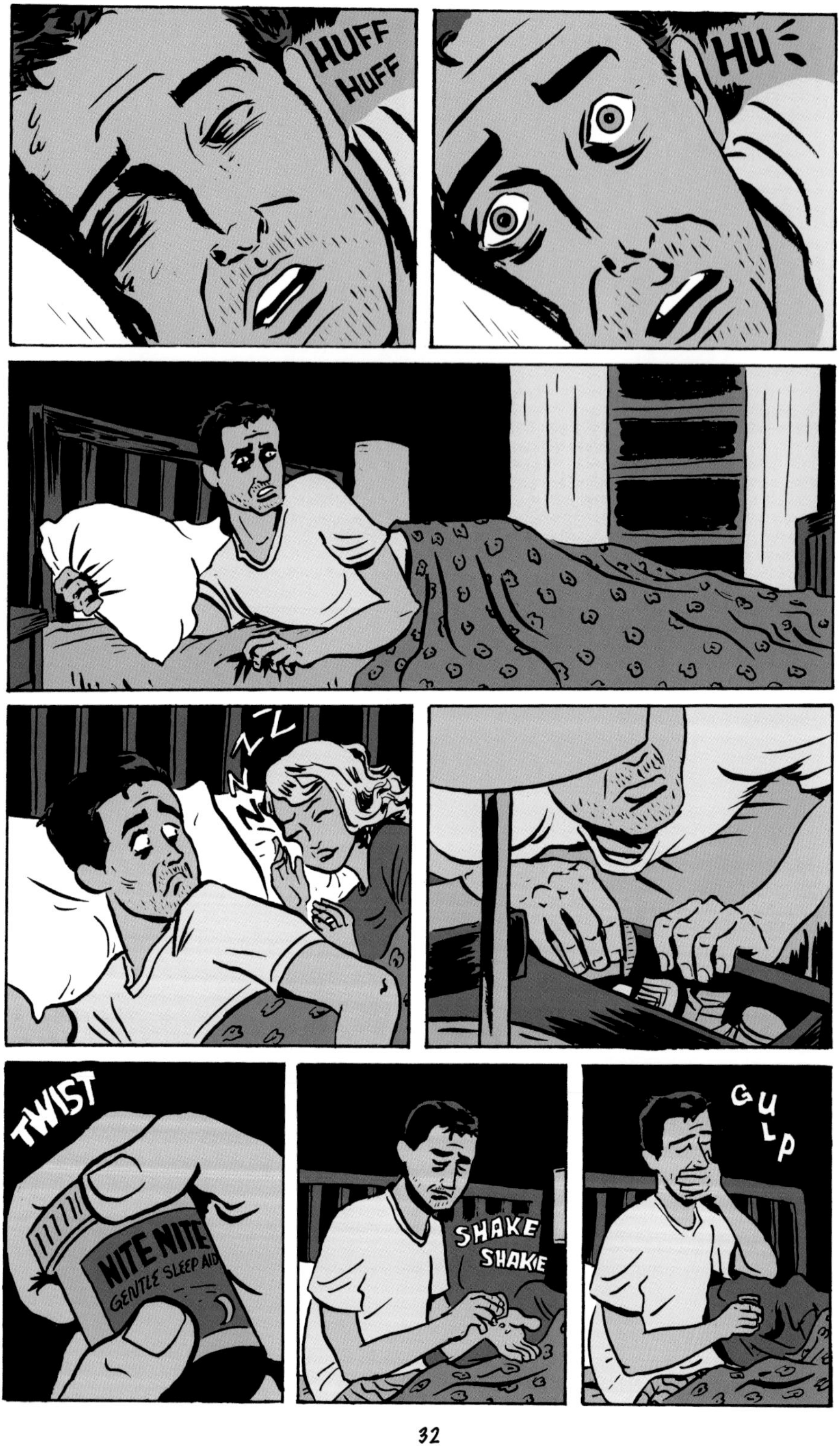
HUFF
HUFF
HU
Z
Z
Z
TWIST
NITE NITE
GENTLE SLEEP AID
SHAKE
SHAKE
GULP

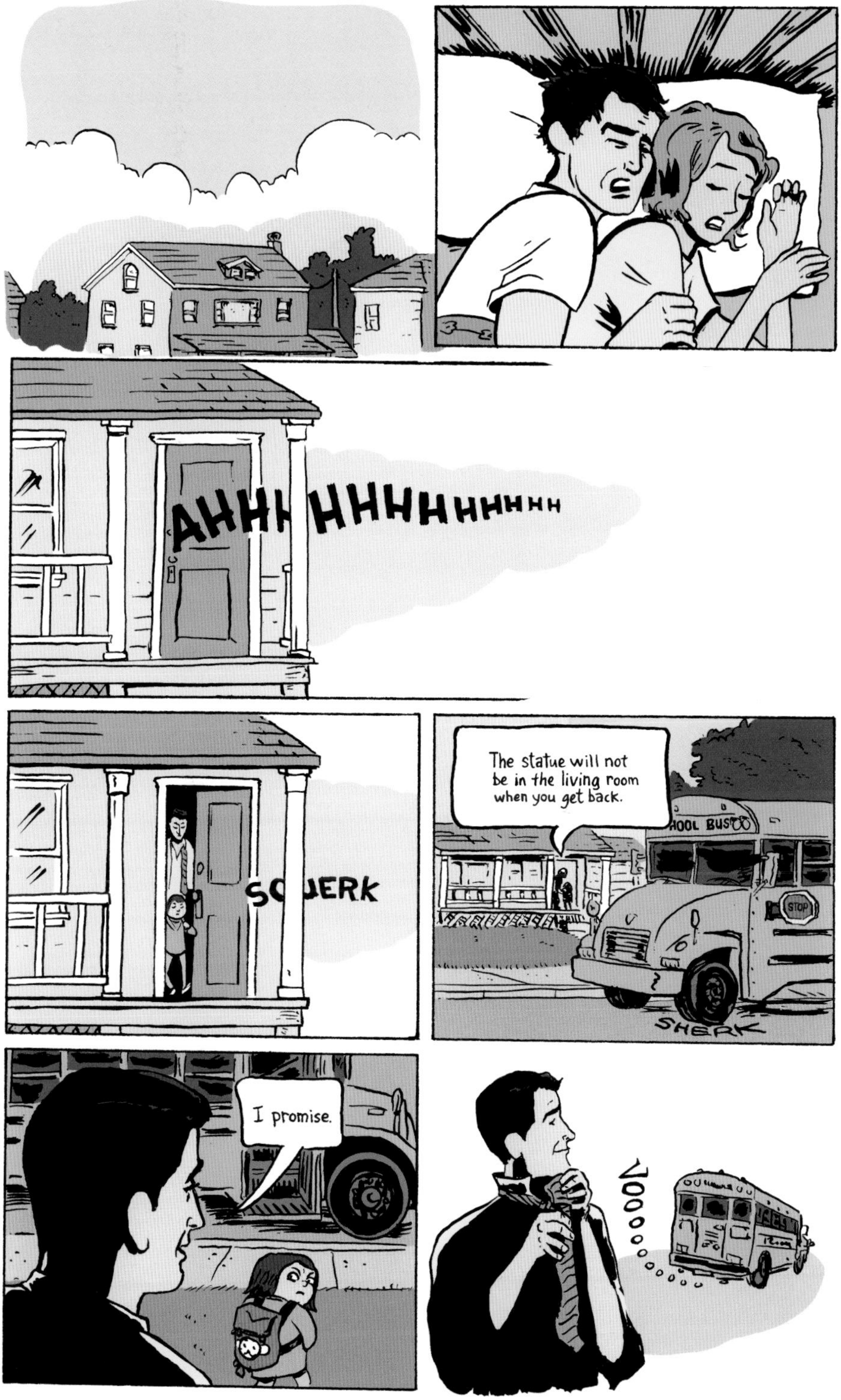
AHHHHHHHHHHH
SQUERK
The statue will not be in the living room when you get back.
SCHOOL BUS
STOP
SHERK
I promise.
VOOOOOOOOO

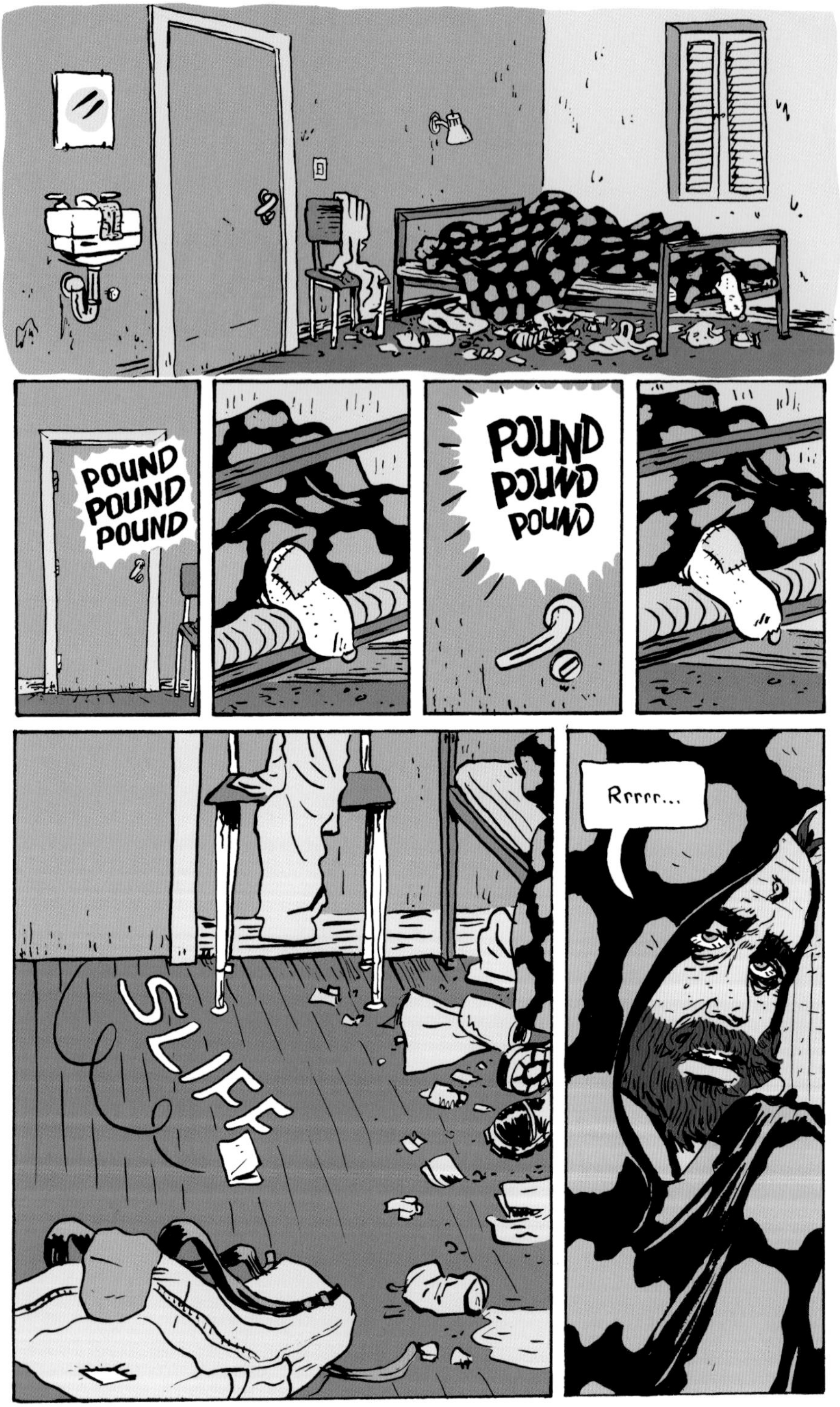
POUND
POUND
POUND
POUND
POUND
POUND
SLIFF
Rrrrr...

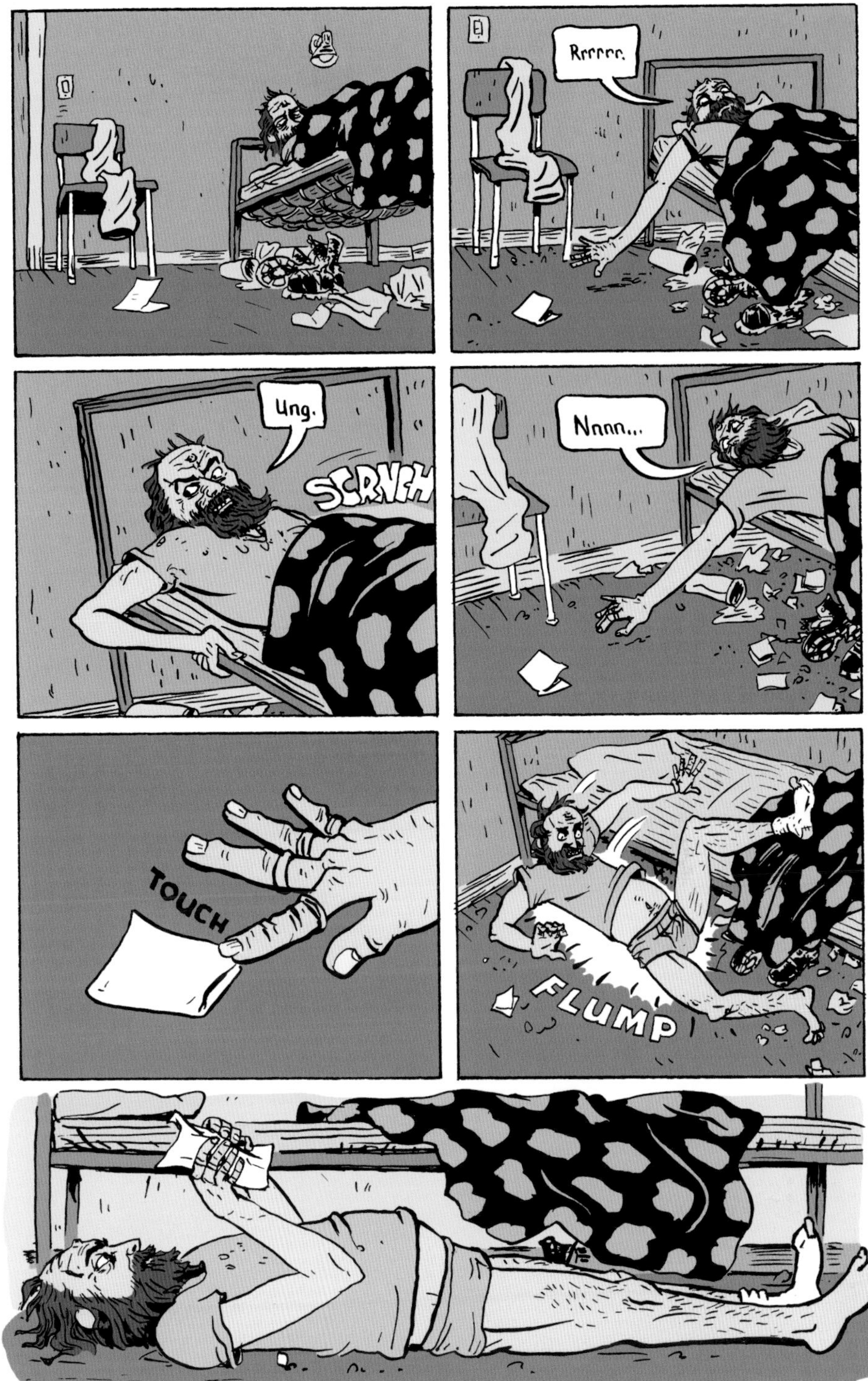
Rrrrrr.
Ung.
SCRNCH
Nnnn...
TOUCH
FLUMP

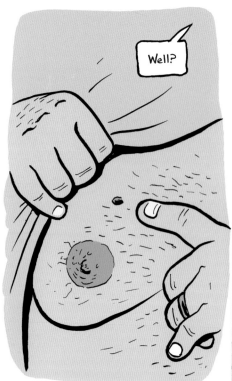

Well?

Do you think it's just a mole or some kind of melanoma?

Mr. Drayson, **PLEASE**...

You need to ask a doctor, not a benefits administrator.

But--

RING

Please, Mr. Drayson. See a doctor about your bosom.

Mole.

Tim Johnston.

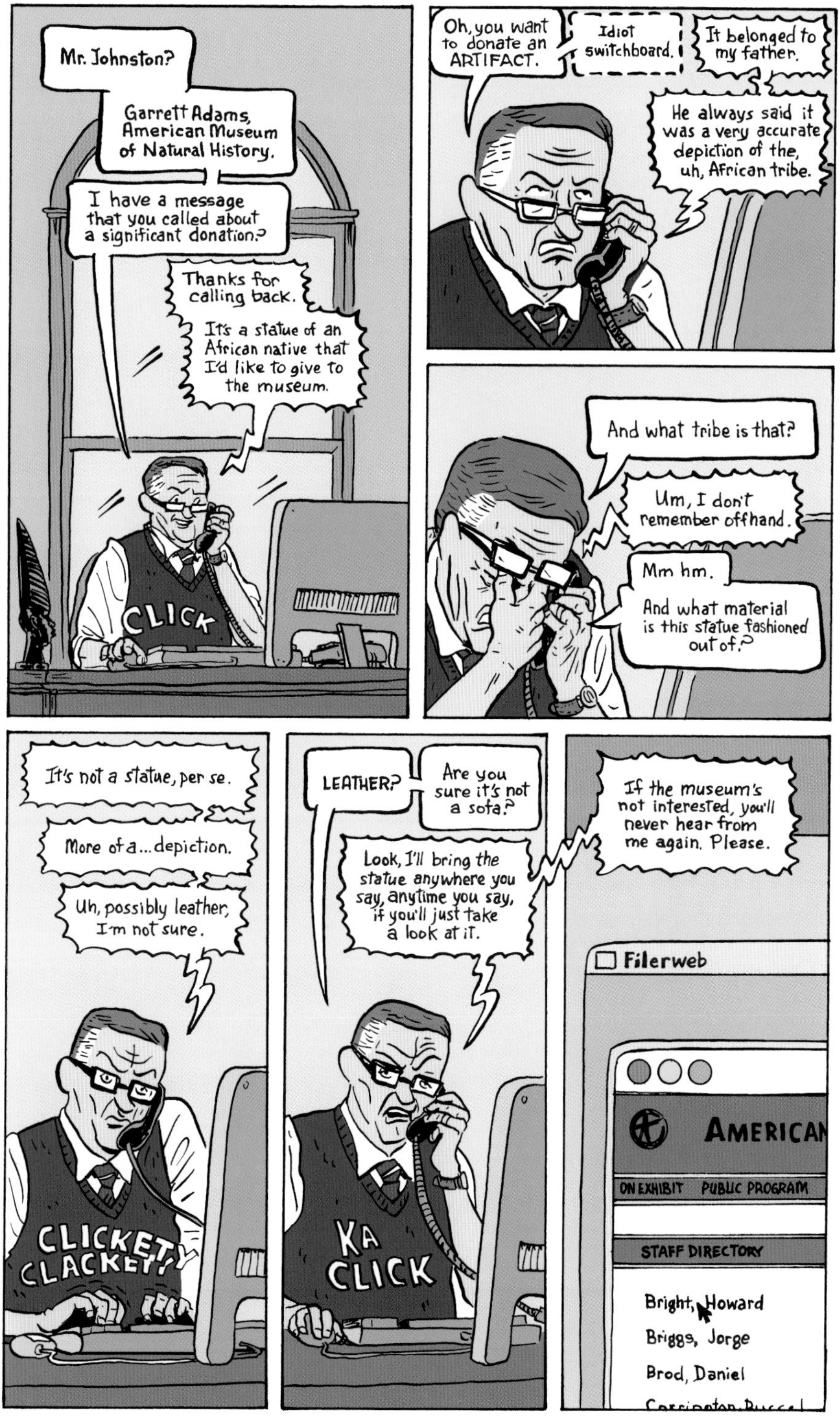

Mr. Johnston?
Garrett Adams, American Museum of Natural History.
I have a message that you called about a significant donation?
Thanks for calling back.
It's a statue of an African native that I'd like to give to the museum.
CLICK
Oh, you want to donate an ARTIFACT.
Idiot switchboard.
It belonged to my father.
He always said it was a very accurate depiction of the, uh, African tribe.
And what tribe is that?
Um, I don't remember offhand.
Mm hm.
And what material is this statue fashioned out of?
It's not a statue, per se.
More of a... depiction.
Uh, possibly leather, I'm not sure.
CLICKETY CLACKETY
LEATHER?
Are you sure it's not a sofa?
Look, I'll bring the statue anywhere you say, anytime you say, if you'll just take a look at it.
KA CLICK
If the museum's not interested, you'll never hear from me again. Please.
Filerweb
AMERICAN
ON EXHIBIT
PUBLIC PROGRAM
STAFF DIRECTORY
Bright, Howard
Briggs, Jorge
Brod, Daniel

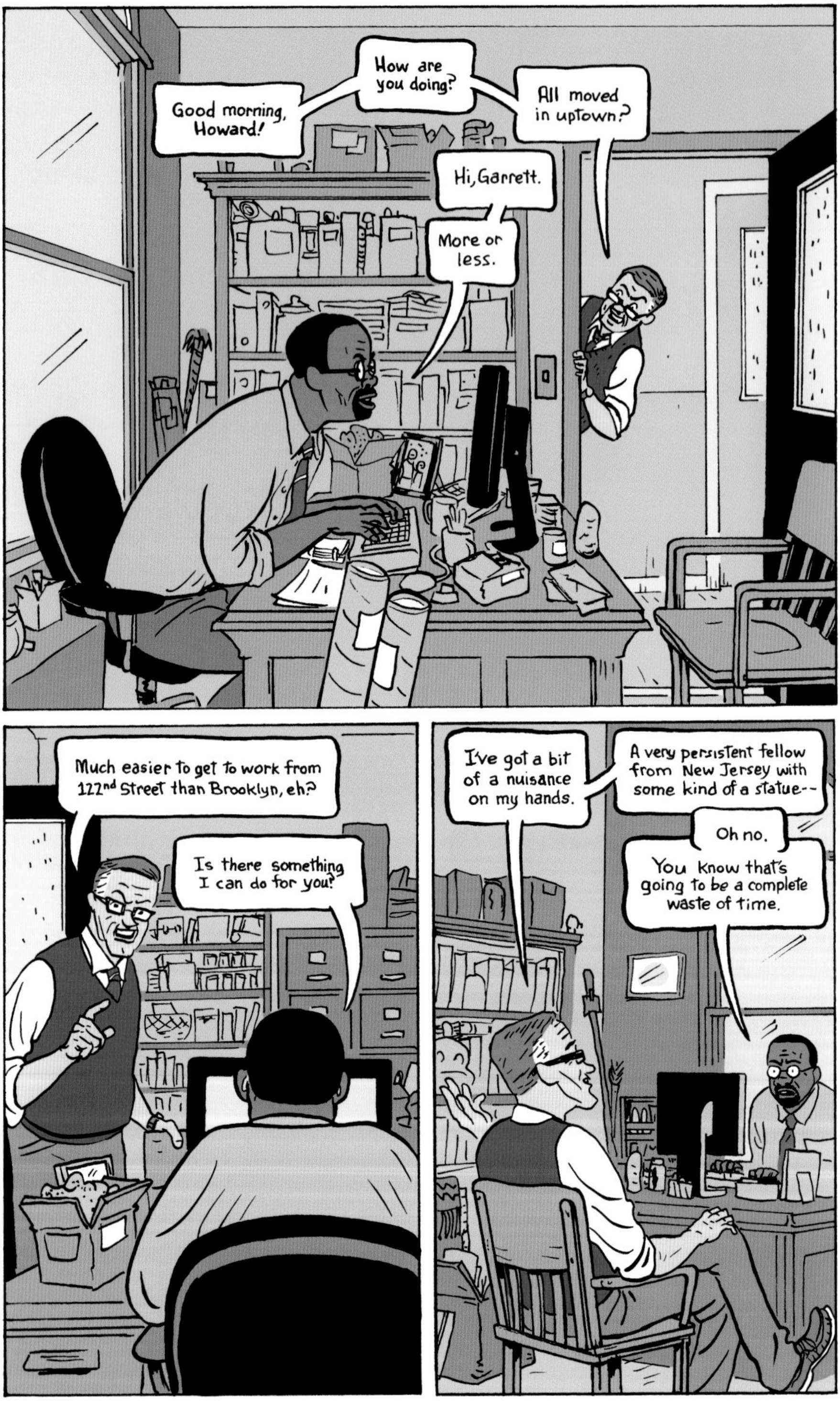
Good morning, Howard!
How are you doing?
All moved in uptown?
Hi, Garrett.
More or less.
Much easier to get to work from 122nd Street than Brooklyn, eh?
Is there something I can do for you?
I've got a bit of a nuisance on my hands.
A very persistent fellow from New Jersey with some kind of a statue--
Oh no.
You know that's going to be a complete waste of time.

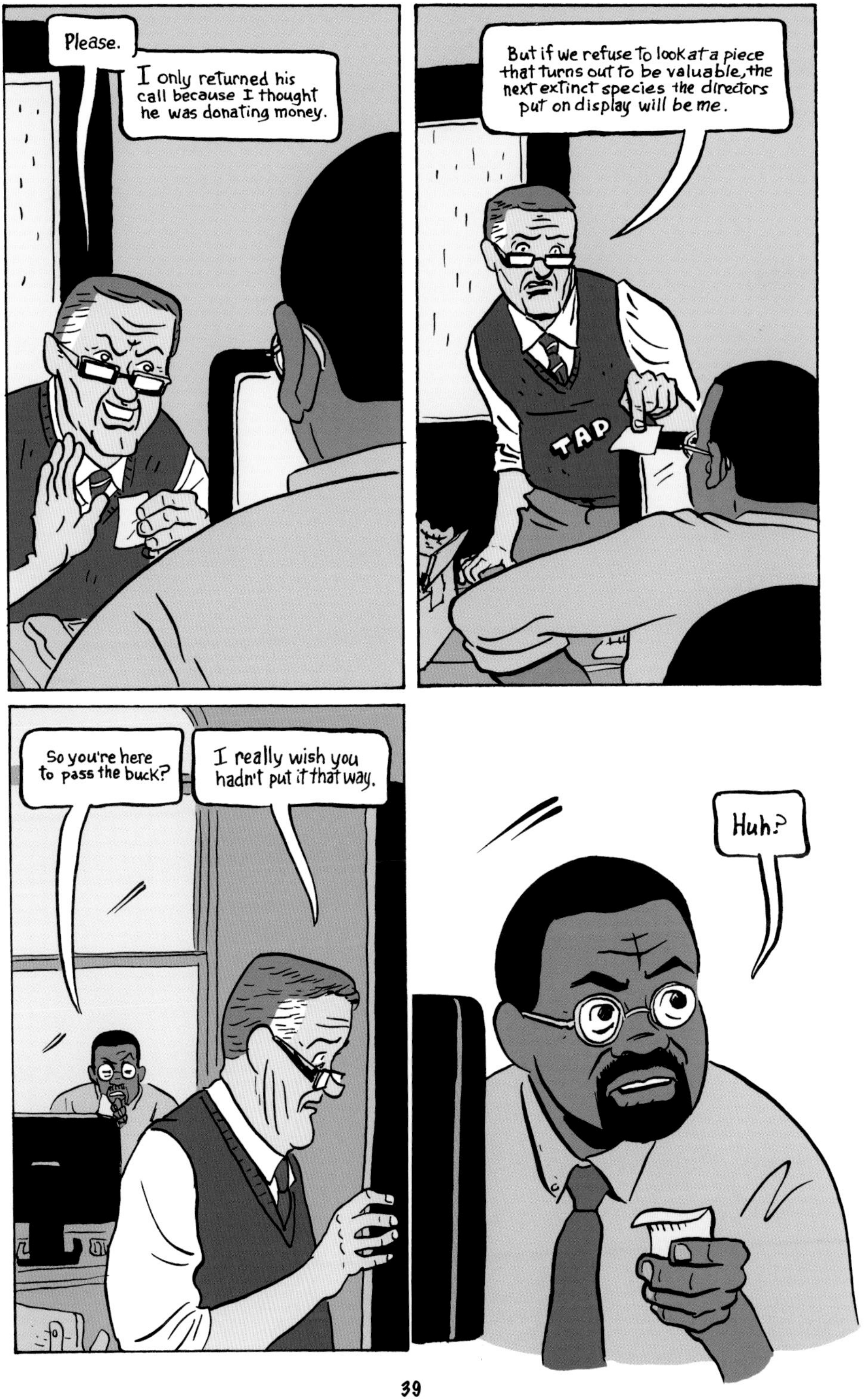
Please.
I only returned his call because I thought he was donating money.
But if we refuse to look at a piece that turns out to be valuable, the next extinct species the directors put on display will be me.
TAP
So you're here to pass the buck?
I really wish you hadn't put it that way.
Huh?

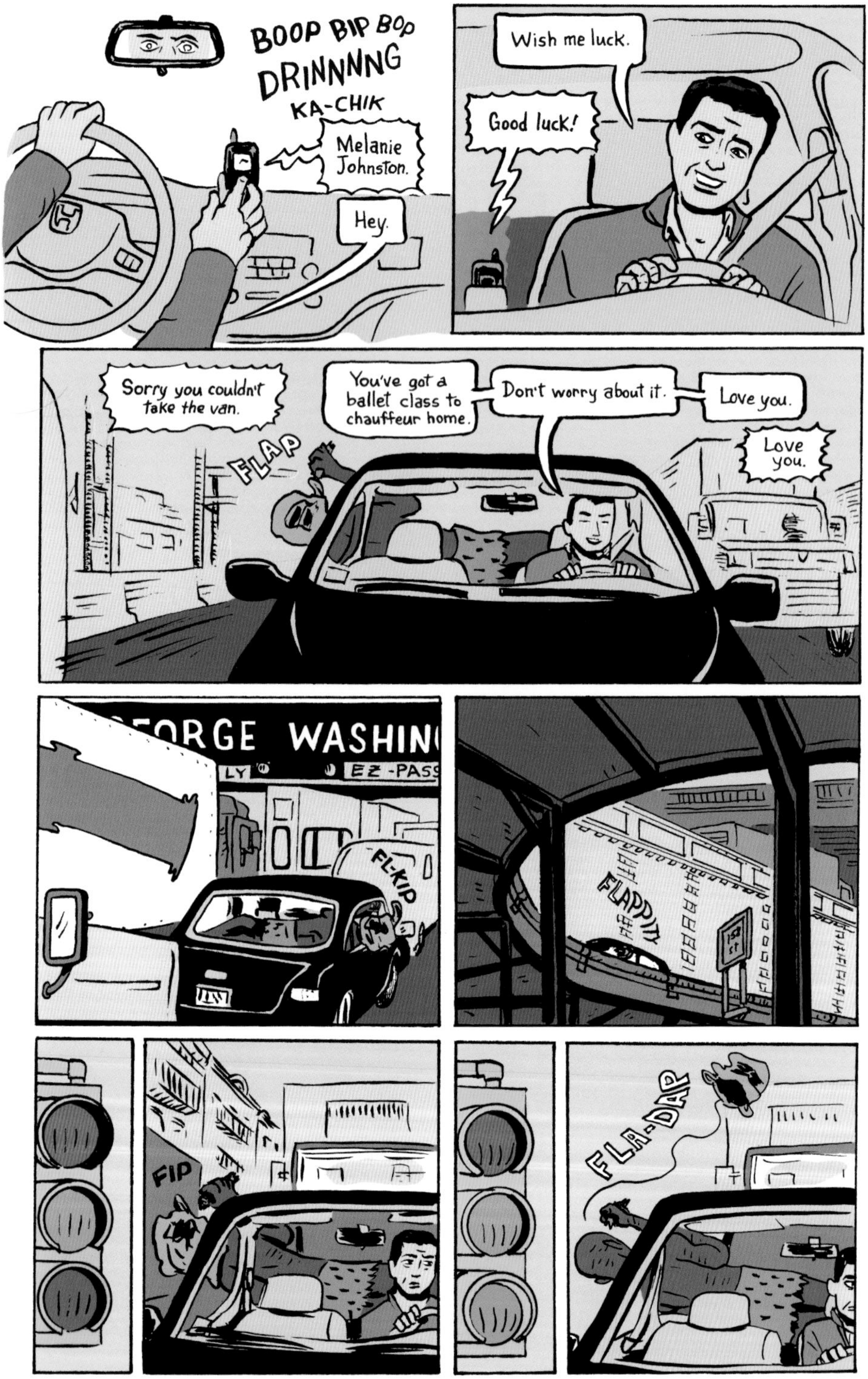
BOOP BIP BOP
DRINNNNG
KA-CHIK
Melanie Johnston.
Hey.
Wish me luck.
Good luck!
Sorry you couldn't take the van.
You've got a ballet class to chauffeur home.
Don't worry about it.
Love you.
Love you.
FLAP
GEORGE WASHIN
EZ-PASS
FL-KIP
FLAPPITY
FIP
FLA-DAR

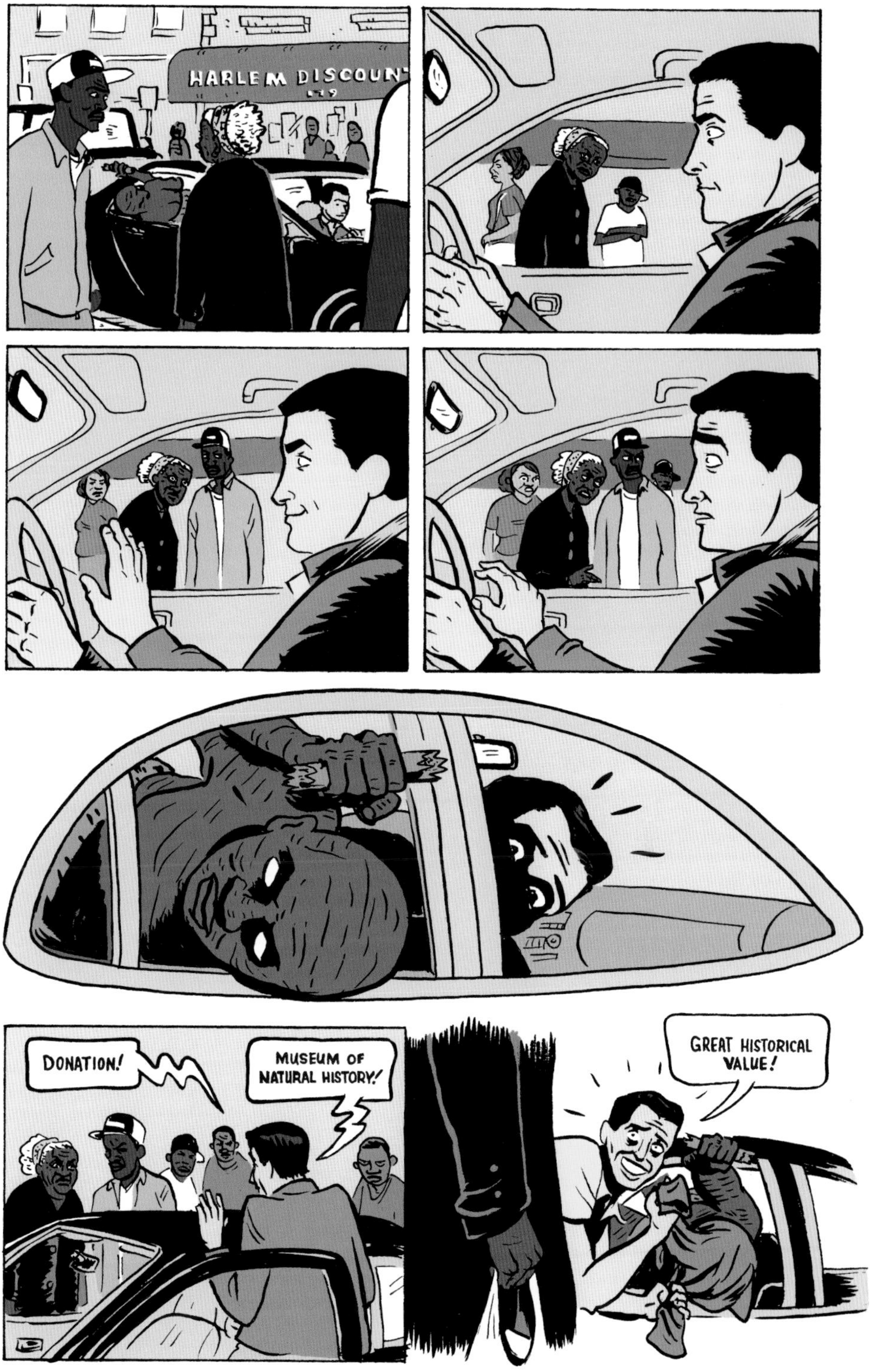
HARLEM DISCOUNT
DONATION!
MUSEUM OF NATURAL HISTORY!
GREAT HISTORICAL VALUE!

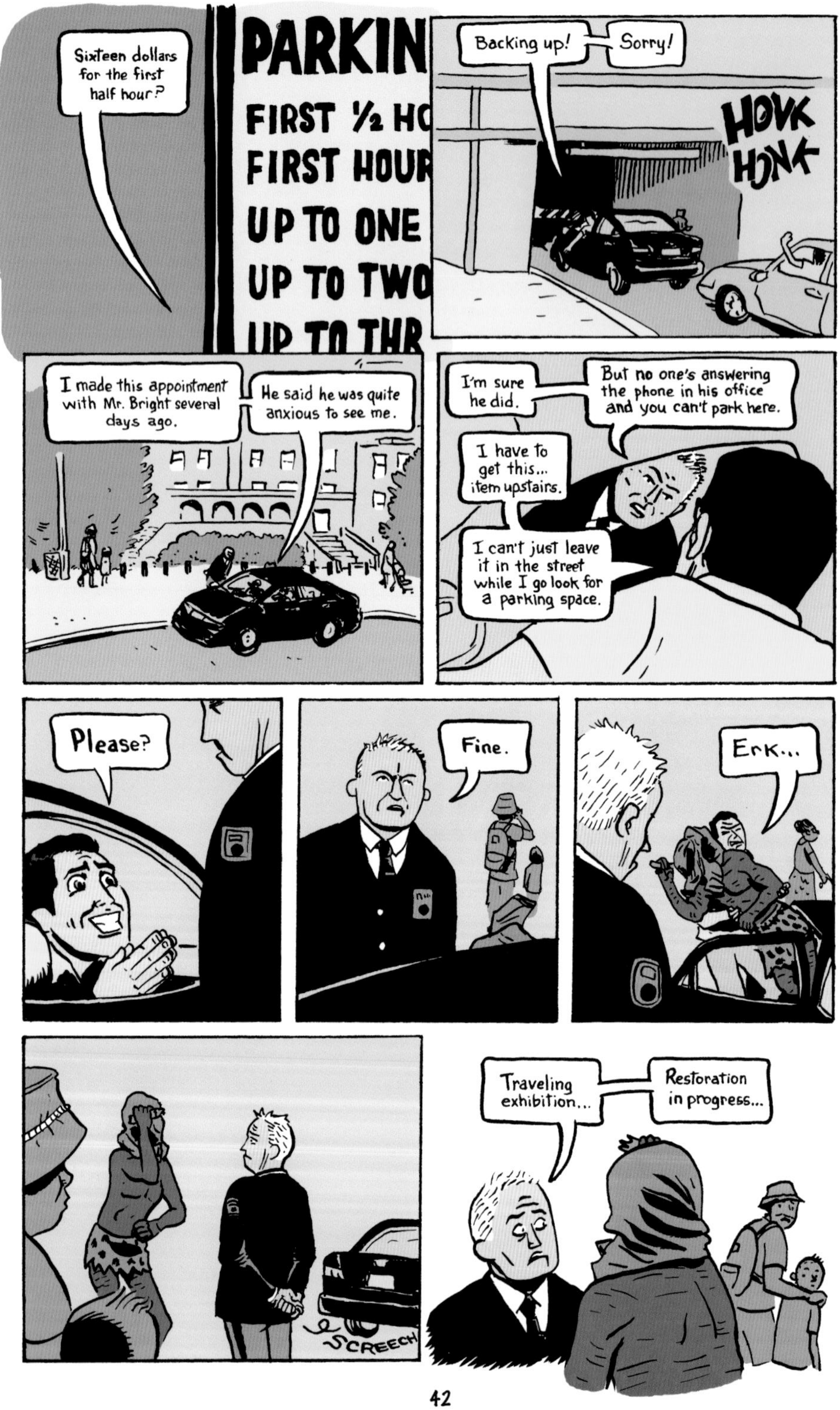

Sixteen dollars for the first half hour?
PARKIN
FIRST ½ HO
FIRST HOUR
UP TO ONE
UP TO TWO
UP TO THR
Backing up!
Sorry!
HONK
HONK
I made this appointment with Mr. Bright several days ago.
He said he was quite anxious to see me.
I'm sure he did.
But no one's answering the phone in his office and you can't park here.
I have to get this... item upstairs.
I can't just leave it in the street while I go look for a parking space.
Please?
Fine.
Erk...
SCREECH
Traveling exhibition...
Restoration in progress...

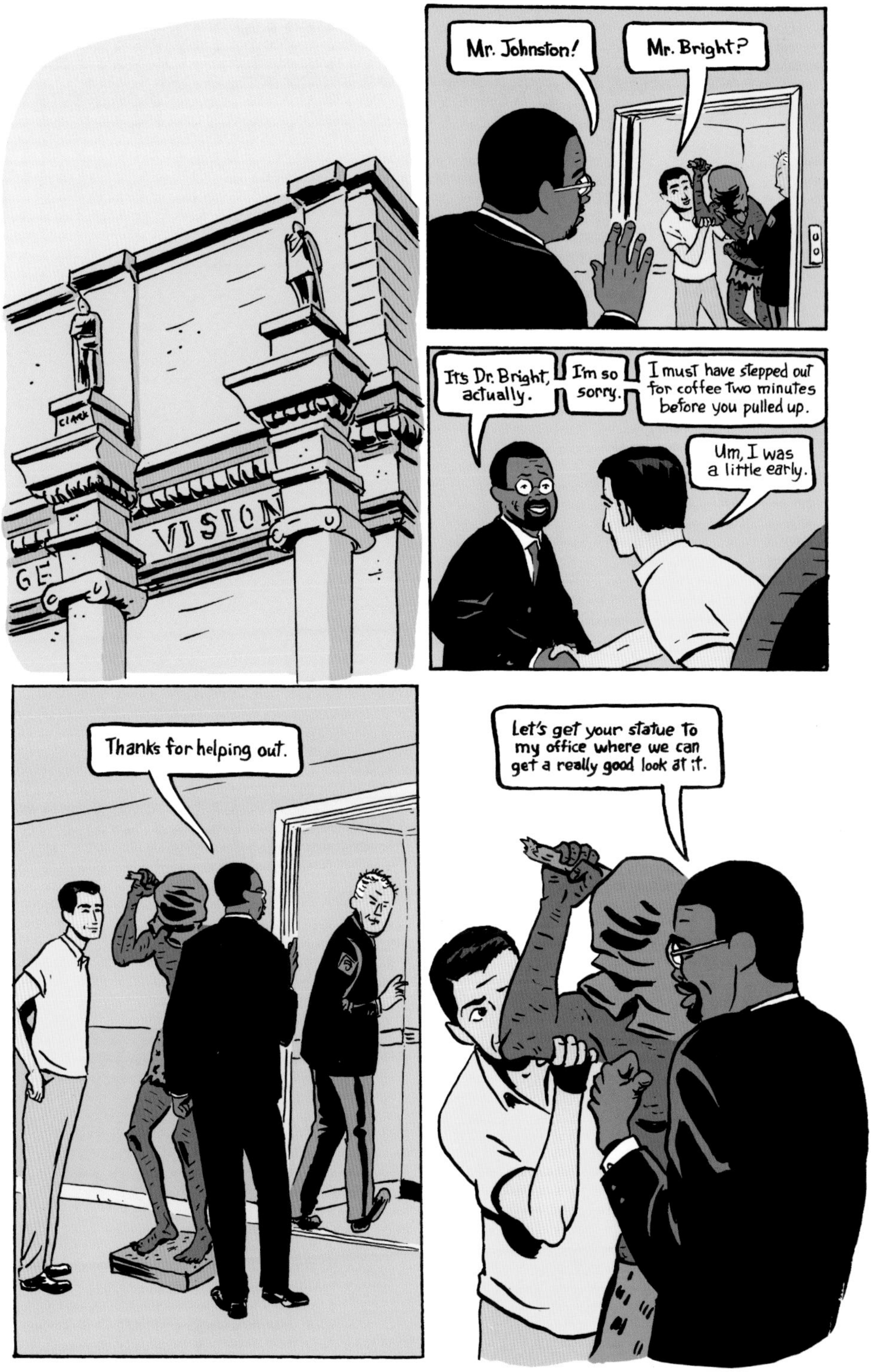
GE
VISION
CLARK
Mr. Johnston!
Mr. Bright?
It's Dr. Bright, actually.
I'm so sorry.
I must have stepped out for coffee two minutes before you pulled up.
Um, I was a little early.
Thanks for helping out.
Let's get your statue to my office where we can get a really good look at it.

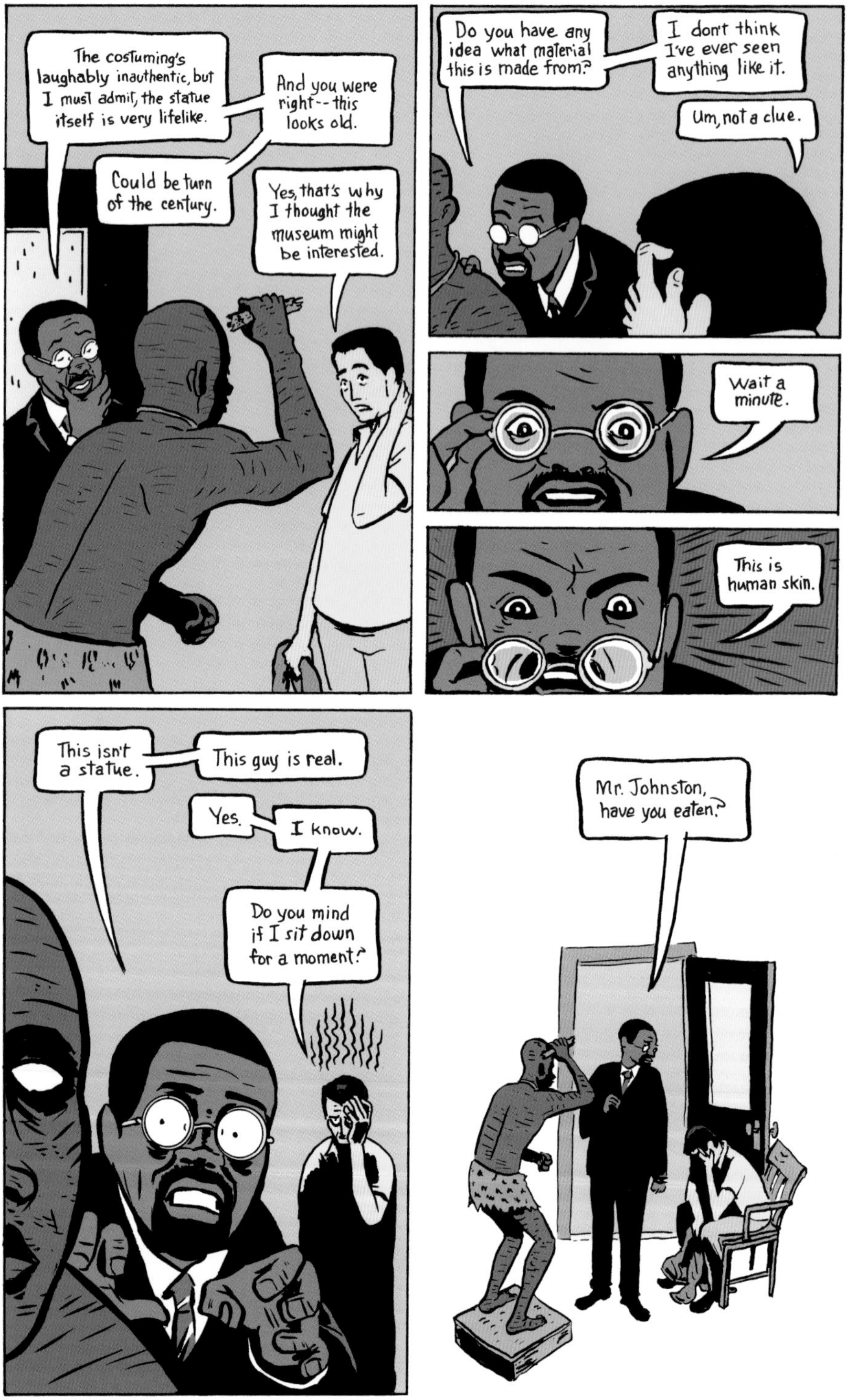
The costuming's laughably inauthentic, but I must admit, the statue itself is very lifelike.
And you were right -- this looks old.
Could be turn of the century.
Yes, that's why I thought the museum might be interested.
Do you have any idea what material this is made from?
I don't think I've ever seen anything like it.
Um, not a clue.
Wait a minute.
This is human skin.
This isn't a statue.
This guy is real.
Yes.
I know.
Do you mind if I sit down for a moment?
Mr. Johnston, have you eaten?

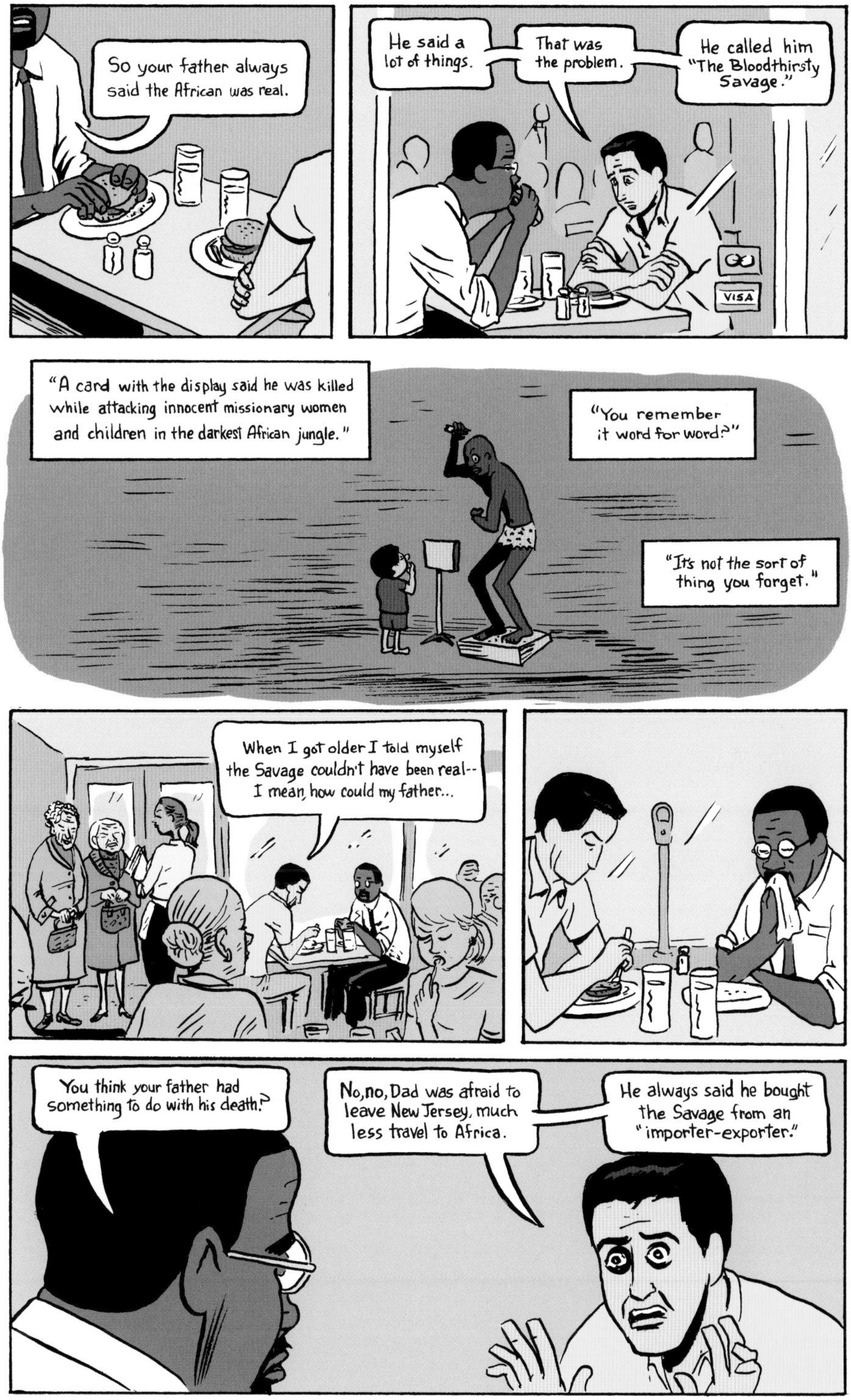

So your father always said the African was real.
He said a lot of things.
That was the problem.
He called him "The Bloodthirsty Savage."
VISA
"A card with the display said he was killed while attacking innocent missionary women and children in the darkest African jungle."
"You remember it word for word?"
"It's not the sort of thing you forget."
When I got older I told myself the Savage couldn't have been real-- I mean, how could my father...
You think your father had something to do with his death?
No, no, Dad was afraid to leave New Jersey, much less travel to Africa.
He always said he bought the Savage from an "importer-exporter."

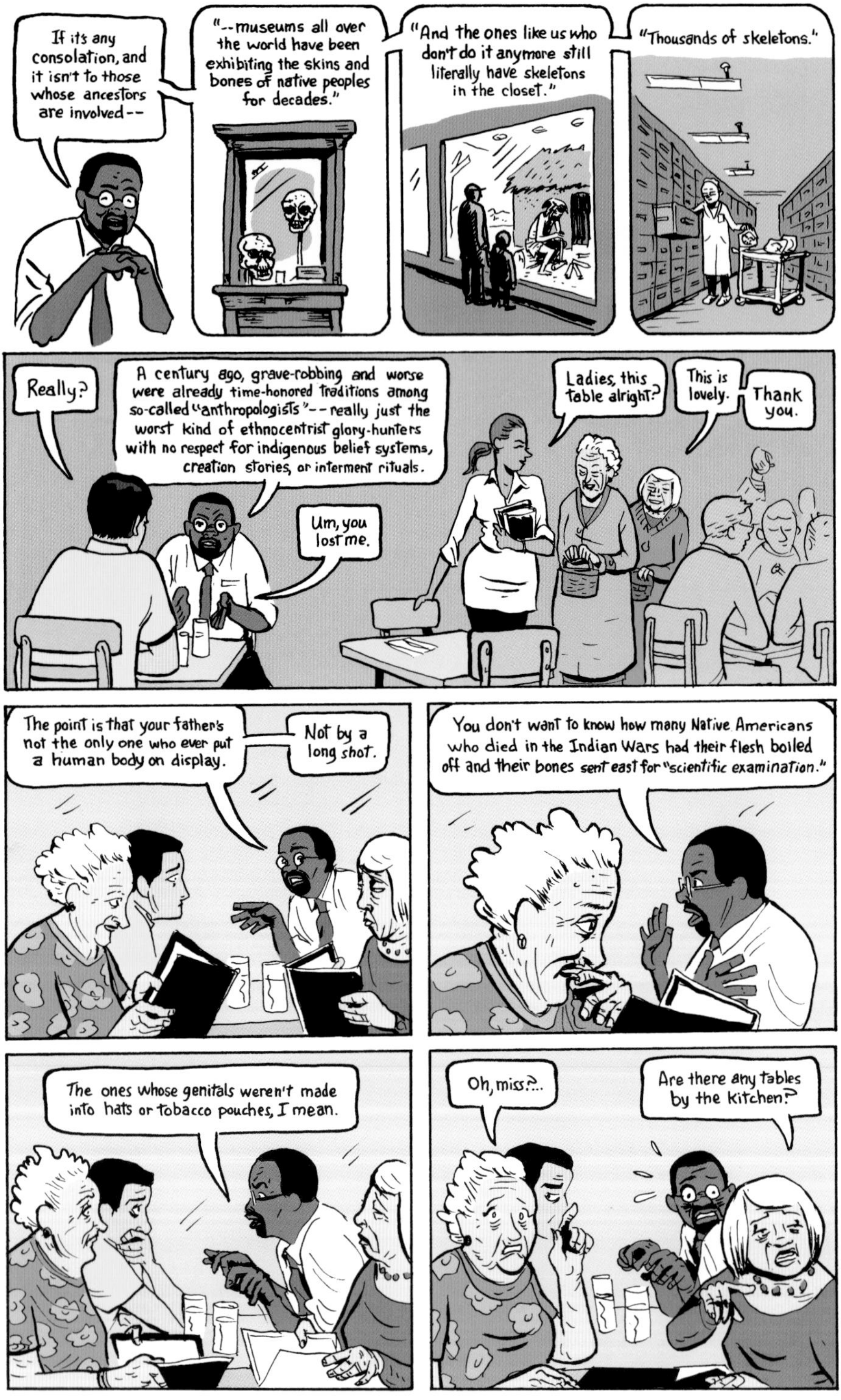
If it's any consolation, and it isn't to those whose ancestors are involved--
"--museums all over the world have been exhibiting the skins and bones of native peoples for decades."
"And the ones like us who don't do it anymore still literally have skeletons in the closet."
"Thousands of skeletons."
Really?
A century ago, grave-robbing and worse were already time-honored traditions among so-called "anthropologists"--really just the worst kind of ethnocentrist glory-hunters with no respect for indigenous belief systems, creation stories, or interment rituals.
Um, you lost me.
Ladies, this table alright?
This is lovely.
Thank you.
The point is that your father's not the only one who ever put a human body on display.
Not by a long shot.
You don't want to know how many Native Americans who died in the Indian Wars had their flesh boiled off and their bones sent east for "scientific examination."
The ones whose genitals weren't made into hats or tobacco pouches, I mean.
Oh, miss?...
Are there any tables by the kitchen?

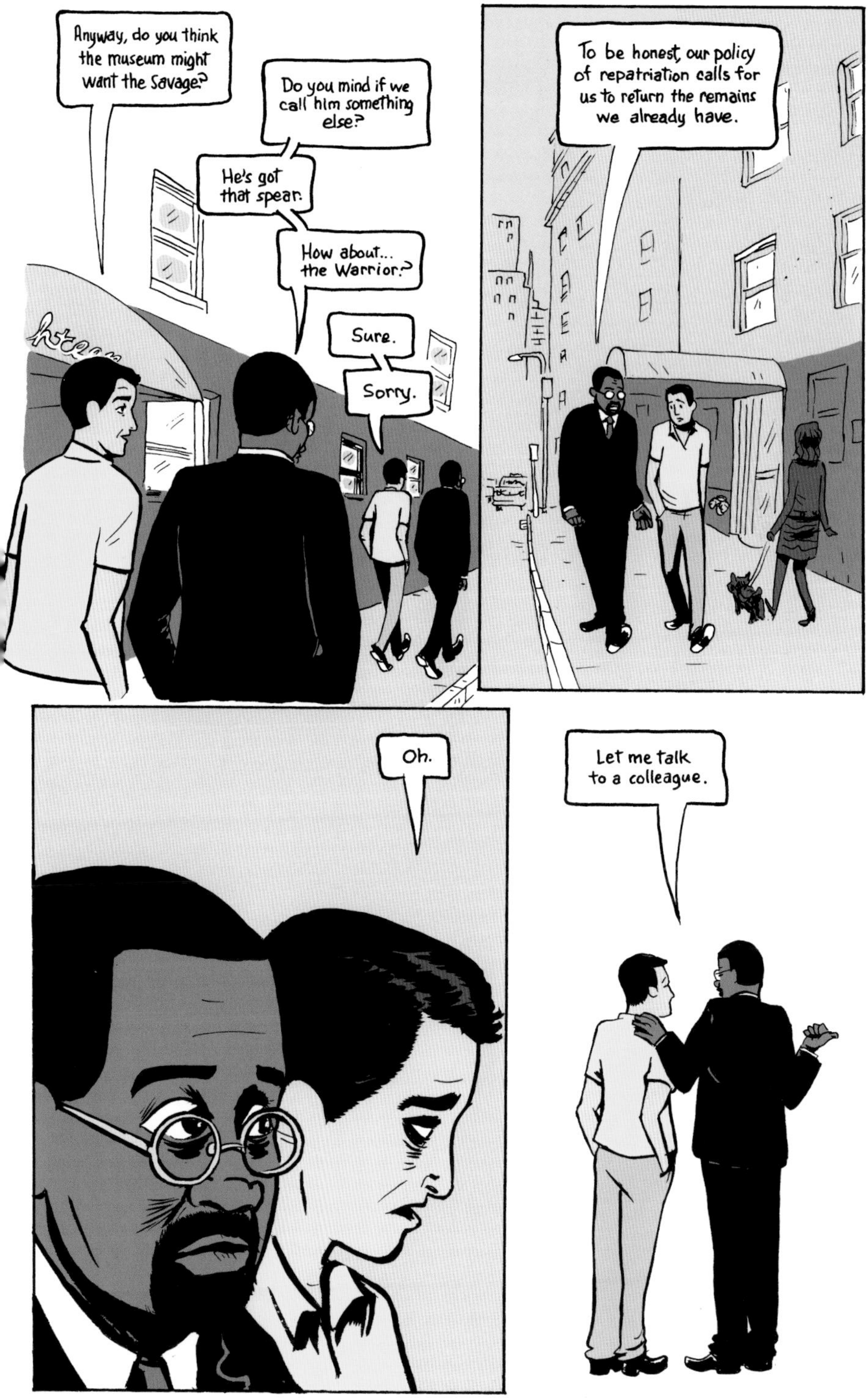
Anyway, do you think the museum might want the Savage?
Do you mind if we call him something else?
He's got that spear.
How about... the Warrior?
Sure.
Sorry.
To be honest, our policy of repatriation calls for us to return the remains we already have.
Oh.
Let me talk to a colleague.

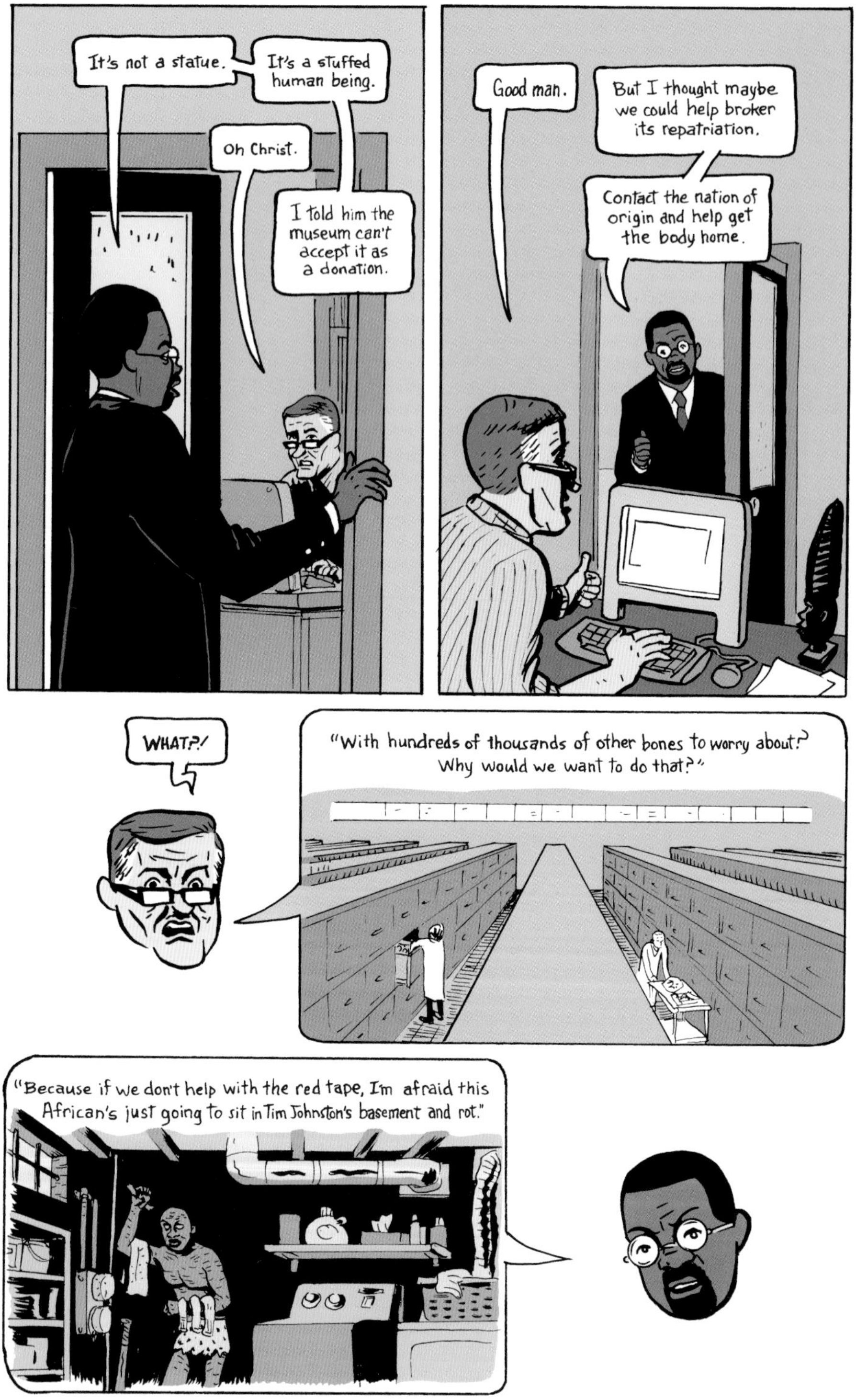
It's not a statue.
It's a stuffed human being.
Oh Christ.
I told him the museum can't accept it as a donation.
Good man.
But I thought maybe we could help broker its repatriation.
Contact the nation of origin and help get the body home.
WHAT?!
"With hundreds of thousands of other bones to worry about? Why would we want to do that?"
"Because if we don't help with the red tape, I'm afraid this African's just going to sit in Tim Johnston's basement and rot."

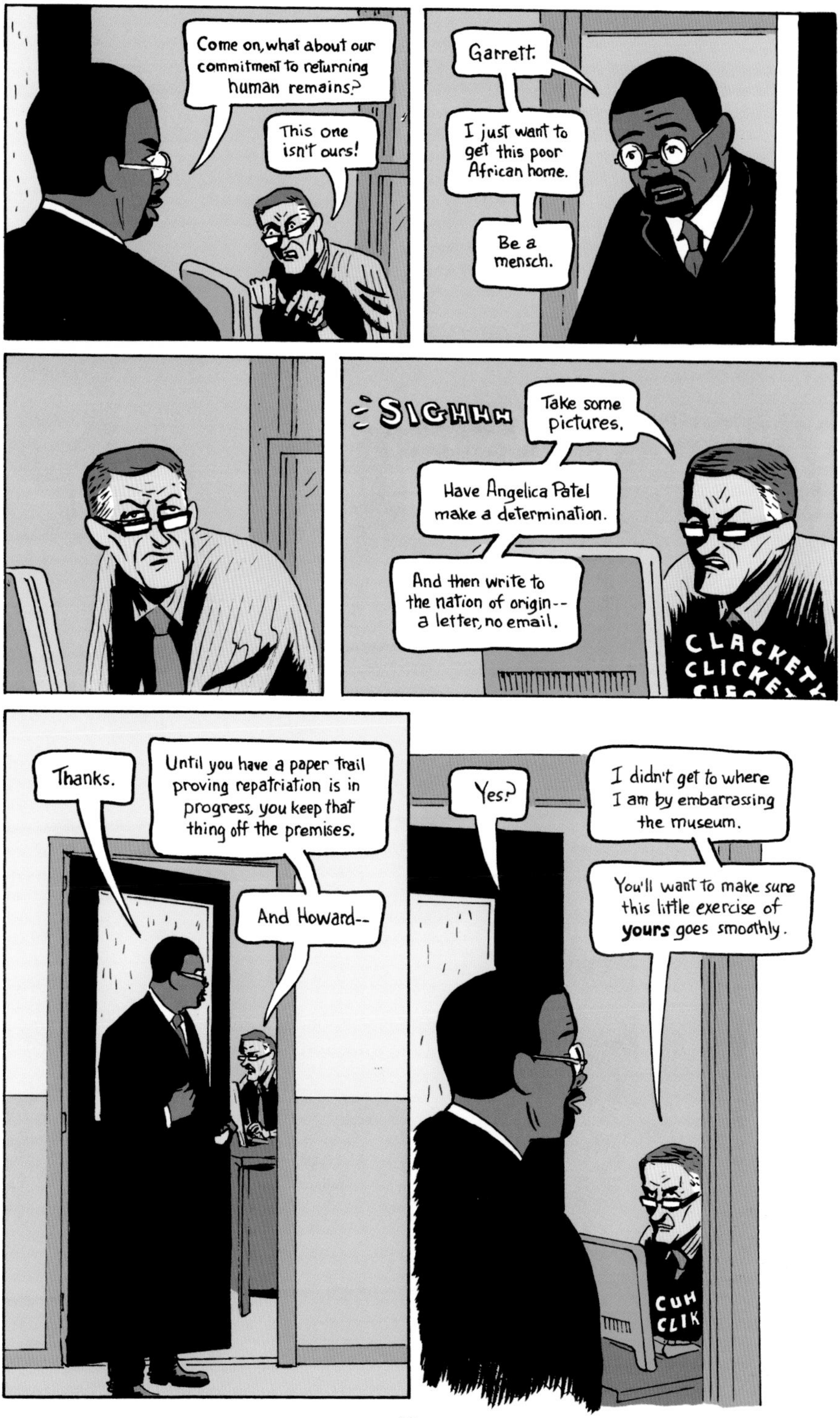
Come on, what about our commitment to returning human remains?
This one isn't ours!
Garrett.
I just want to get this poor African home.
Be a mensch.
SIGHHH
Take some pictures.
Have Angelica Patel make a determination.
And then write to the nation of origin-- a letter, no email.
CLACKETY CLICKETY
Thanks.
Until you have a paper trail proving repatriation is in progress, you keep that thing off the premises.
And Howard--
Yes?
I didn't get to where I am by embarrassing the museum.
You'll want to make sure this little exercise of **yours** goes smoothly.
CUH CLIK

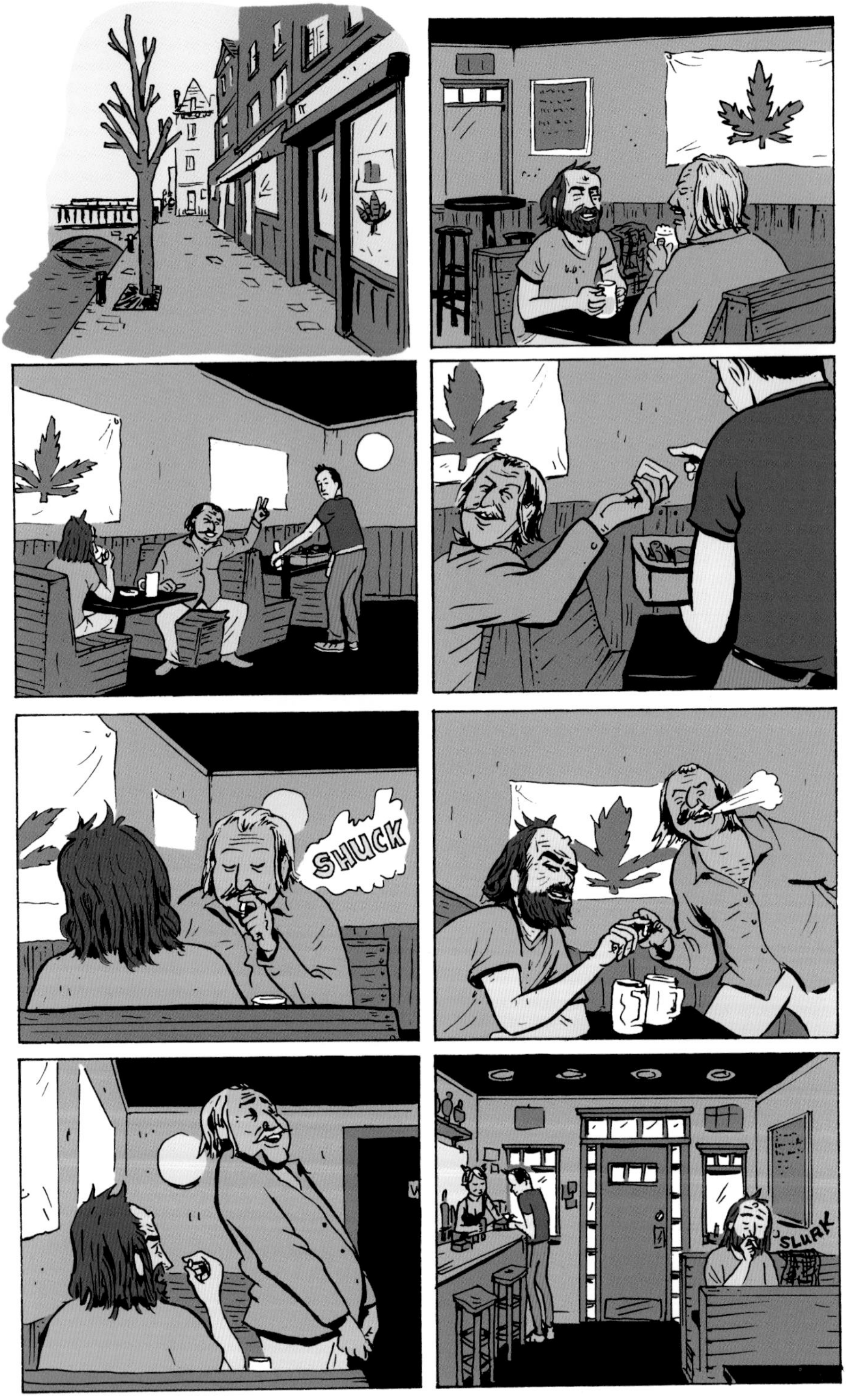
SHUCK
SLURK

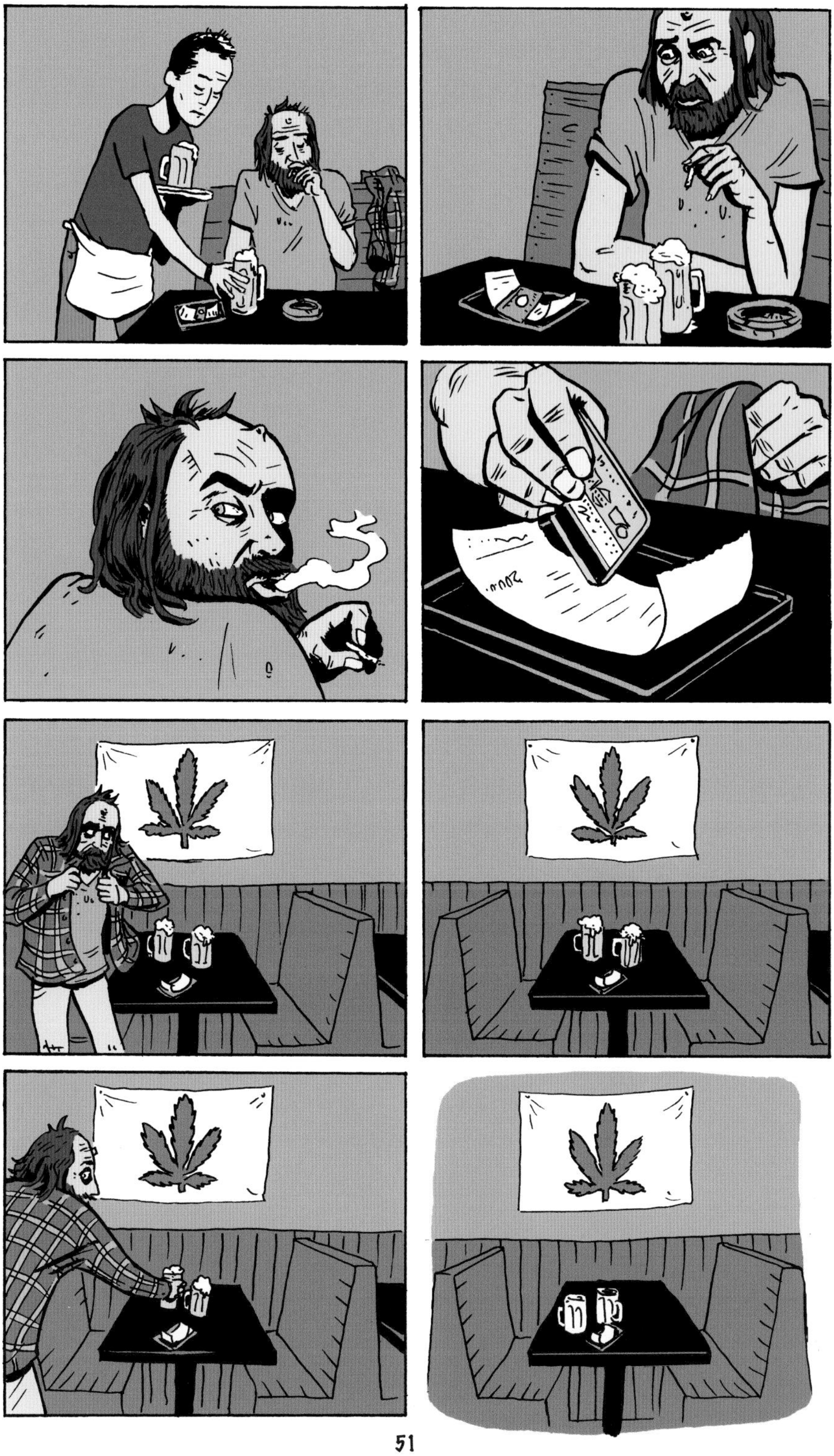

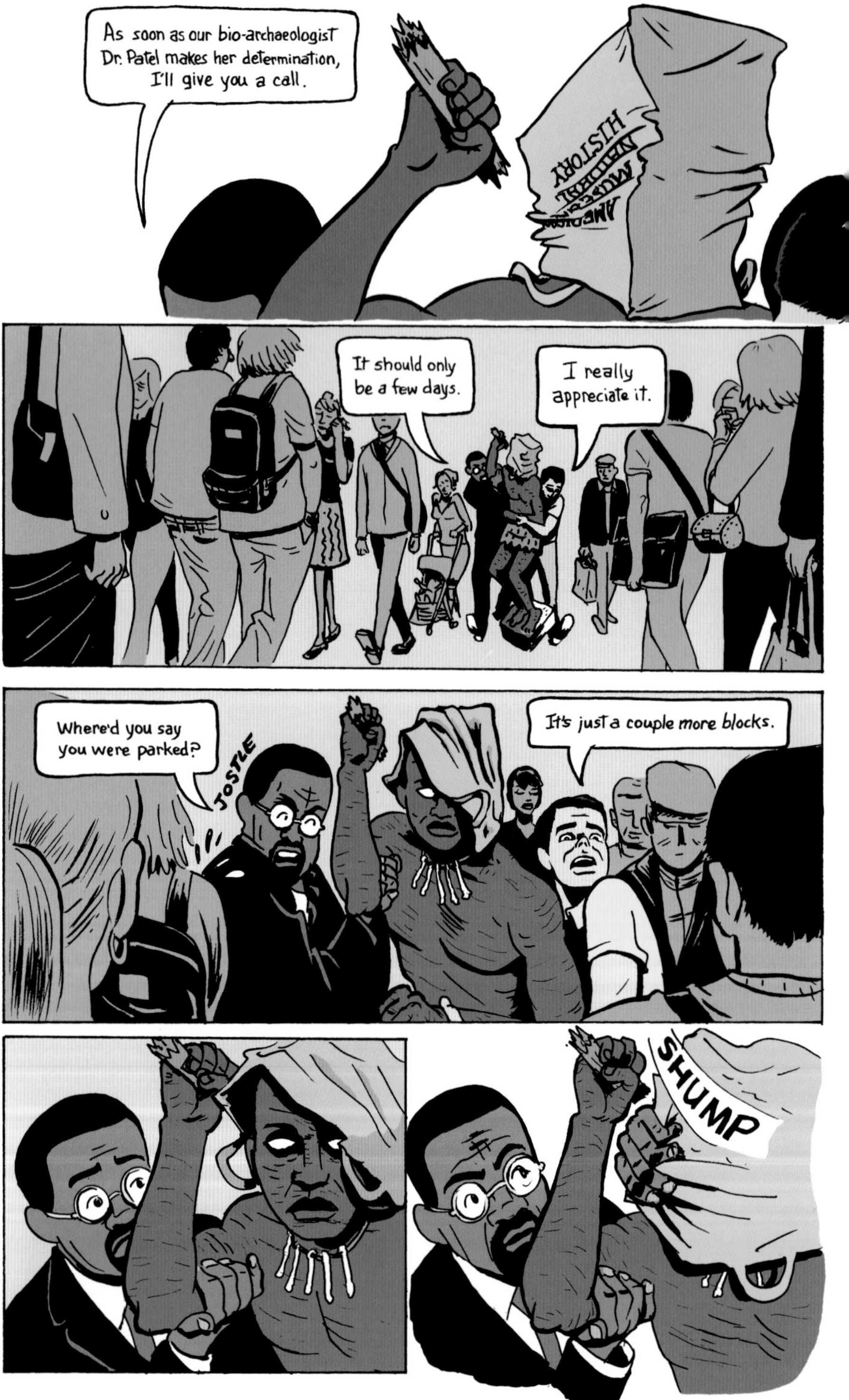
As soon as our bio-archaeologist Dr. Patel makes her determination, I'll give you a call.
AMERICAN MUSEUM NATURAL HISTORY
It should only be a few days.
I really appreciate it.
Where'd you say you were parked?
JOSTLE
It's just a couple more blocks.
SHUMP

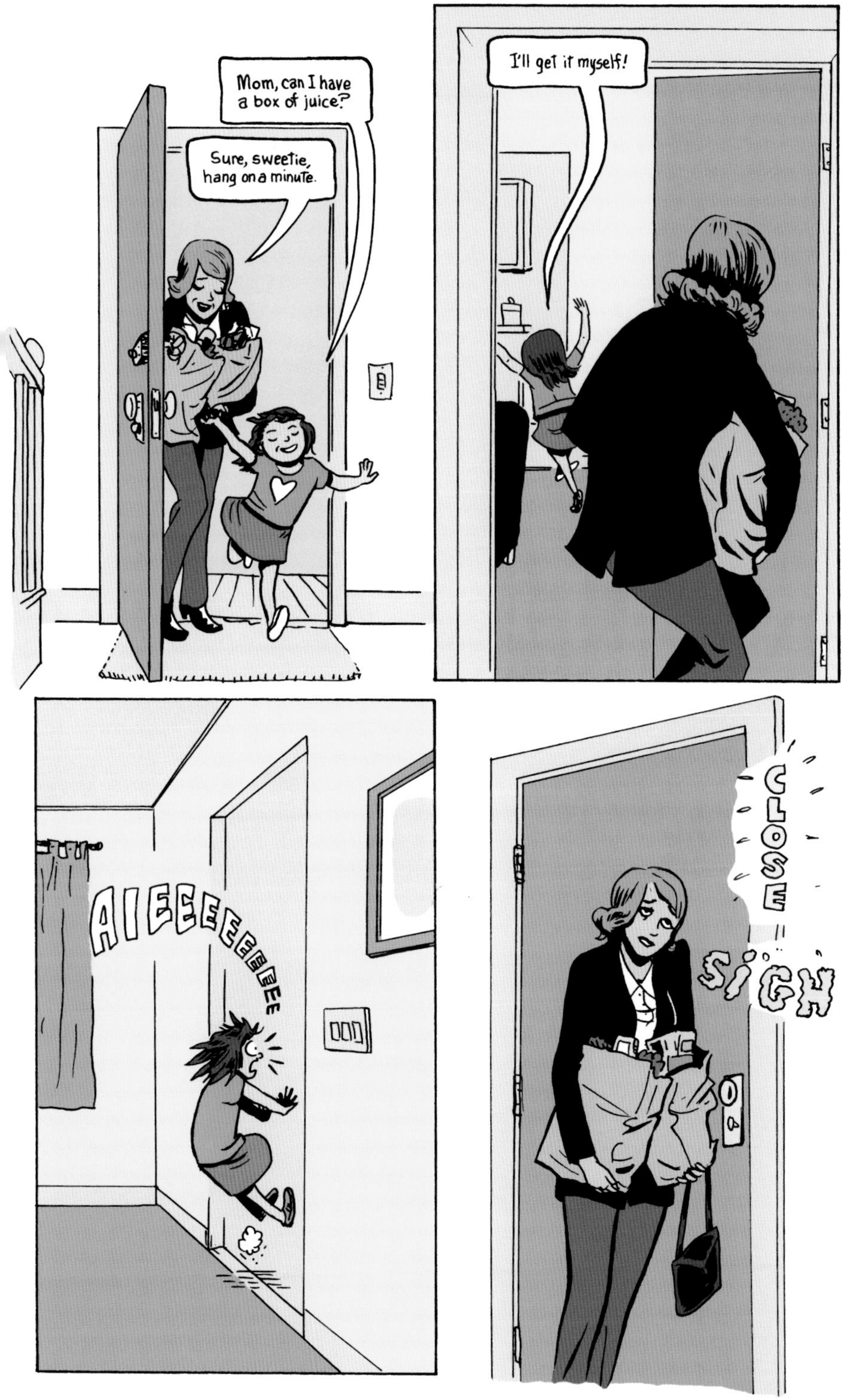
Mom, can I have a box of juice?
Sure, sweetie, hang on a minute.
I'll get it myself!
AIEEEEEEEEEE
CLOSE
SIGH

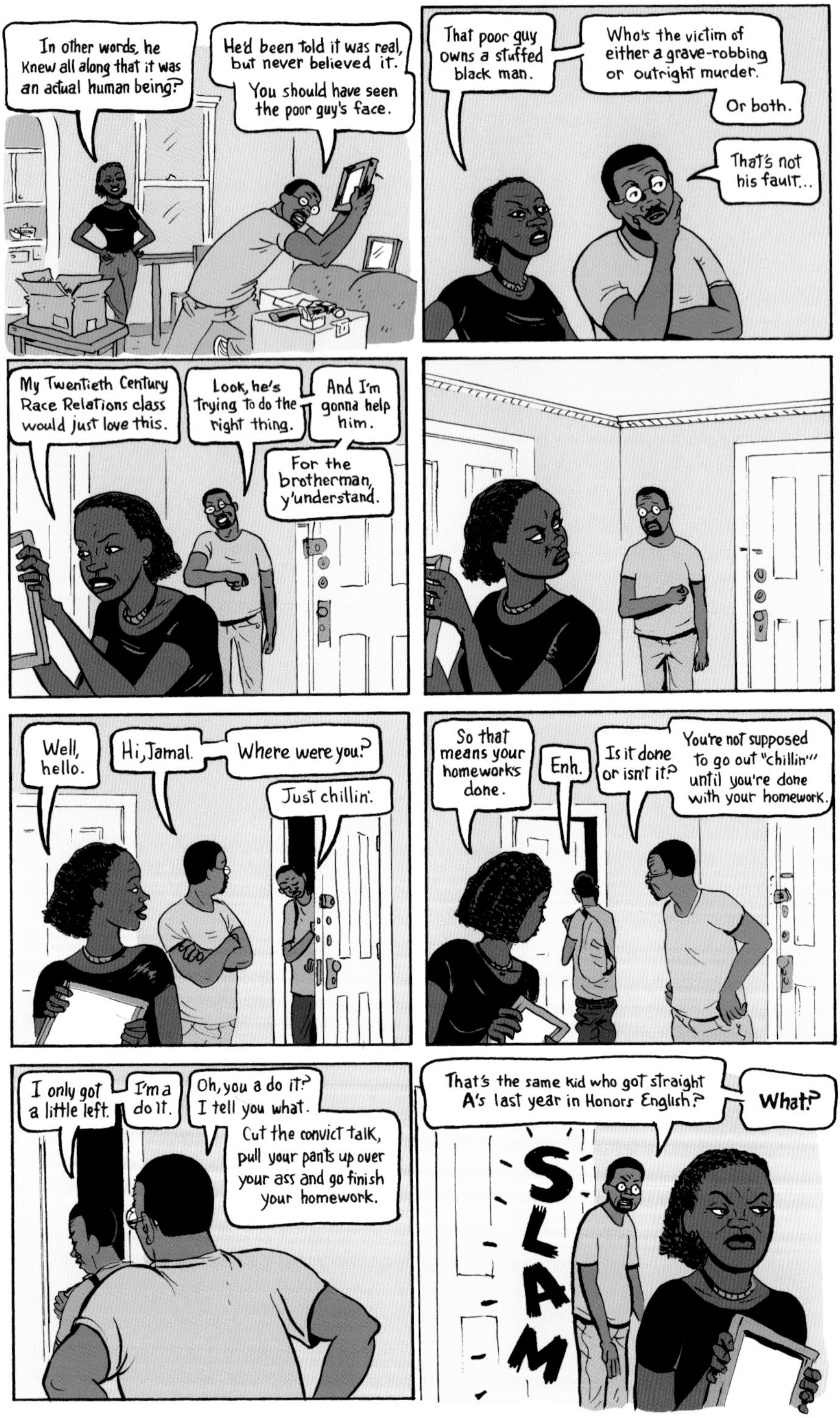

In other words, he Knew all along that it was an actual human being?
He'd been told it was real, but never believed it.
You should have seen the poor guy's face.
That poor guy owns a stuffed black man.
Who's the victim of either a grave-robbing or outright murder.
Or both.
That's not his fault...
My Twentieth Century Race Relations class would just love this.
Look, he's trying to do the right thing.
And I'm gonna help him.
For the brotherman, y'understand.
Well, hello.
Hi, Jamal.
Where were you?
Just chillin'.
So that means your homework's done.
Enh.
Is it done or isn't it?
You're not supposed to go out "chillin'" until you're done with your homework.
I only got a little left.
I'm a do it.
Oh, you a do it? I tell you what.
Cut the convict talk, pull your pants up over your ass and go finish your homework.
That's the same kid who got straight A's last year in Honors English?
What?
SLAM

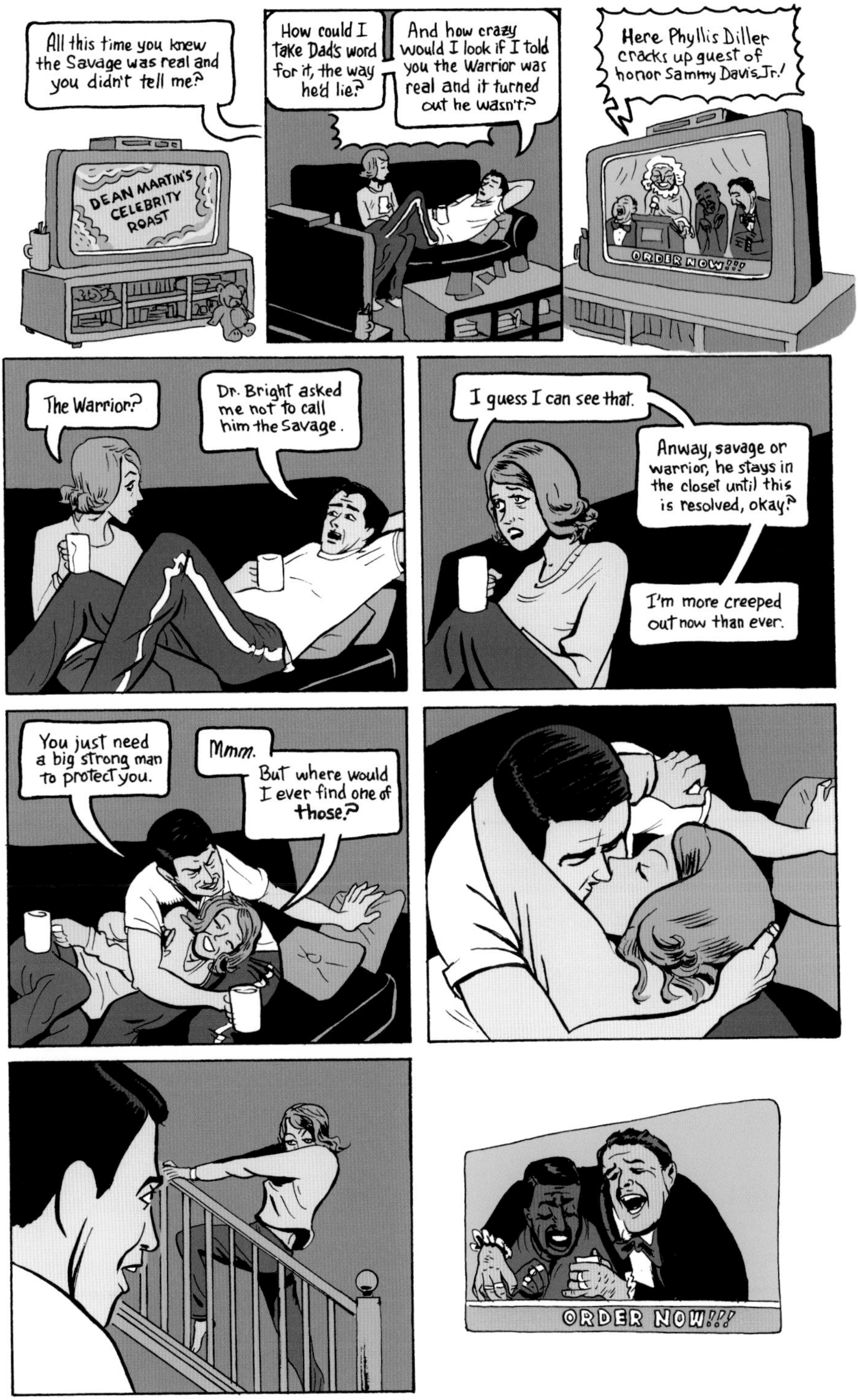
All this time you knew the Savage was real and you didn't tell me?
DEAN MARTIN'S CELEBRITY ROAST
How could I take Dad's word for it, the way he'd lie?
And how crazy would I look if I told you the Warrior was real and it turned out he wasn't?
Here Phyllis Diller cracks up guest of honor Sammy Davis Jr.!
ORDER NOW!!!
The Warrior?
Dr. Bright asked me not to call him the Savage.
I guess I can see that.
Anway, savage or warrior, he stays in the closet until this is resolved, okay?
I'm more creeped out now than ever.
You just need a big strong man to protect you.
Mmm.
But where would I ever find one of those?
ORDER NOW!!!

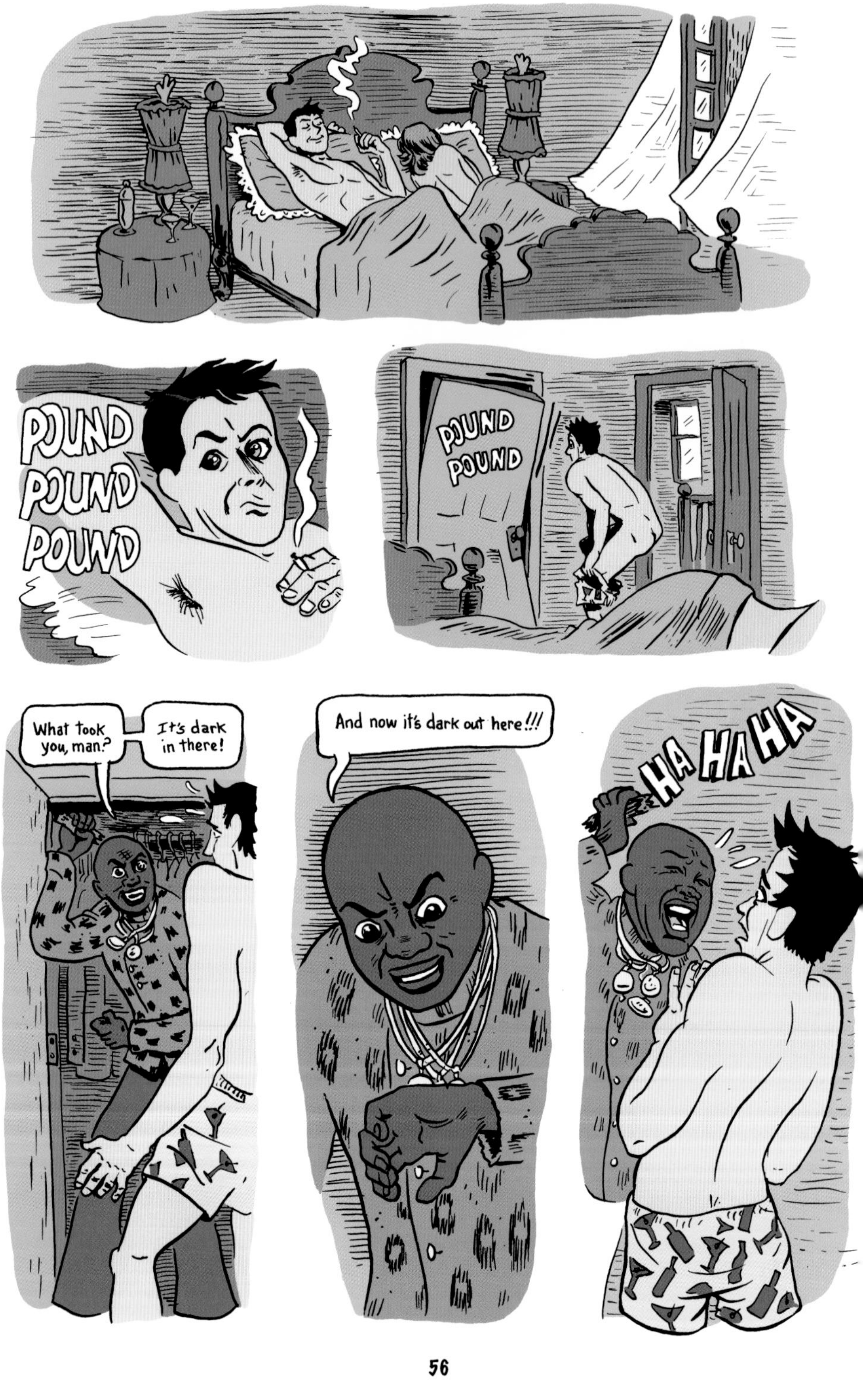
POUND
POUND
POUND
POUND
POUND
POUND
POUND
What took you, man?
It's dark in there!
And now it's dark out here!!!
HA HA HA HA

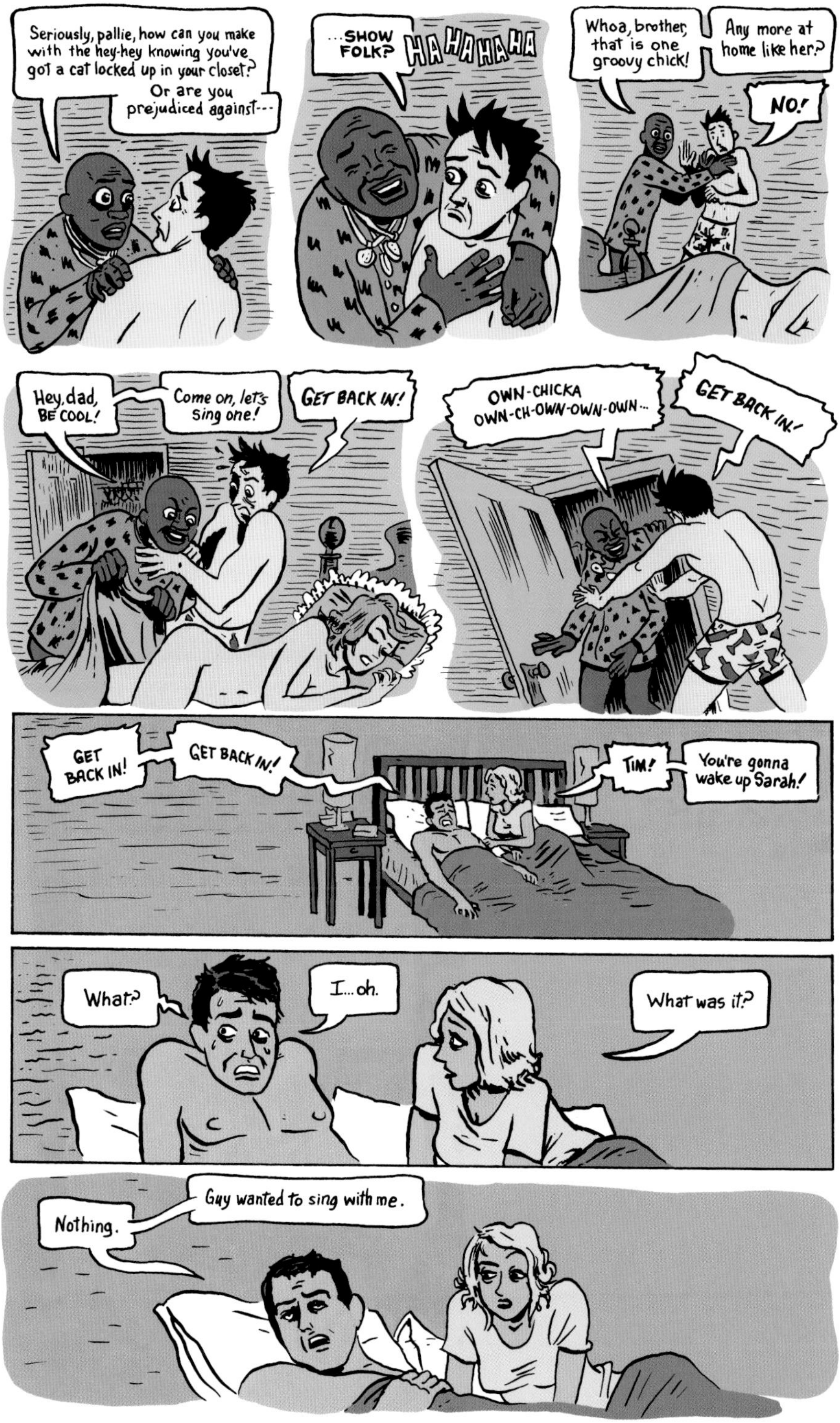
Seriously, pallie, how can you make with the hey-hey knowing you've got a cat locked up in your closet?
Or are you prejudiced against---
...SHOW FOLK?
HAHAHAHA
Whoa, brother, that is one groovy chick!
Any more at home like her?
NO!
Hey, dad, BE COOL!
Come on, let's sing one!
GET BACK IN!
OWN-CHICKA OWN-CH-OWN-OWN-OWN...
GET BACK IN!
GET BACK IN!
GET BACK IN!
TIM!
You're gonna wake up Sarah!
What?
I...oh.
What was it?
Nothing.
Guy wanted to sing with me.

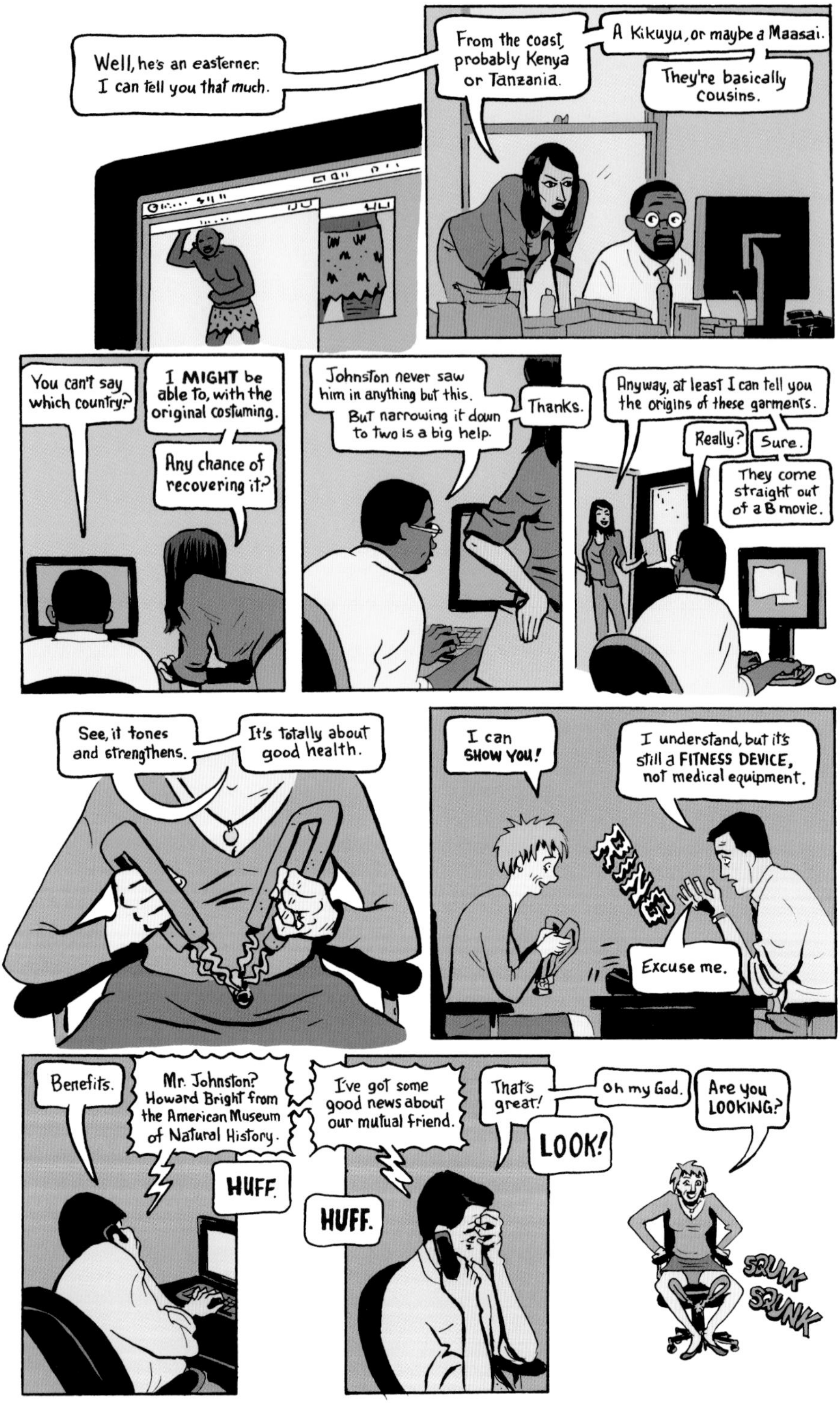
Well, he's an easterner. I can tell you that much.
From the coast, probably Kenya or Tanzania.
A Kikuyu, or maybe a Maasai.
They're basically cousins.
You can't say which country?
I MIGHT be able to, with the original costuming.
Any chance of recovering it?
Johnston never saw him in anything but this.
But narrowing it down to two is a big help.
Thanks.
Anyway, at least I can tell you the origins of these garments.
Really?
Sure.
They come straight out of a B movie.
See, it tones and strengthens.
It's totally about good health.
I can SHOW YOU!
I understand, but it's still a FITNESS DEVICE, not medical equipment.
Excuse me.
Benefits.
Mr. Johnston? Howard Bright from the American Museum of Natural History.
HUFF.
I've got some good news about our mutual friend.
HUFF.
That's great!
Oh my God.
LOOK!
Are you LOOKING?
SQUNK
SQUNK

I'm confused.

If they don't know which country the Warrior's from, how can they send him back?

They can't... yet.

"But they invited both countries to take a look, which proves they intend to."

"So once I sign him over, they can store him at the museum while they're sorting the whole thing out."

Well. I'm glad.

We're not doing the Warrior any favors keeping him here.

POUND POUND POUND

Now who's that?

Why don't they use the doorbell?

Couldn't be.

POUND POUND POUND

POUND POUND POUND POUND

POU

TIMMY!

IT'S ME!

IT'S ME!

Ollie? I mean Red Wolf?

FREE!

Jasmine thought you were in Costa Rica.

I was for a while. Then Tibet.

But you know, no disrepect to the Costa Ricans, or the Tibettos, but I'm all about self-discovery.

Come on, Sarah, let's go see if Sesame Street is on.

At NIGHT?

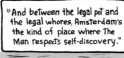

"And between the legal pot and the legal whores, Amsterdam's the kind of place where The Man respects self-discovery."

Anyway, I came as quick as I could.

I'm sure you want to get Dad buried and everything

Um, Ollie.

Free, I mean.

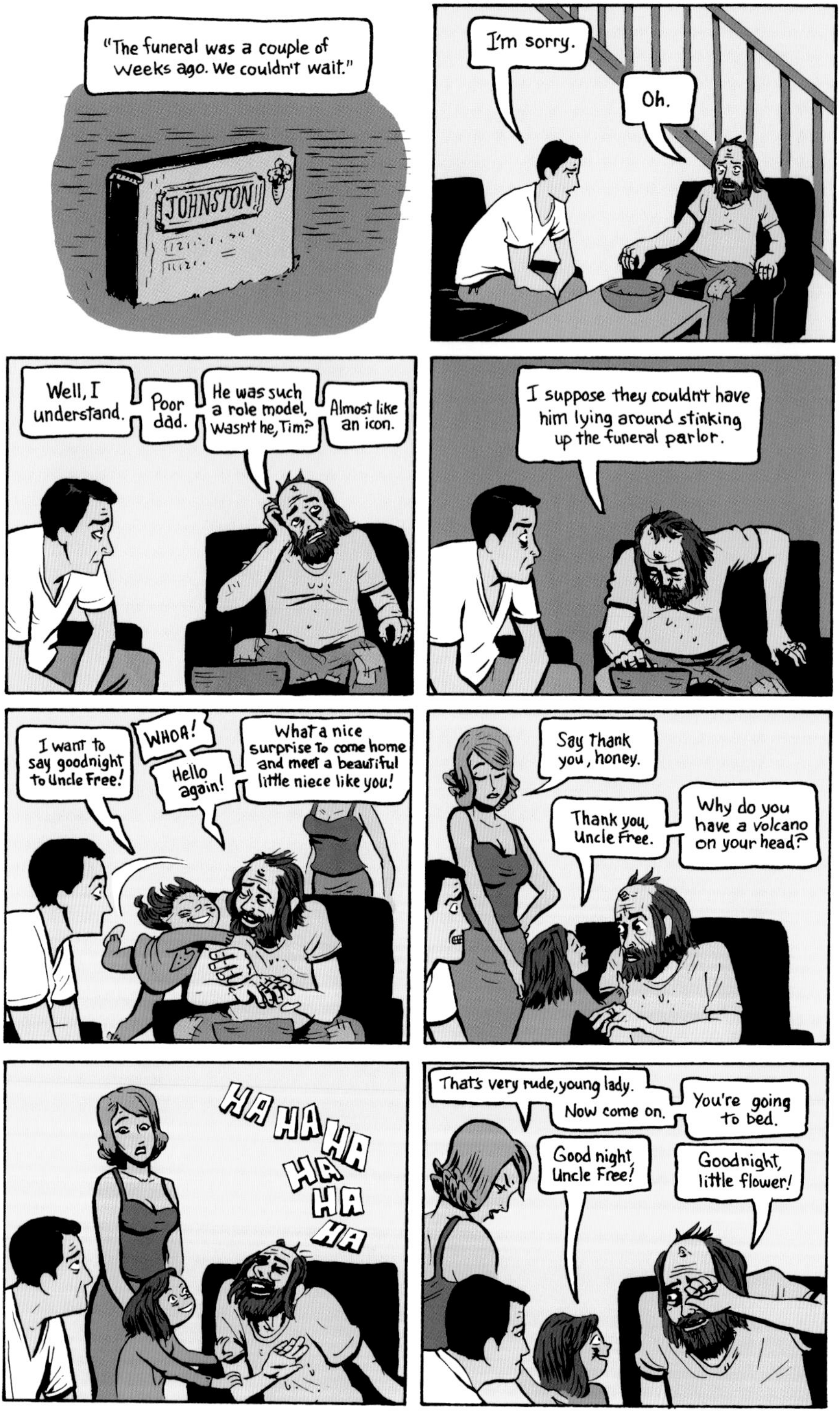
"The funeral was a couple of weeks ago. We couldn't wait."
JOHNSTON
I'm sorry.
Oh.
Well, I understand.
Poor dad.
He was such a role model, wasn't he, Tim?
Almost like an icon.
I suppose they couldn't have him lying around stinking up the funeral parlor.
I want to say goodnight to Uncle Free!
WHOA!
Hello again!
What a nice surprise to come home and meet a beautiful little niece like you!
Say thank you, honey.
Thank you, Uncle Free.
Why do you have a volcano on your head?
HA HA HA HA HA HA HA
That's very rude, young lady.
Now come on.
You're going to bed.
Good night, Uncle Free!
Goodnight, little flower!

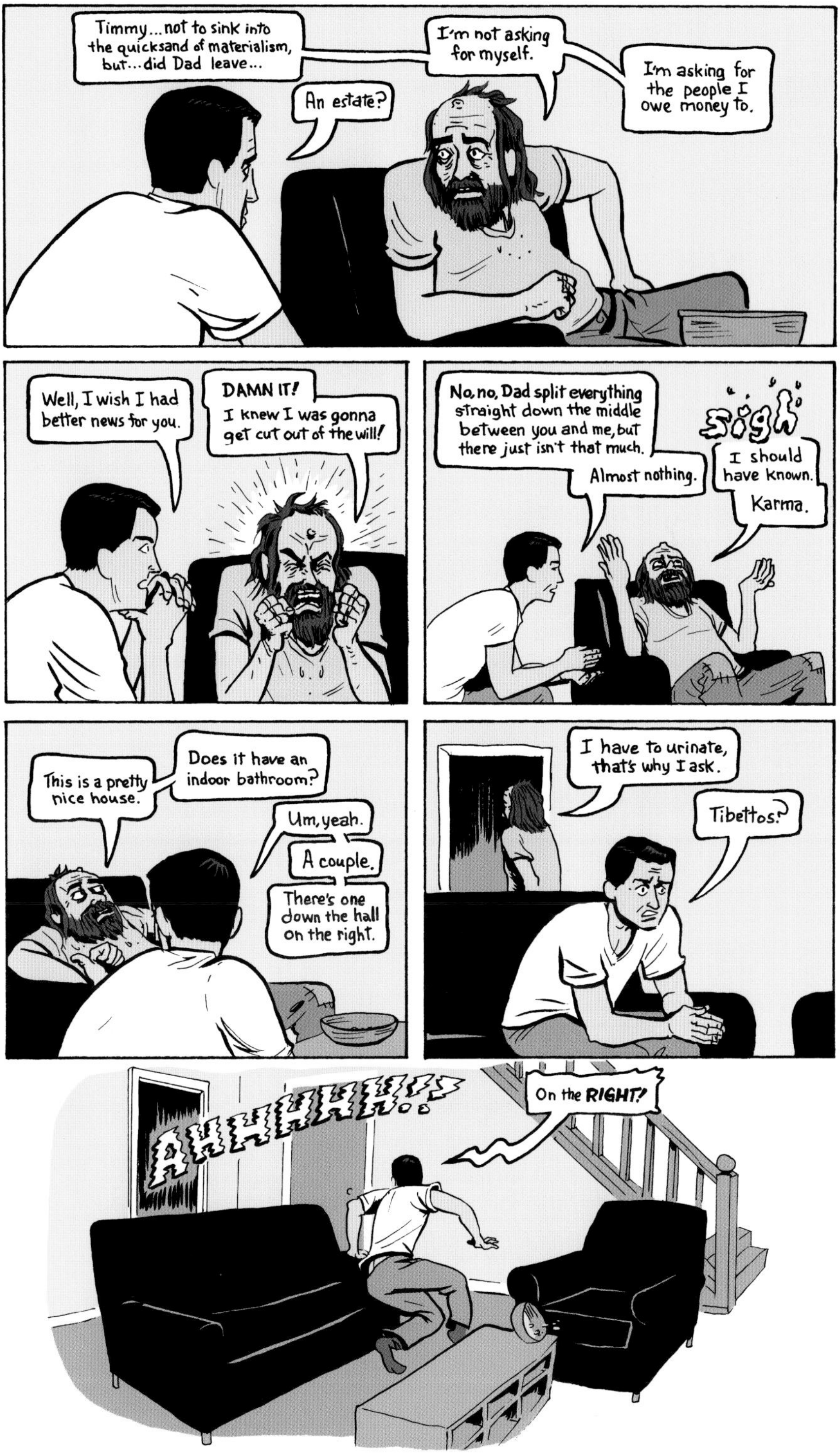
Timmy...not to sink into the quicksand of materialism, but...did Dad leave...
I'm not asking for myself.
I'm asking for the people I owe money to.
An estate?
Well, I wish I had better news for you.
DAMN IT!
I knew I was gonna get cut out of the will!
No, no, Dad split everything straight down the middle between you and me, but there just isn't that much.
Almost nothing.
sigh
I should have known.
Karma.
This is a pretty nice house.
Does it have an indoor bathroom?
Um, yeah.
A couple.
There's one down the hall on the right.
I have to urinate, that's why I ask.
Tibettos?
AHHHHH!!
On the RIGHT!

I should have told you he was in the closet.

I'm sorry, Ollie.

I mean Free. What happened to Red Wolf, anyway?

EAT NOW DINER

The world's sped up, Timmy.

Free's faster.

You have to understand.

I've honed my consciousness to a razor's edge.

The tiniest stimulus can send me into heightened recall.

SQURK

Heightened recall?

What's the layman's term... flashbacks.

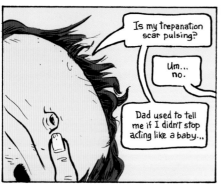

Is my trepanation scar pulsing?

Um... no.

Dad used to tell me if I didn't stop acting like a baby...

"...the Savage would tie me to a stake and slit me open so his pet tigers could feast on my intestines."

Ugh.

I got off easy.

Dad was a real sadistic bastard, you know that?

But before you said...

He damn near drove my mom insane.

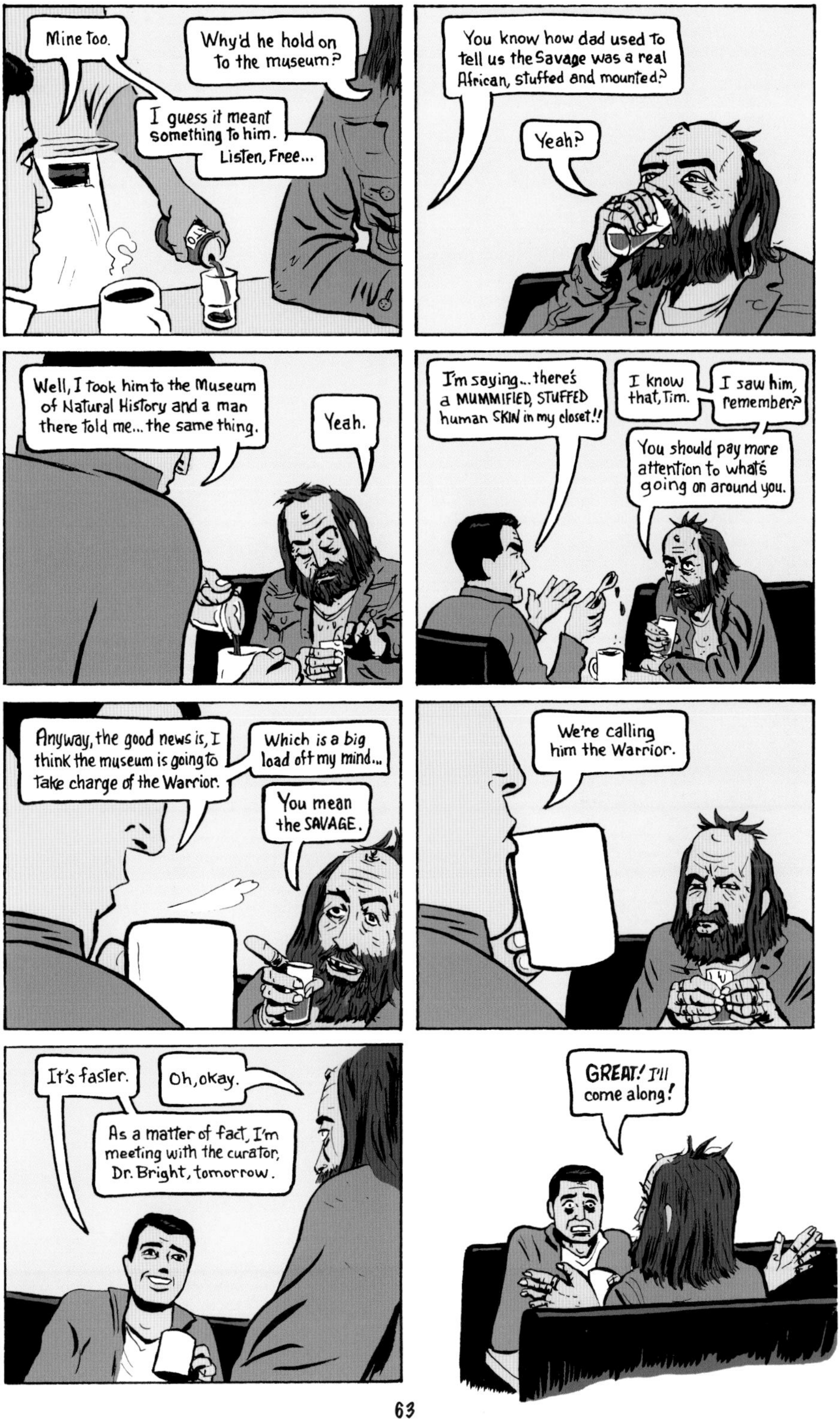
Mine too.
Why'd he hold on to the museum?
I guess it meant something to him.
Listen, Free...
You know how dad used to tell us the Savage was a real African, stuffed and mounted?
Yeah?
Well, I took him to the Museum of Natural History and a man there told me... the same thing.
Yeah.
I'm saying... there's a MUMMIFIED, STUFFED human SKIN in my closet!!
I know that, Tim.
I saw him, remember?
You should pay more attention to what's going on around you.
Anyway, the good news is, I think the museum is going to take charge of the Warrior.
Which is a big load off my mind...
You mean the SAVAGE.
We're calling him the Warrior.
It's faster.
Oh, okay.
As a matter of fact, I'm meeting with the curator, Dr. Bright, tomorrow.
GREAT! I'll come along!

Your presence today is an unexpected plus, Mr. Johnston.

It will expedite things nicely.

It usually does.

I'm a problem solver.

And call me Free.

Now as you know, the AMNH has begun the repatriation process by entering into correspondence with likely nations of origin.

So once you have reviewed and signed these documents and waivers, we can take the item into protective custody, as it were.

Thank you so much.

Yes.

I just have one little question.

What is repenetration? Because I have to tell you, it sounds a little unhygienic.

Repatriation.

That just means returning the Warrior to his country of origin.

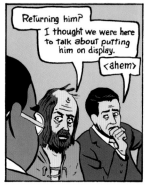

Returning him?

I thought we were here to talk about putting him on display.

<ahem>

I probably should have explained better.

They're going to send the Warrior back to Africa to be buried in his homeland.

But then no one will get to see him!

That's more or less the point, Mr...Free.

We're trying to restore the dignity taken from him when he was stuffed and sold to your father as a curio.

What about my father's dignity?

Excuse me?

"My father hated selling suits. Monday mornings the light in his eyes would just go out."

"But on weekends, when he unlocked the door to the Museum of the Rare and Curious, that was the only time I ever saw him happy."

I'm glad your father enjoyed his hobby, Mr. Johnston, but the Warrior was and IS a human being.

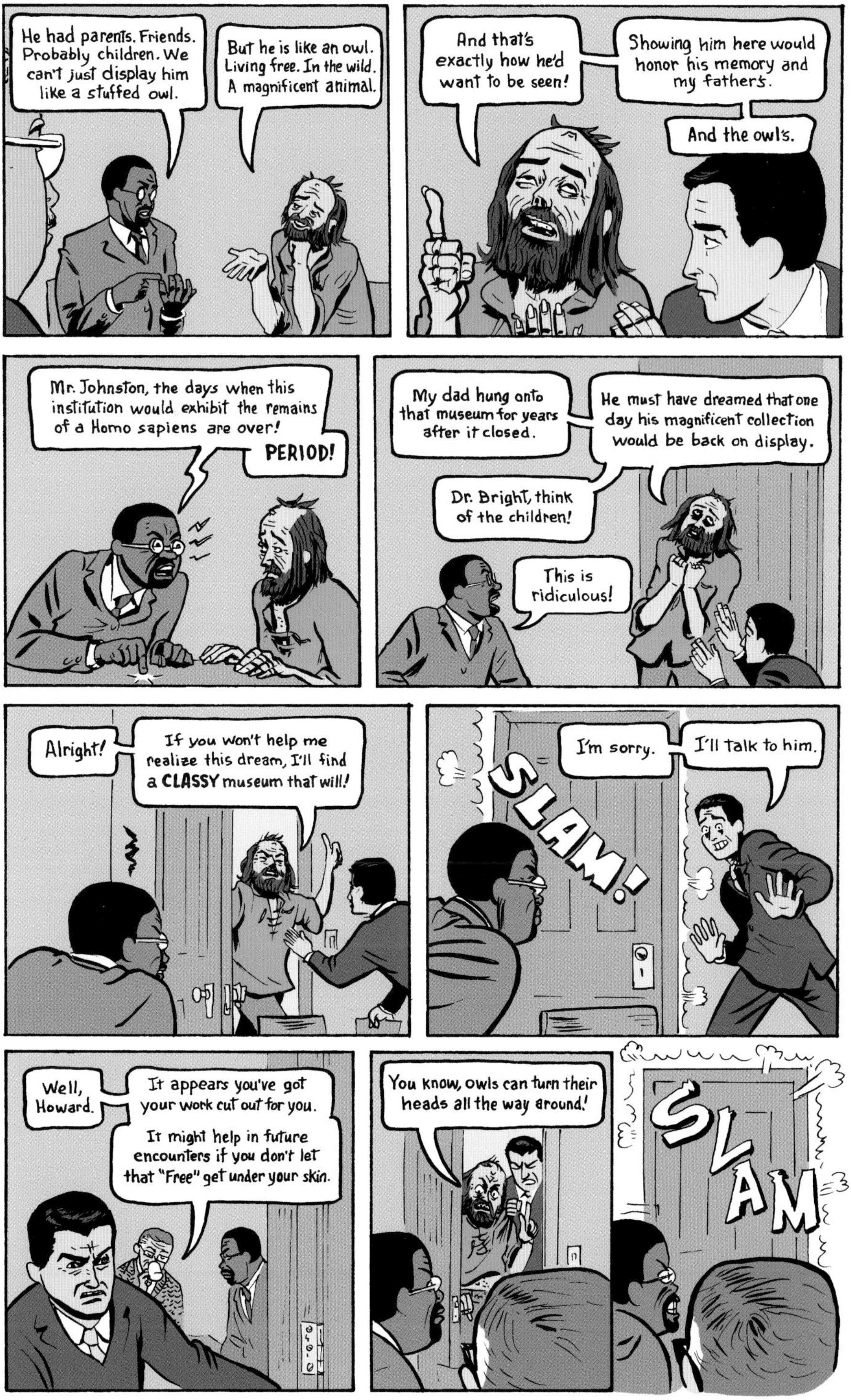
He had parents. Friends. Probably children. We can't just display him like a stuffed owl.
But he is like an owl. Living free. In the wild. A magnificent animal.
And that's exactly how he'd want to be seen!
Showing him here would honor his memory and my father's.
And the owl's.
Mr. Johnston, the days when this institution would exhibit the remains of a Homo sapiens are over!
PERIOD!
My dad hung onto that museum for years after it closed.
He must have dreamed that one day his magnificent collection would be back on display.
Dr. Bright, think of the children!
This is ridiculous!
Alright!
If you won't help me realize this dream, I'll find a CLASSY museum that will!
SLAM!
I'm sorry.
I'll talk to him.
Well, Howard.
It appears you've got your work cut out for you.
It might help in future encounters if you don't let that "Free" get under your skin.
You know, owls can turn their heads all the way around!
SLAM

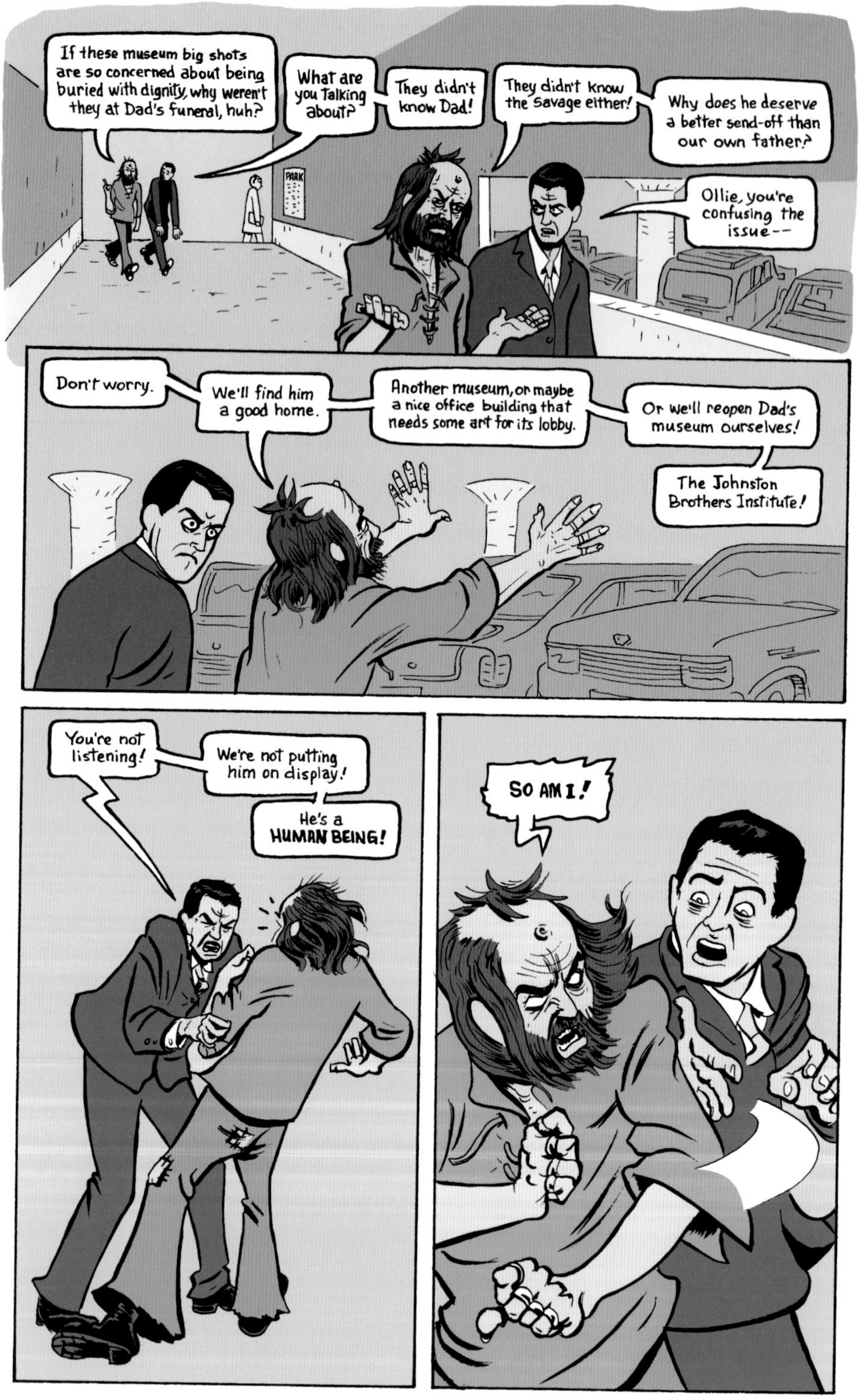
If these museum big shots are so concerned about being buried with dignity, why weren't they at Dad's funeral, huh?
What are you talking about?
They didn't know Dad!
They didn't know the savage either!
Why does he deserve a better send-off than our own father?
Ollie, you're confusing the issue--
PARK
Don't worry.
We'll find him a good home.
Another museum, or maybe a nice office building that needs some art for its lobby.
Or we'll reopen Dad's museum ourselves!
The Johnston Brothers Institute!
You're not listening!
We're not putting him on display!
He's a HUMAN BEING!
SO AM I!

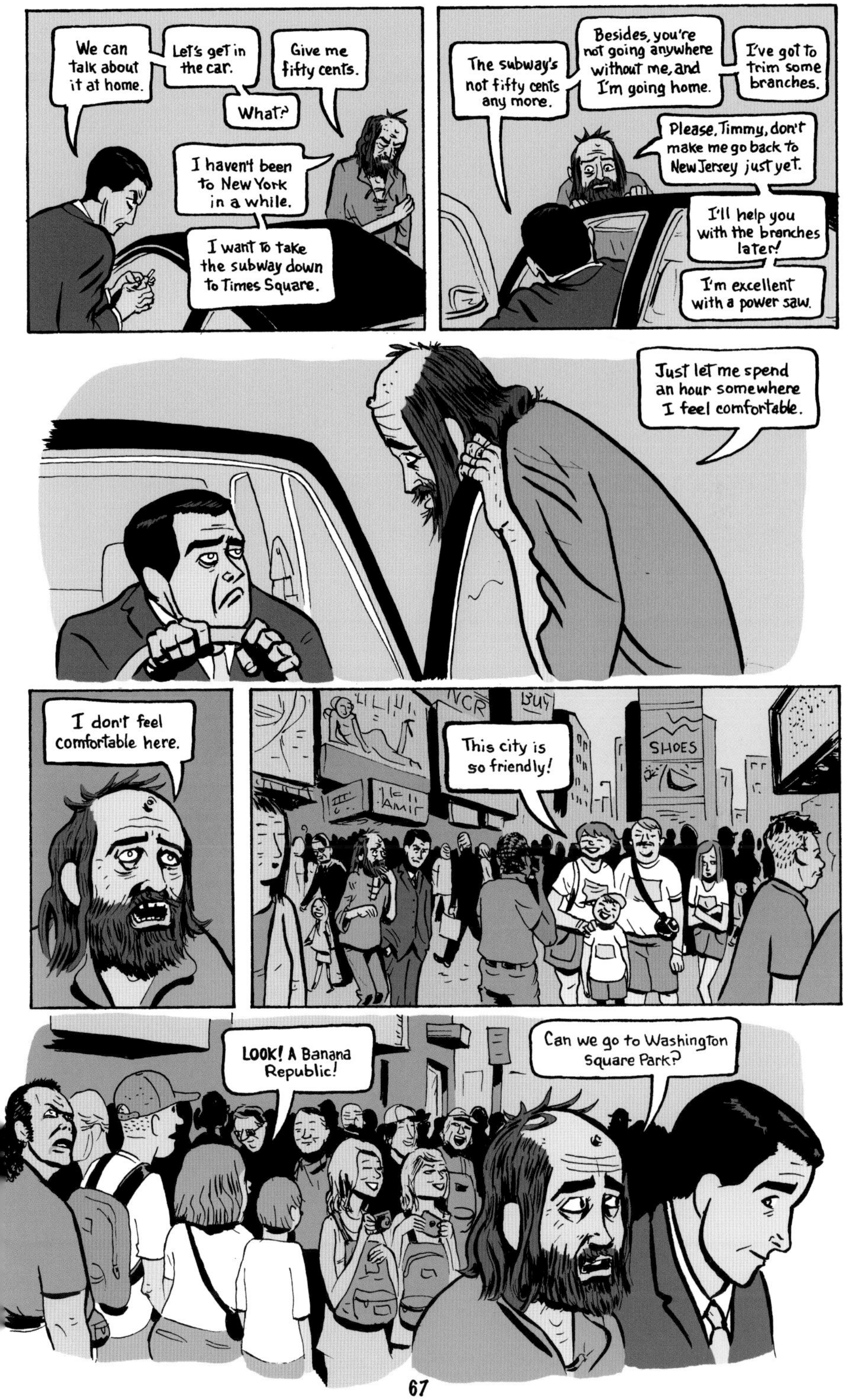
We can talk about it at home.
Let's get in the car.
Give me fifty cents.
What?
I haven't been to New York in a while.
I want to take the subway down to Times Square.
The subway's not fifty cents any more.
Besides, you're not going anywhere without me, and I'm going home.
I've got to trim some branches.
Please, Timmy, don't make me go back to New Jersey just yet.
I'll help you with the branches later!
I'm excellent with a power saw.
Just let me spend an hour somewhere I feel comfortable.
I don't feel comfortable here.
NCR
BUY
SHOES
AMIR
This city is so friendly!
LOOK! A Banana Republic!
Can we go to Washington Square Park?

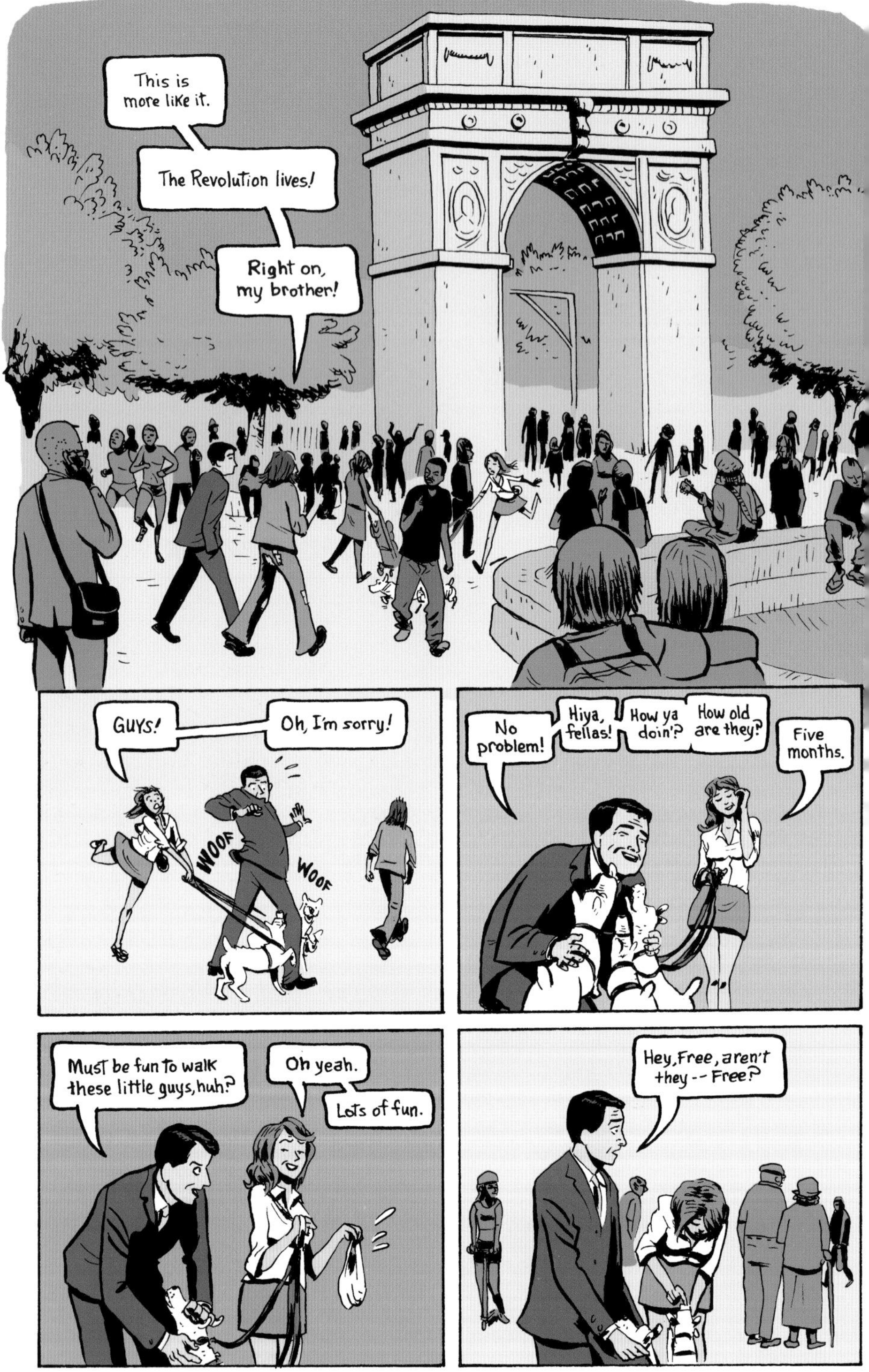
This is more like it.
The Revolution lives!
Right on, my brother!
GUYS!
Oh, I'm sorry!
WOOF
WOOF
No problem!
Hiya, fellas!
How ya doin'?
How old are they?
Five months.
Must be fun to walk these little guys, huh?
Oh yeah.
Lots of fun.
Hey, Free, aren't they -- Free?

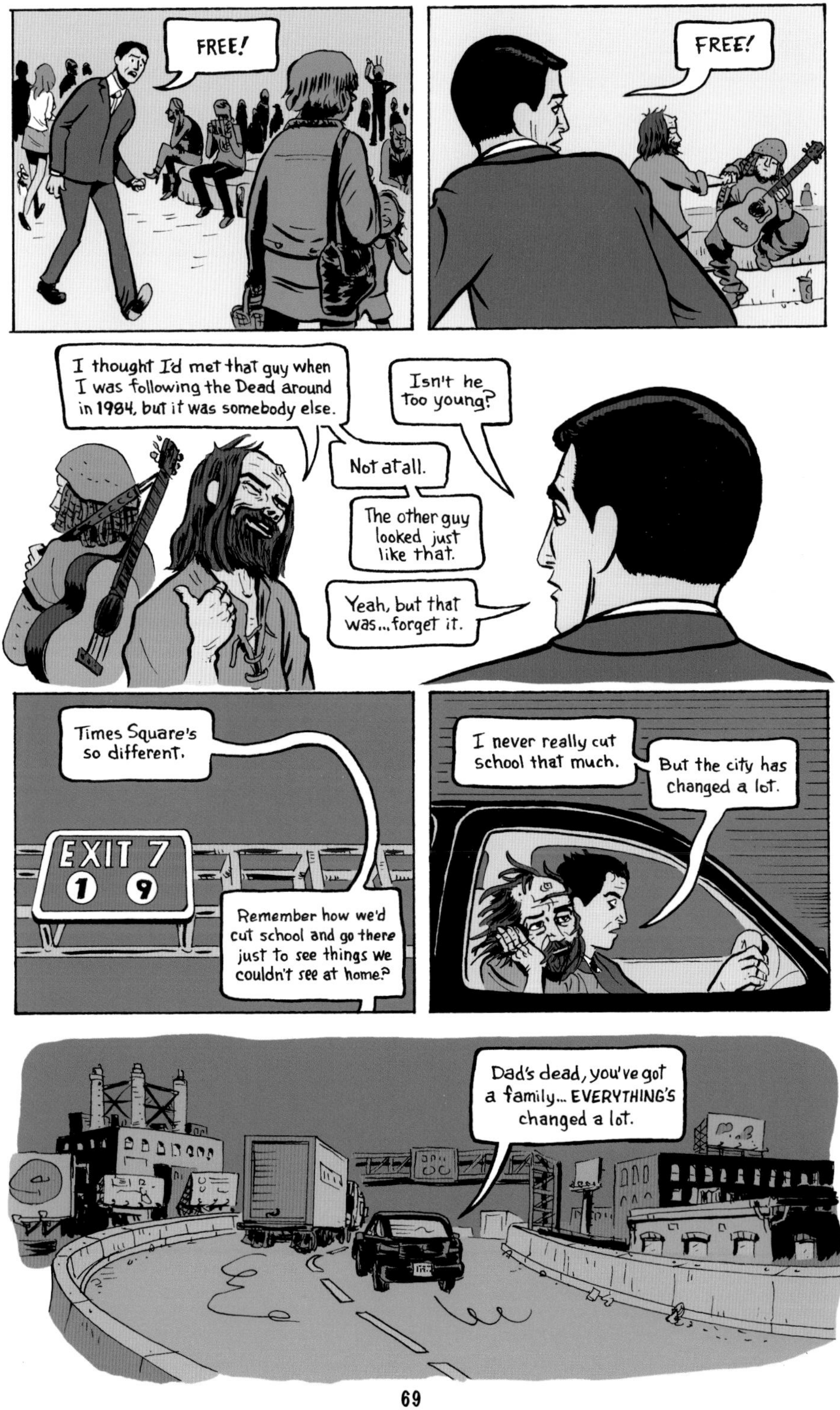
FREE!
FREE!
I thought I'd met that guy when I was following the Dead around in 1984, but it was somebody else.
Isn't he too young?
Not at all.
The other guy looked just like that.
Yeah, but that was... forget it.
Times Square's so different.
Remember how we'd cut school and go there just to see things we couldn't see at home?
EXIT 7
1 9
I never really cut school that much.
But the city has changed a lot.
Dad's dead, you've got a family... EVERYTHING'S changed a lot.

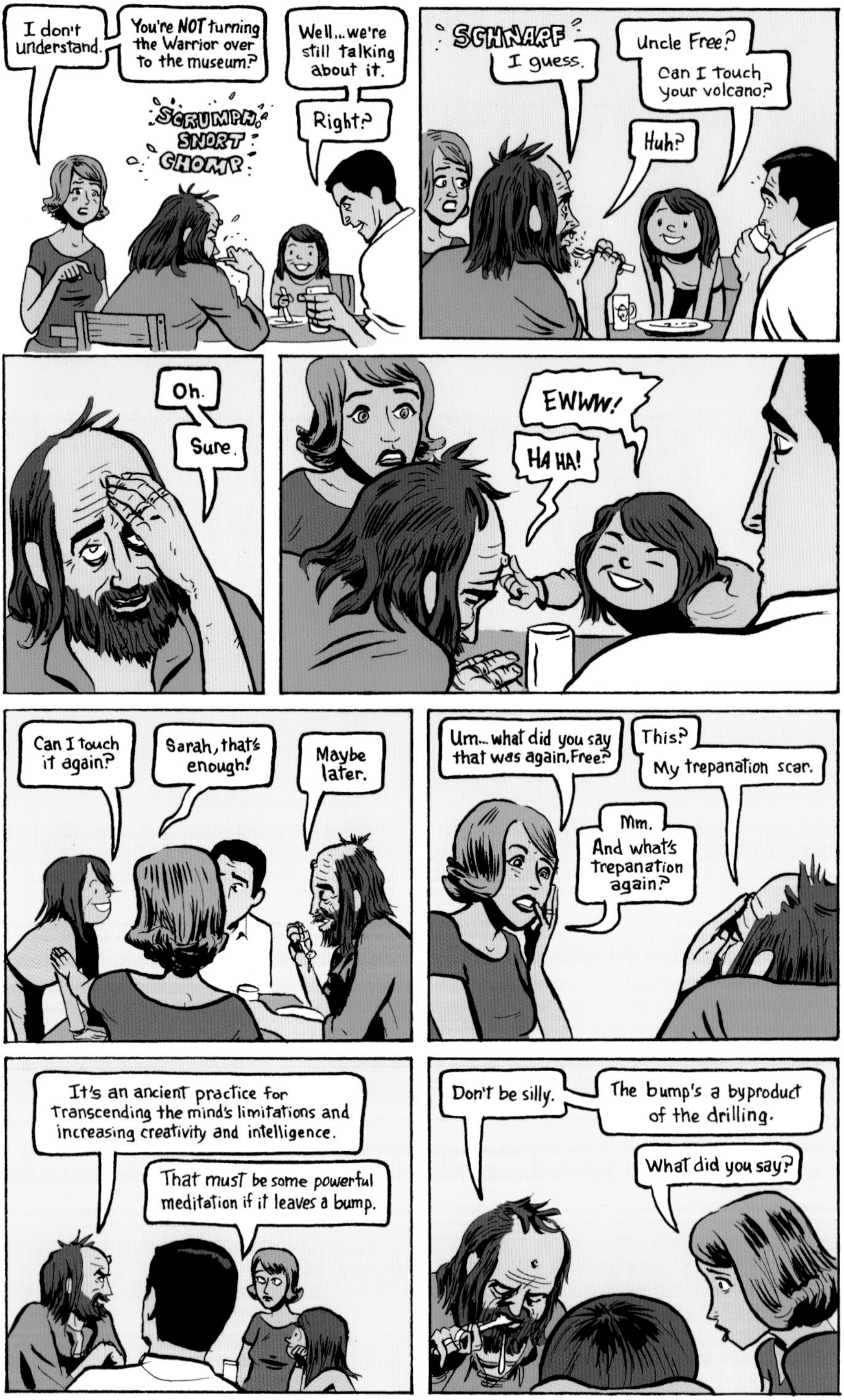
I don't understand.
You're NOT turning the Warrior over to the museum?
SCRUMPH SNORT CHOMP
Well... we're still talking about it.
Right?
SCHNARF
I guess.
Uncle Free?
Can I touch your volcano?
Huh?
Oh.
Sure.
EWWW!
HA HA!
Can I touch it again?
Sarah, that's enough!
Maybe later.
Um... what did you say that was again, Free?
This?
My trepanation scar.
Mm.
And what's trepanation again?
It's an ancient practice for transcending the mind's limitations and increasing creativity and intelligence.
That must be some powerful meditation if it leaves a bump.
Don't be silly.
The bump's a byproduct of the drilling.
What did you say?

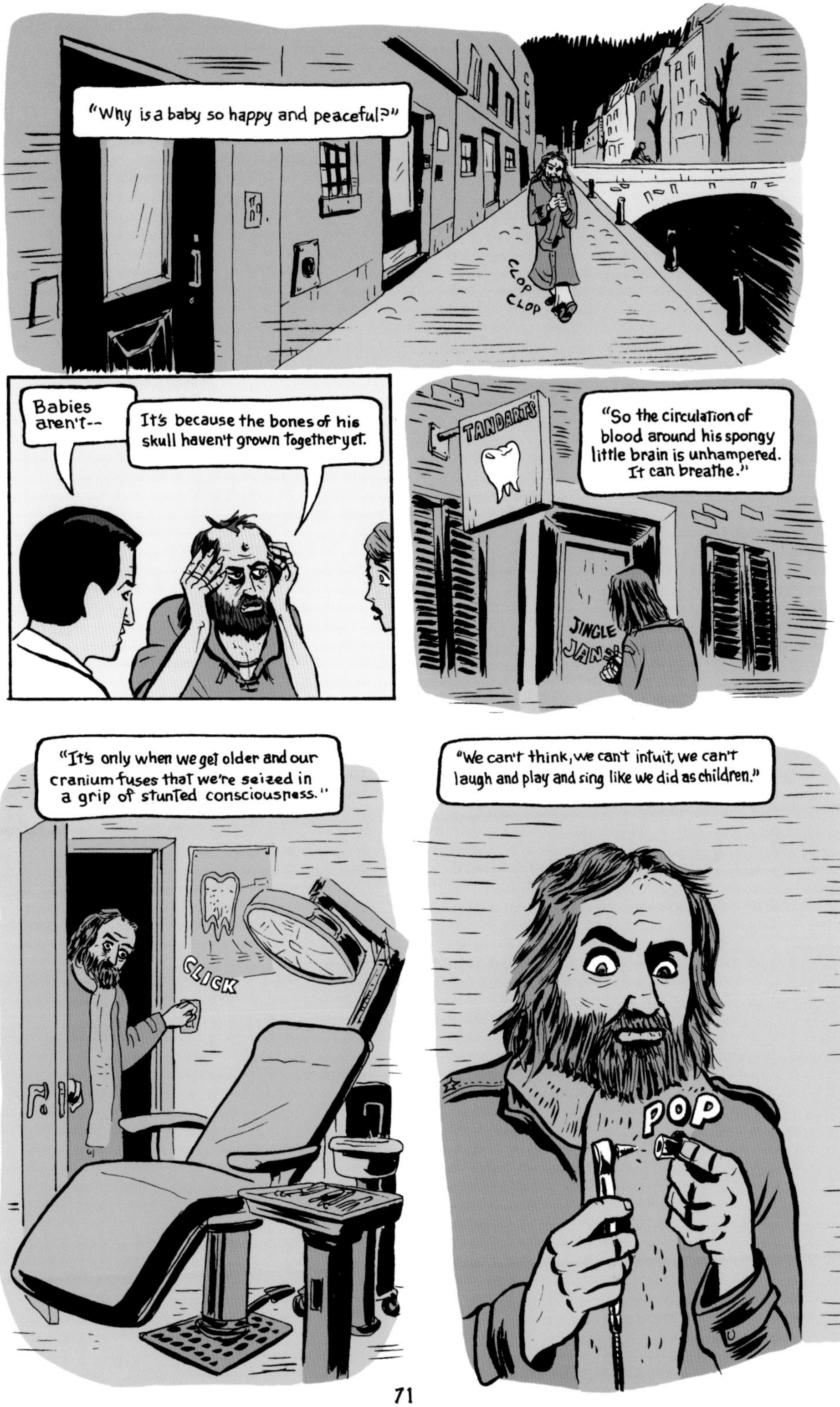
"Why is a baby so happy and peaceful?"
CLOP CLOP
Babies aren't--
It's because the bones of his skull haven't grown together yet.
TANDARTS
"So the circulation of blood around his spongy little brain is unhampered. It can breathe."
JINGLE JAN
"It's only when we get older and our cranium fuses that we're seized in a grip of stunted consciousness."
CLICK
"We can't think, we can't intuit, we can't laugh and play and sing like we did as children."
POP

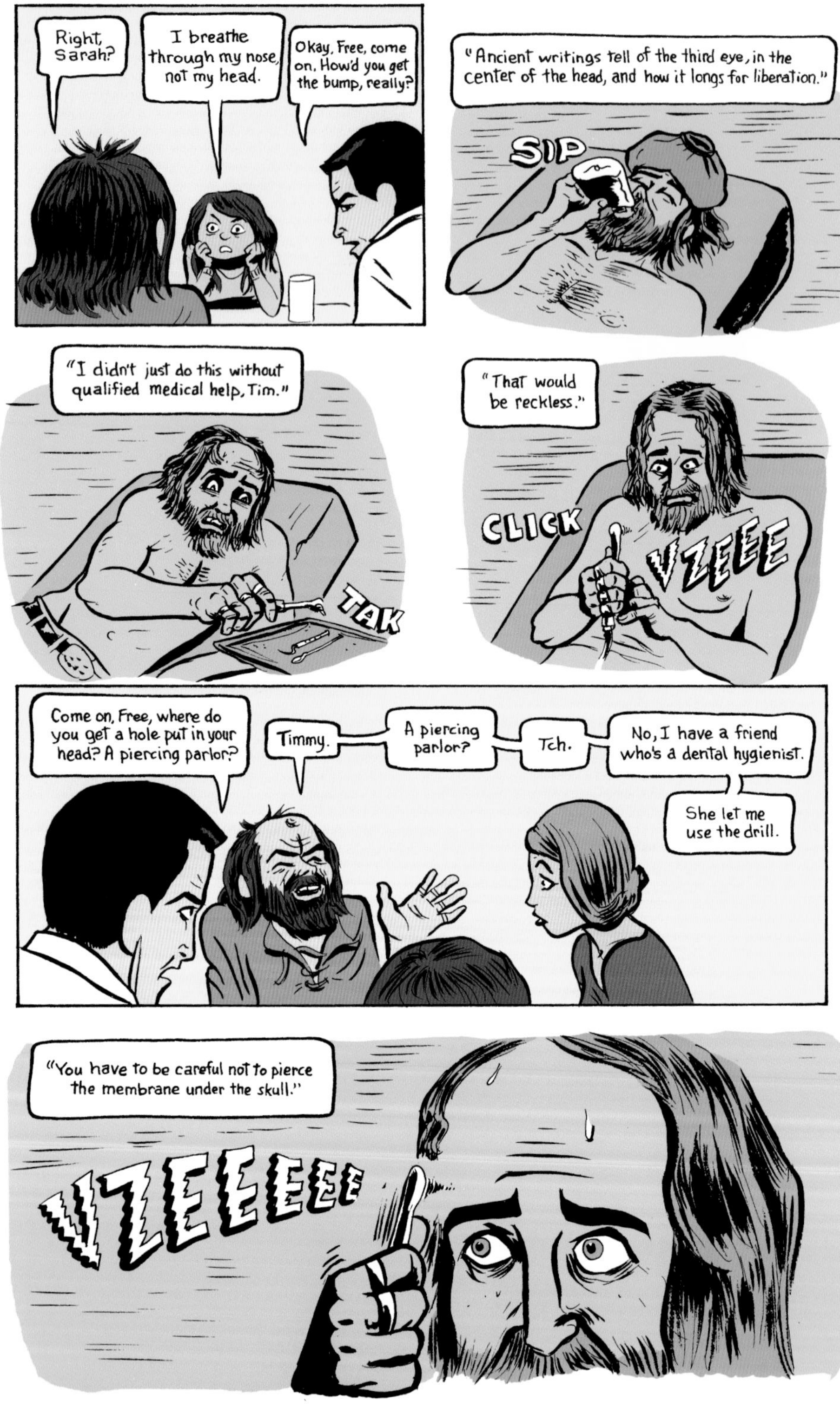
Right, Sarah?
I breathe through my nose, not my head.
Okay, Free, come on. How'd you get the bump, really?
"Ancient writings tell of the third eye, in the center of the head, and how it longs for liberation."
SIP
"I didn't just do this without qualified medical help, Tim."
TAK
"That would be reckless."
CLICK
VZEEE
Come on, Free, where do you get a hole put in your head? A piercing parlor?
Timmy.
A piercing parlor?
Tch.
No, I have a friend who's a dental hygienist.
She let me use the drill.
"You have to be careful not to pierce the membrane under the skull."
VZEEEEEE

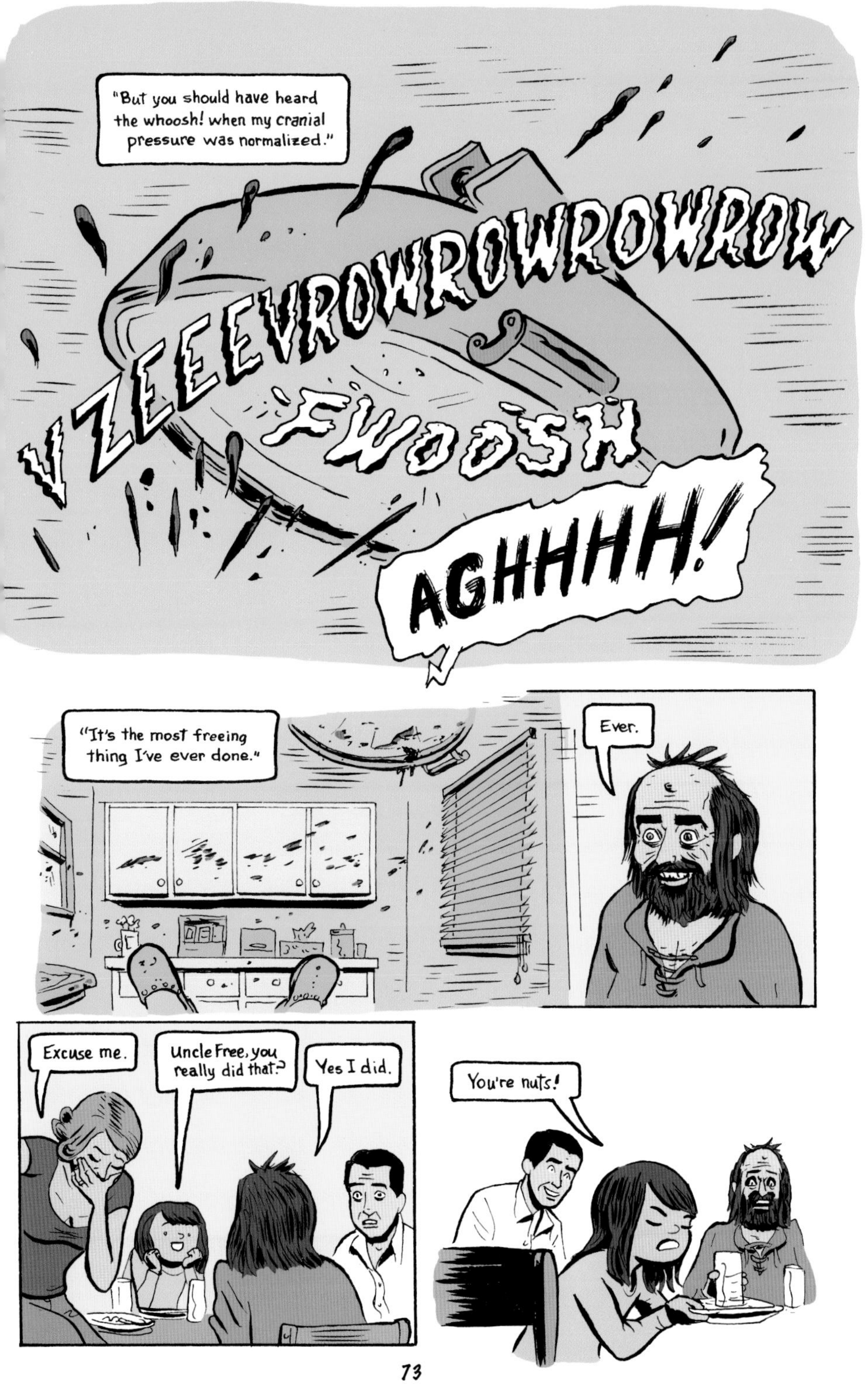
"But you should have heard the whoosh! when my cranial pressure was normalized."
VZEEEVROWROWROWROWROW
FWOOSH
AGHHHH!
"It's the most freeing thing I've ever done."
Ever.
Excuse me.
Uncle Free, you really did that?
Yes I did.
You're nuts!

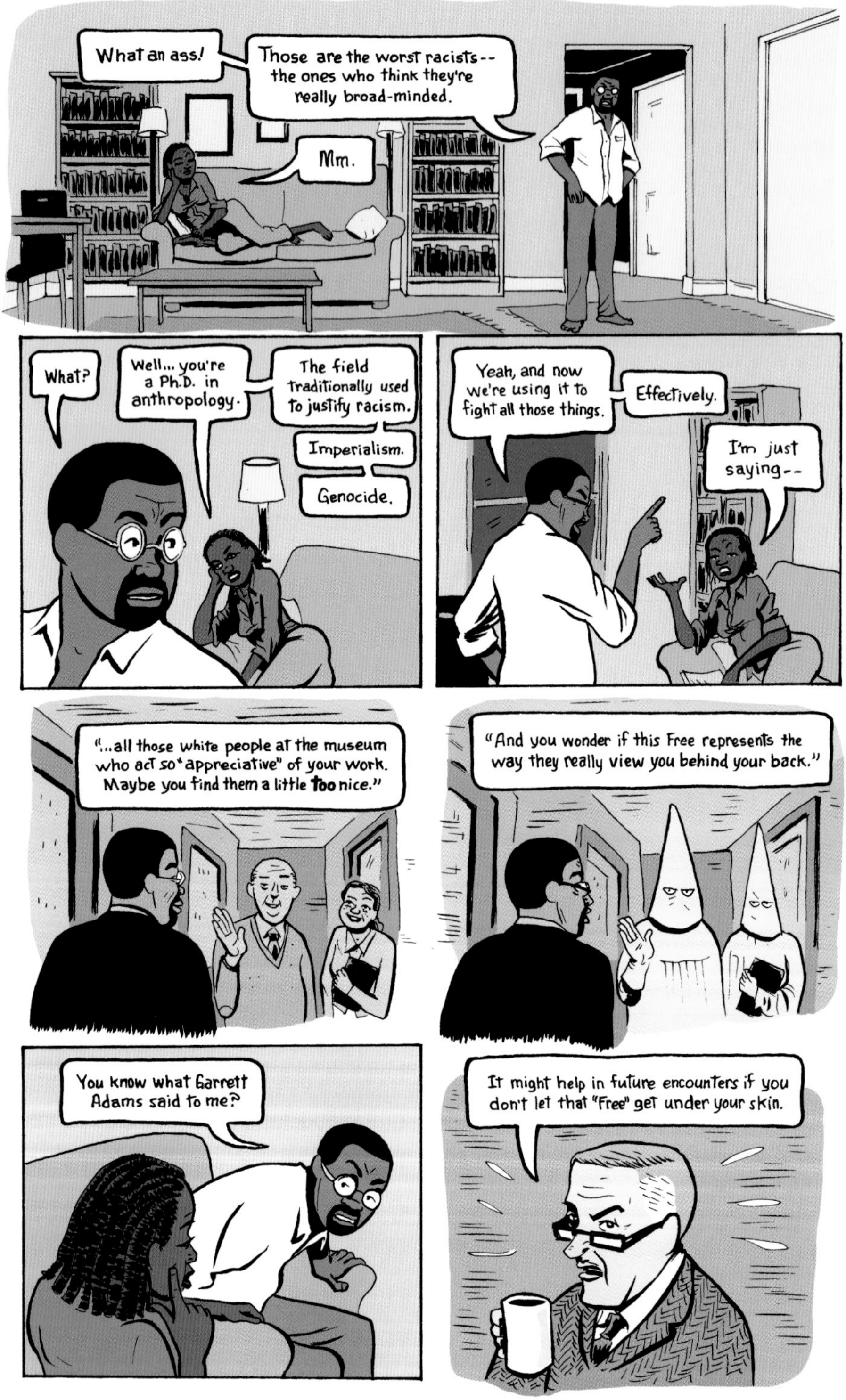
What an ass!
Those are the worst racists-- the ones who think they're really broad-minded.
Mm.
What?
Well... you're a Ph.D. in anthropology.
The field traditionally used to justify racism.
Imperialism.
Genocide.
Yeah, and now we're using it to fight all those things.
Effectively.
I'm just saying--
"...all those white people at the museum who act so "appreciative" of your work. Maybe you find them a little **too** nice."
"And you wonder if this Free represents the way they really view you behind your back."
You know what Garrett Adams said to me?
It might help in future encounters if you don't let that "Free" get under your skin.

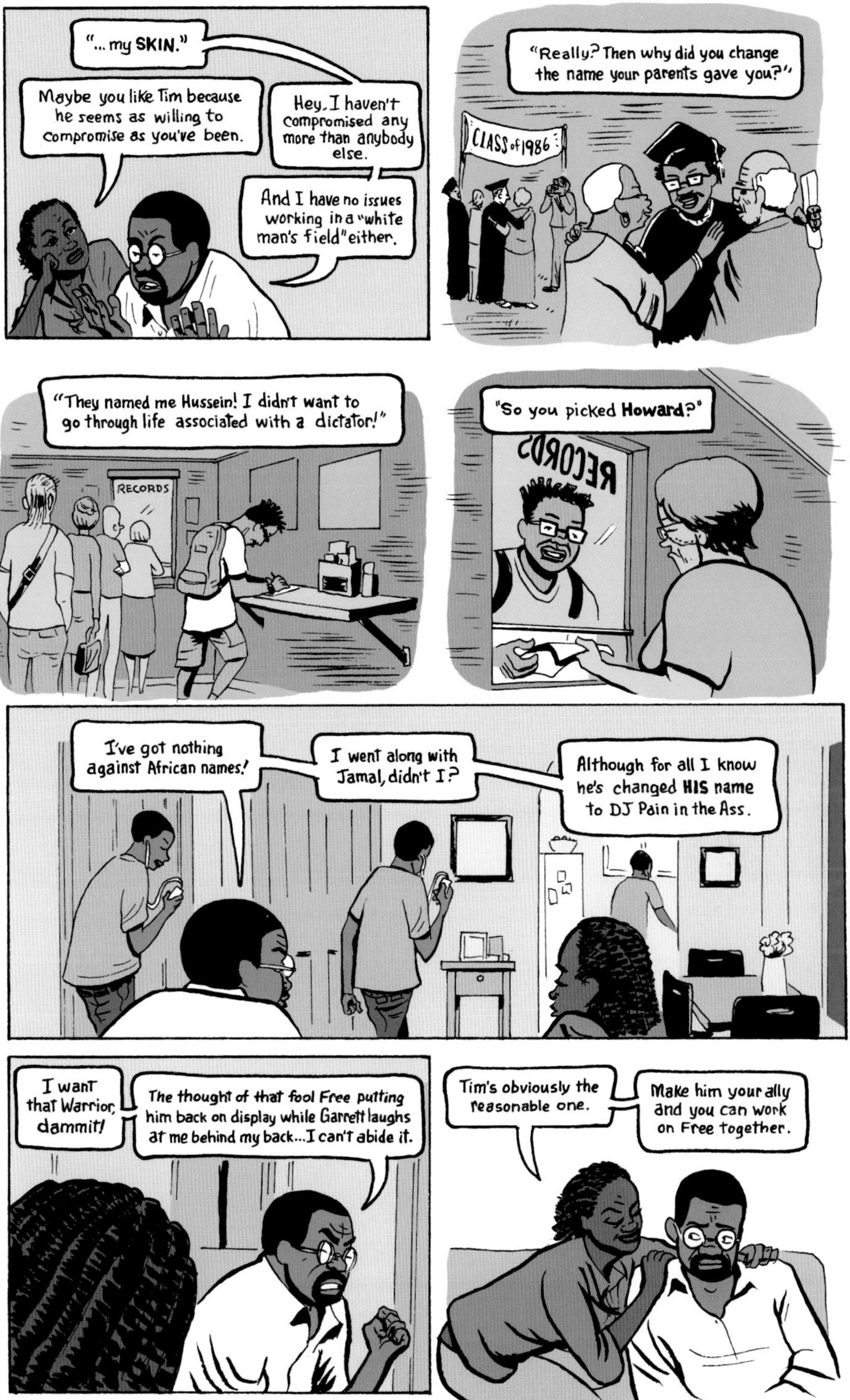
"... my SKIN."
Maybe you like Tim because he seems as willing to compromise as you've been.
Hey, I haven't compromised any more than anybody else.
And I have no issues working in a "white man's field" either.
"Really? Then why did you change the name your parents gave you?"
CLASS of 1986
"They named me Hussein! I didn't want to go through life associated with a dictator!"
RECORDS
"So you picked Howard?"
RECORDS
I've got nothing against African names!
I went along with Jamal, didn't I?
Although for all I know he's changed HIS name to DJ Pain in the Ass.
I want that Warrior, dammit!
The thought of that fool Free putting him back on display while Garrett laughs at me behind my back... I can't abide it.
Tim's obviously the reasonable one.
Make him your ally and you can work on Free together.

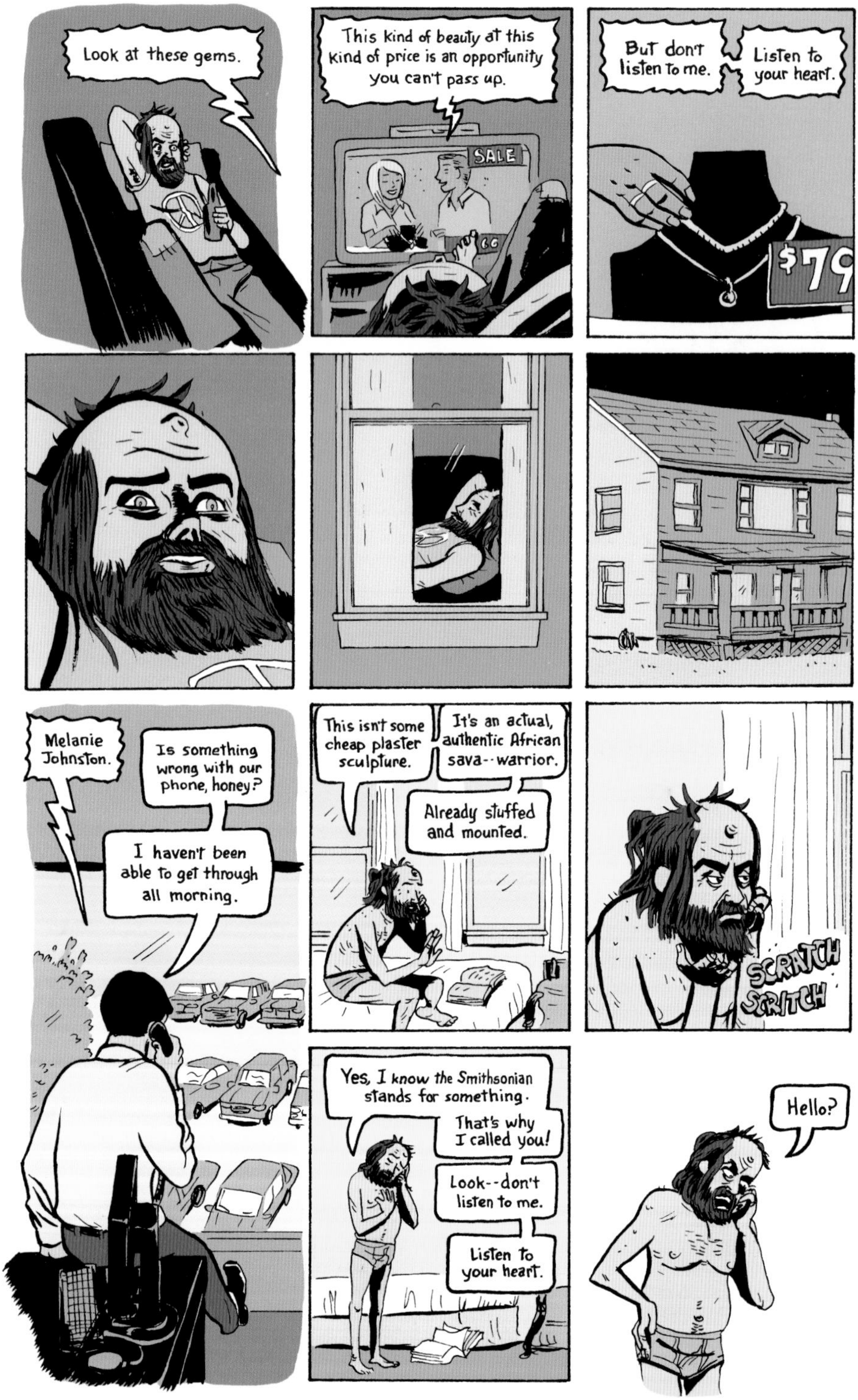
Look at these gems.
This kind of beauty at this kind of price is an opportunity you can't pass up.
SALE
But don't listen to me.
Listen to your heart.
$79
Melanie Johnston.
Is something wrong with our phone, honey?
I haven't been able to get through all morning.
This isn't some cheap plaster sculpture.
It's an actual, authentic African sava--warrior.
Already stuffed and mounted.
SCRATCH
SCRITCH
Yes, I know the Smithsonian stands for something.
That's why I called you!
Look--don't listen to me.
Listen to your heart.
Hello?

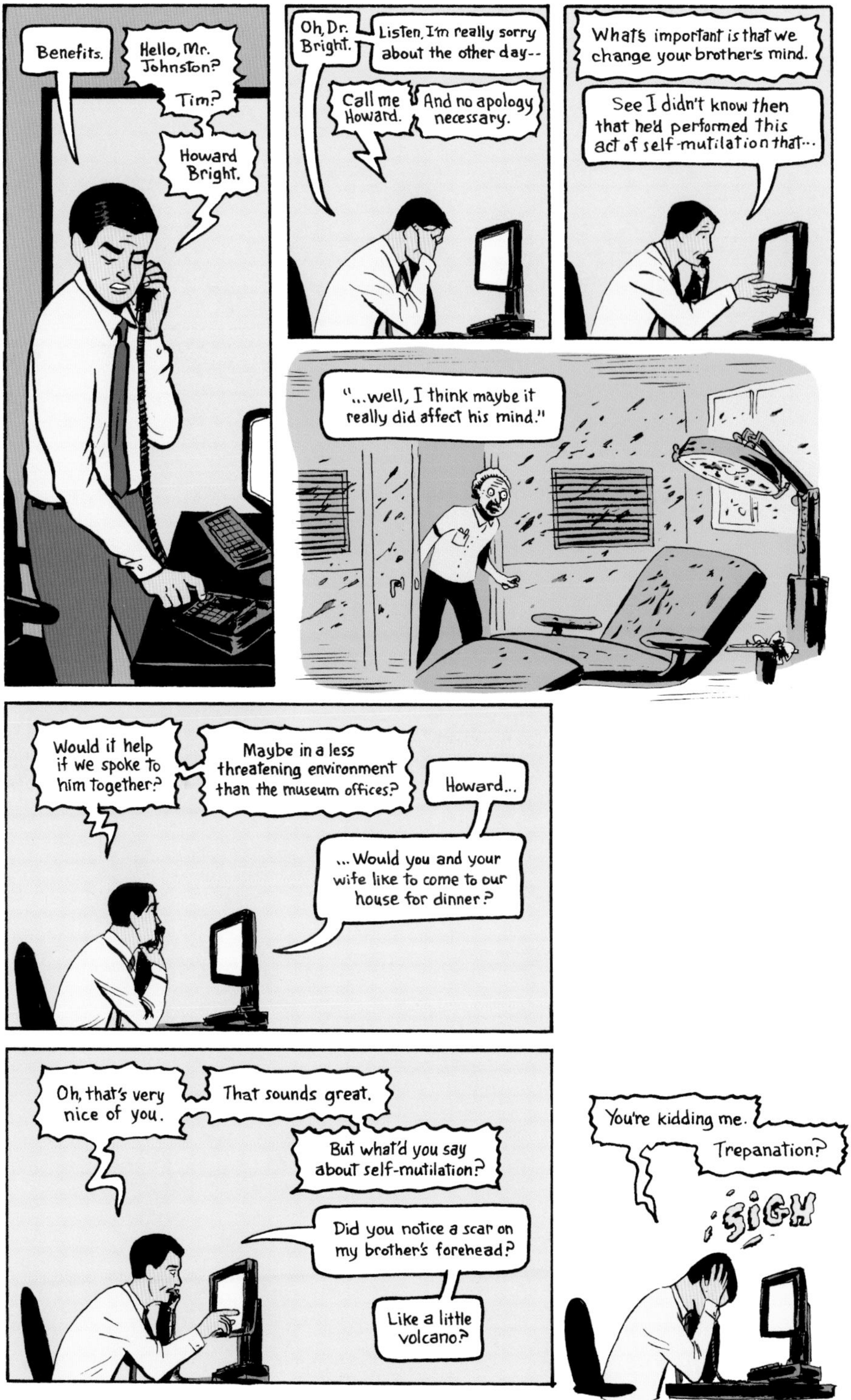
Benefits.
Hello, Mr. Johnston?
Tim?
Howard Bright.
Oh, Dr. Bright.
Listen, I'm really sorry about the other day--
Call me Howard.
And no apology necessary.
What's important is that we change your brother's mind.
See I didn't know then that he'd performed this act of self-mutilation that...
"...well, I think maybe it really did affect his mind."
Would it help if we spoke to him together?
Maybe in a less threatening environment than the museum offices?
Howard...
...Would you and your wife like to come to our house for dinner?
Oh, that's very nice of you.
That sounds great.
But what'd you say about self-mutilation?
Did you notice a scar on my brother's forehead?
Like a little volcano?
You're kidding me.
Trepanation?
SIGH

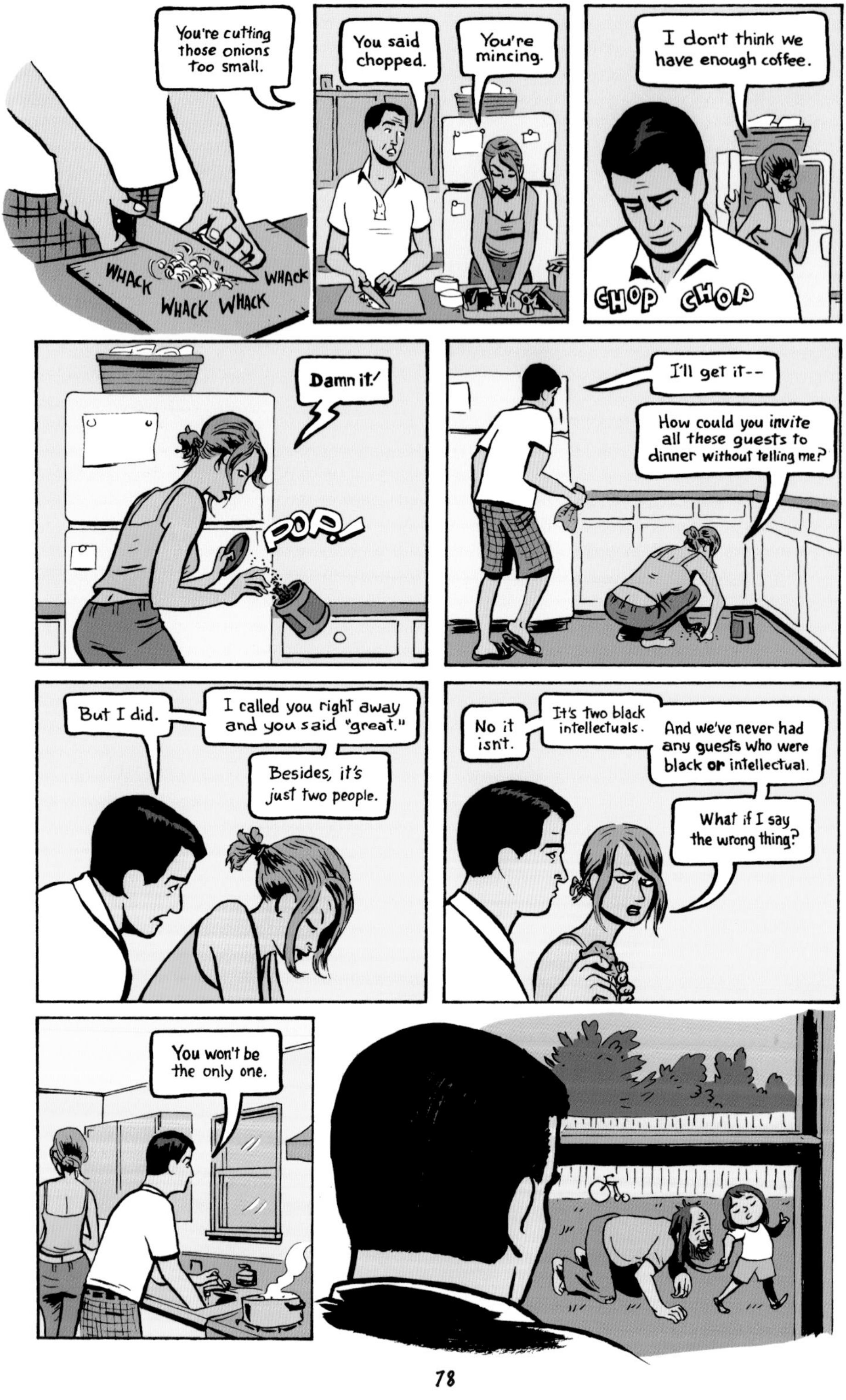

You're cutting those onions too small.
WHACK
WHACK WHACK
WHACK
You said chopped.
You're mincing.
I don't think we have enough coffee.
CHOP CHOP
Damn it!
POP!
I'll get it--
How could you invite all these guests to dinner without telling me?
But I did.
I called you right away and you said "great."
Besides, it's just two people.
No it isn't.
It's two black intellectuals.
And we've never had any guests who were black or intellectual.
What if I say the wrong thing?
You won't be the only one.

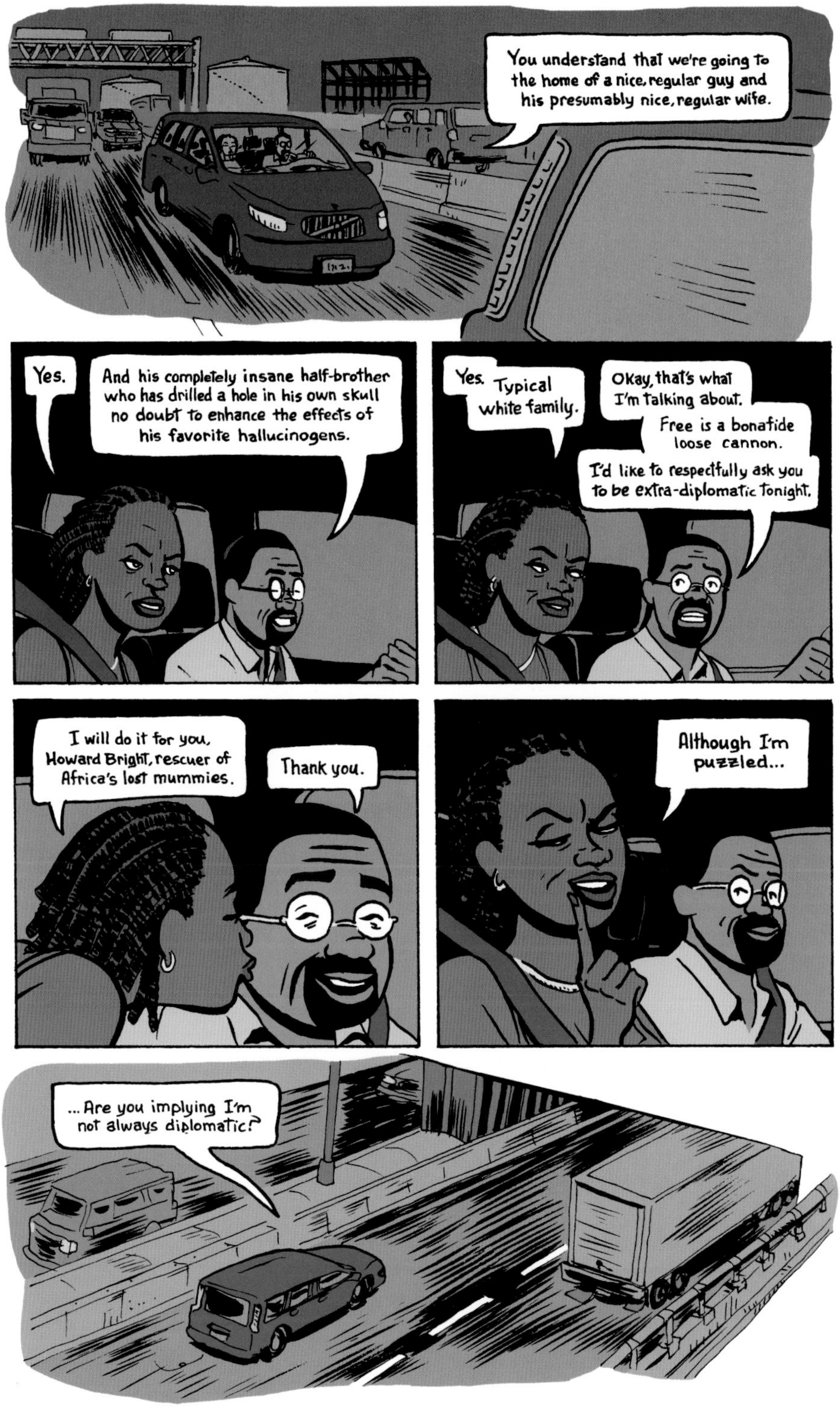
You understand that we're going to the home of a nice, regular guy and his presumably nice, regular wife.
Yes.
And his completely insane half-brother who has drilled a hole in his own skull no doubt to enhance the effects of his favorite hallucinogens.
Yes. Typical white family.
Okay, that's what I'm talking about.
Free is a bonafide loose cannon.
I'd like to respectfully ask you to be extra-diplomatic tonight.
I will do it for you, Howard Bright, rescuer of Africa's lost mummies.
Thank you.
Although I'm puzzled...
...Are you implying I'm not always diplomatic?

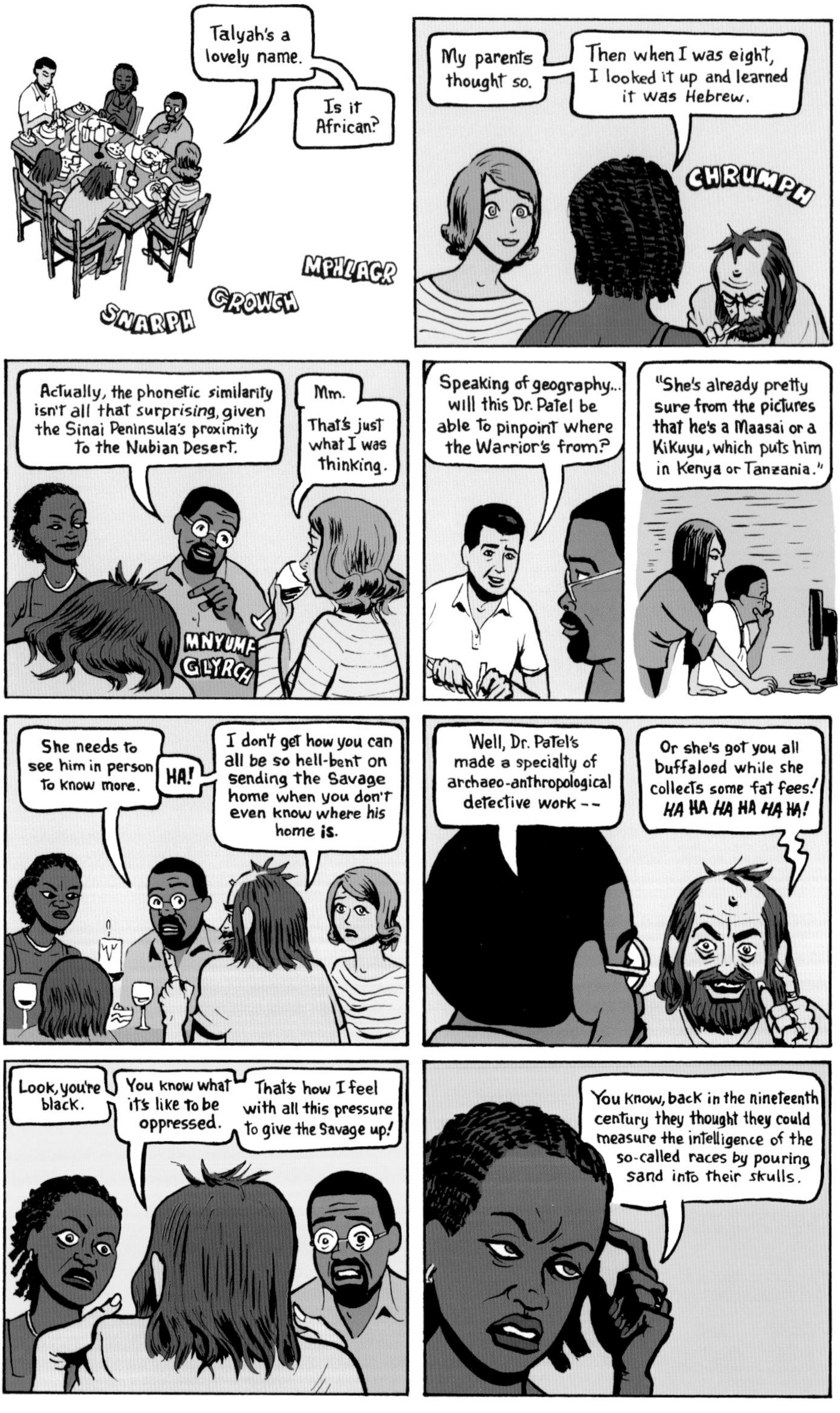
Talyah's a lovely name.
Is it African?
MPHLAGR
GROWCH
SNARPH
My parents thought so.
Then when I was eight, I looked it up and learned it was Hebrew.
CHRUMPH
Actually, the phonetic similarity isn't all that *surprising*, given the Sinai Peninsula's proximity to the Nubian Desert.
Mm.
That's just what I was thinking.
MNYUMF
GLYRCH
Speaking of geography... will this Dr. Patel be able to pinpoint where the Warrior's from?
"She's already pretty sure from the pictures that he's a Maasai or a Kikuyu, which puts him in Kenya or Tanzania."
She needs to see him in person to know more.
HA!
I don't get how you can all be so hell-bent on sending the Savage home when you don't even know where his home **is**.
Well, Dr. Patel's made a specialty of archaeo-anthropological detective work --
Or she's got you all buffaloed while she collects some fat fees! HA HA HA HA HA HA!
Look, you're black.
You know what it's like to be oppressed.
That's how I feel with all this pressure to give the Savage up!
You know, back in the nineteenth century they thought they could measure the intelligence of the so-called races by pouring sand into their skulls.

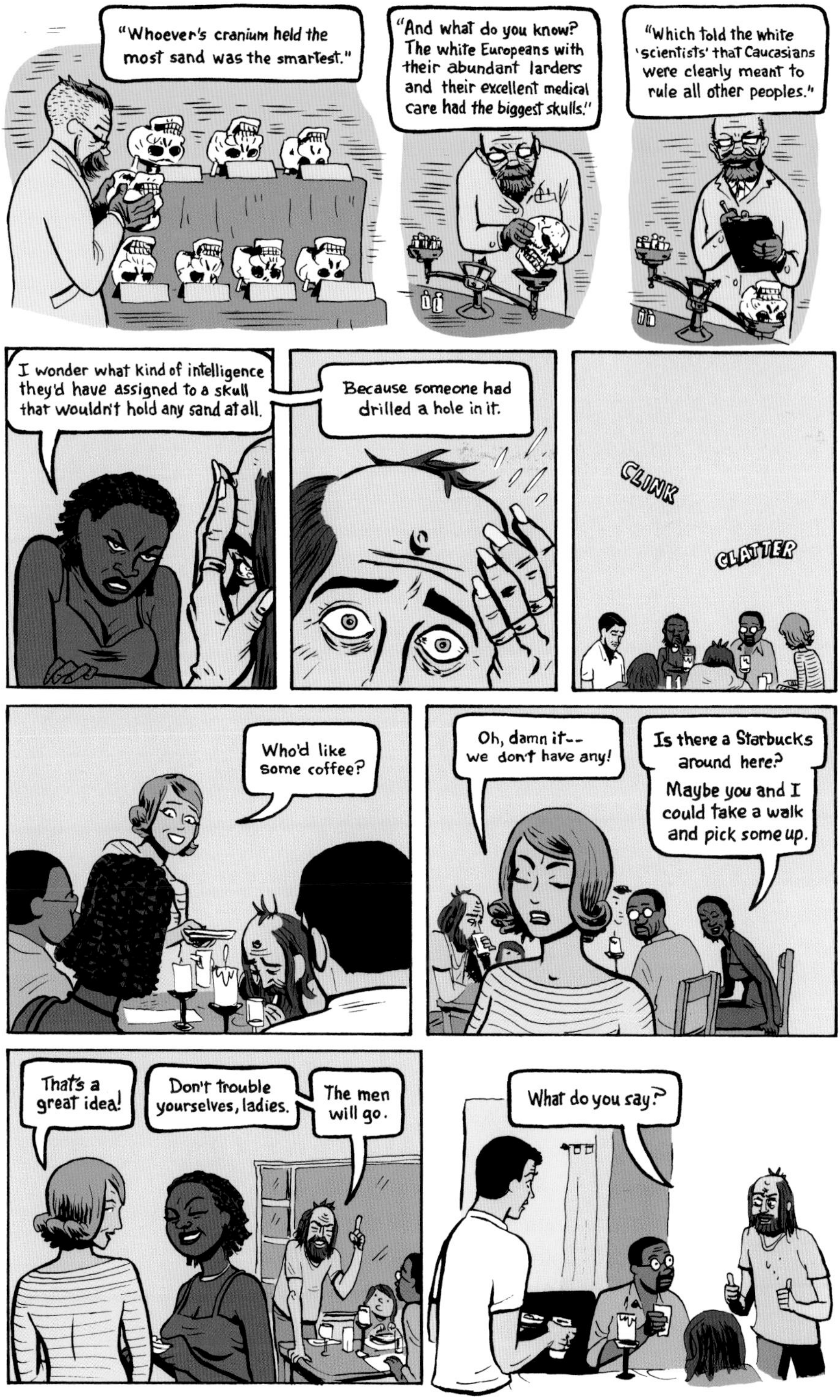
"Whoever's cranium held the most sand was the smartest."
"And what do you know? The white Europeans with their abundant larders and their excellent medical care had the biggest skulls."
"Which told the white 'scientists' that Caucasians were clearly meant to rule all other peoples."
I wonder what kind of intelligence they'd have assigned to a skull that wouldn't hold any sand at all.
Because someone had drilled a hole in it.
CLINK
CLATTER
Who'd like some coffee?
Oh, damn it-- we don't have any!
Is there a Starbucks around here?
Maybe you and I could take a walk and pick some up.
That's a great idea!
Don't trouble yourselves, ladies.
The men will go.
What do you say?

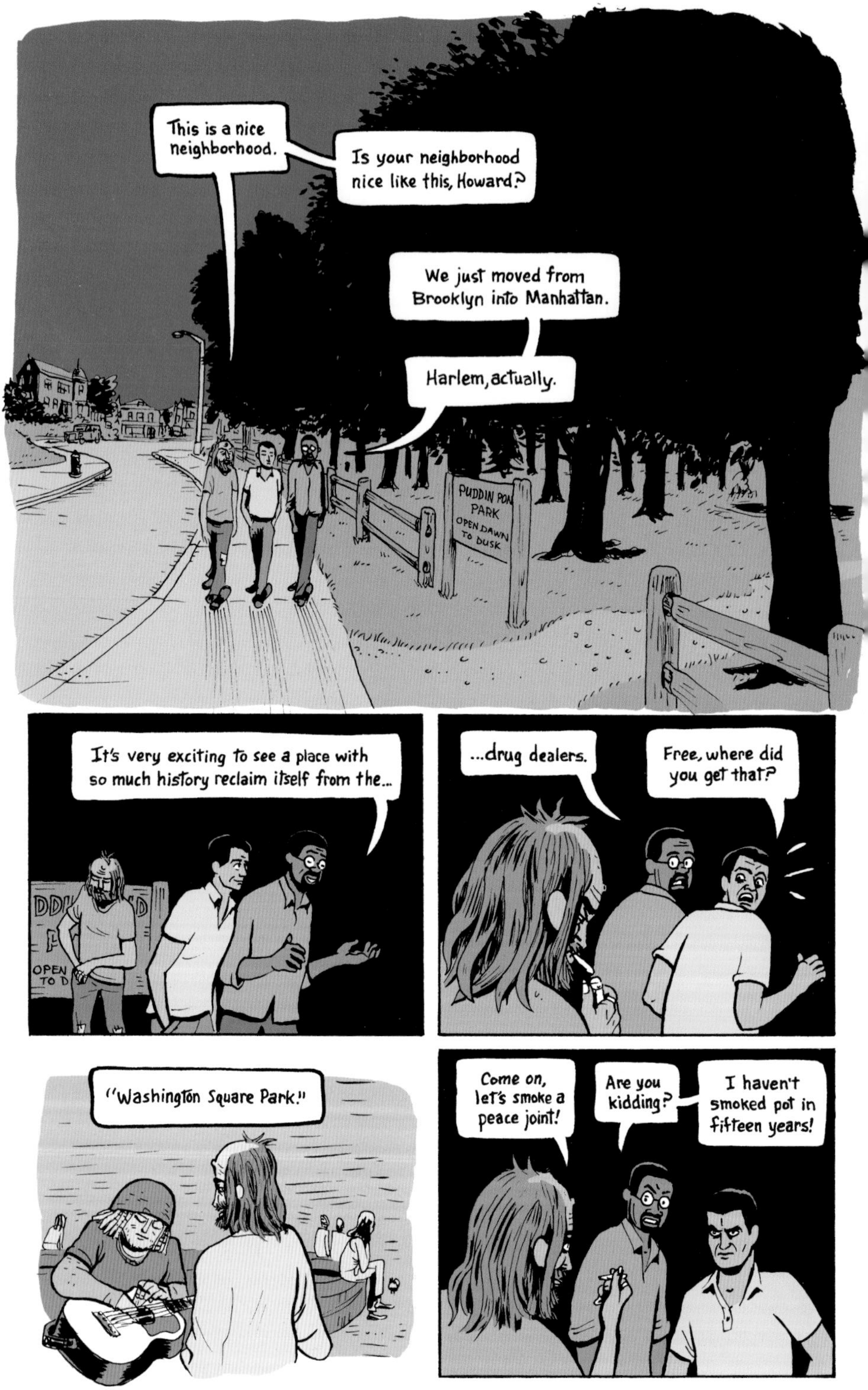

This is a nice neighborhood.
Is your neighborhood nice like this, Howard?
We just moved from Brooklyn into Manhattan.
Harlem, actually.
PUDDIN PON PARK OPEN DAWN TO DUSK
It's very exciting to see a place with so much history reclaim itself from the...
...drug dealers.
Free, where did you get that?
"Washington Square Park."
Come on, let's smoke a peace joint!
Are you kidding?
I haven't smoked pot in fifteen years!

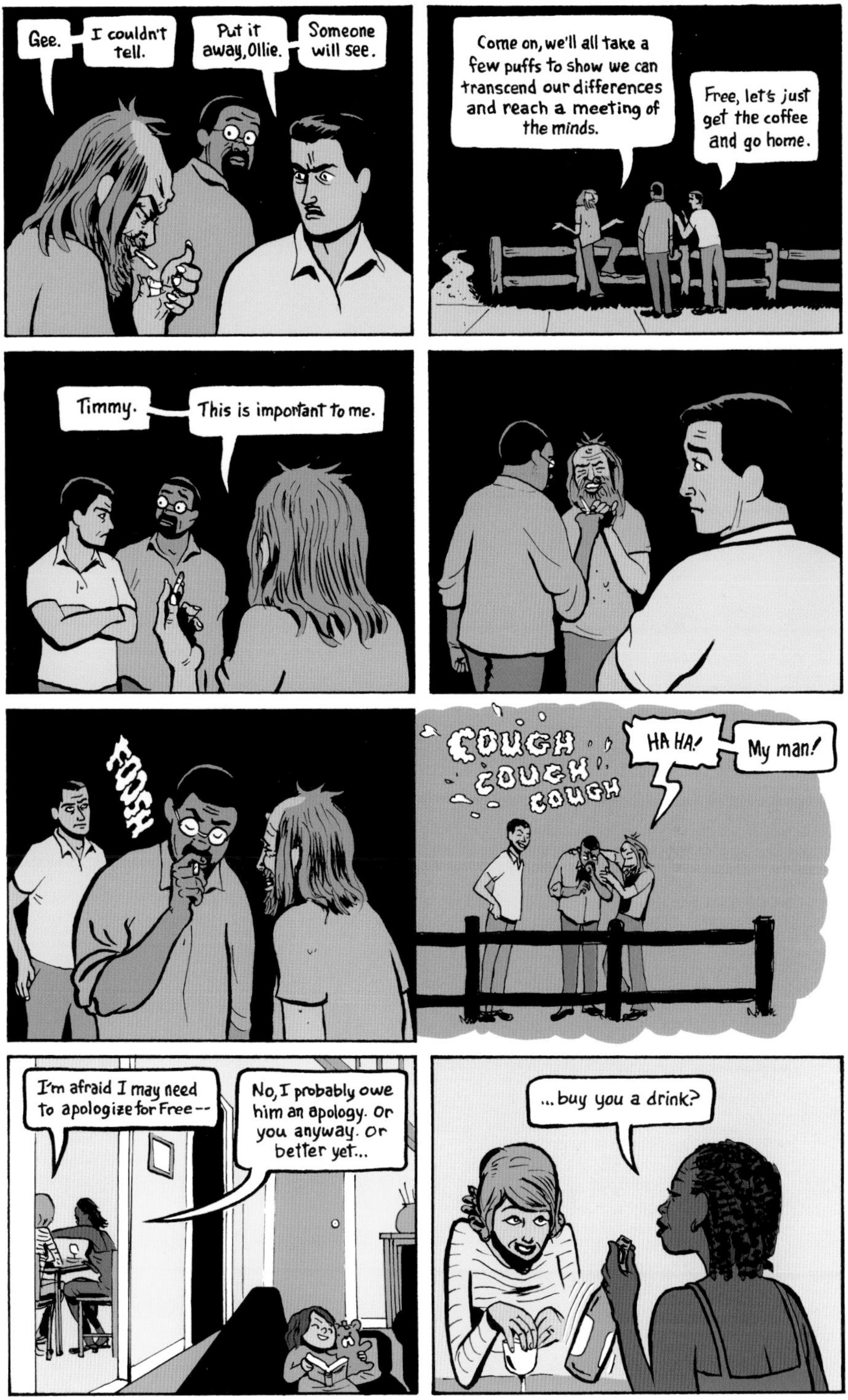
Gee.
I couldn't tell.
Put it away, Ollie.
Someone will see.
Come on, we'll all take a few puffs to show we can transcend our differences and reach a meeting of the minds.
Free, let's just get the coffee and go home.
Timmy.
This is important to me.
FOOSH
COUGH COUGH COUGH
HA HA!
My man!
I'm afraid I may need to apologize for Free--
No, I probably owe him an apology. Or you anyway. Or better yet...
...buy you a drink?

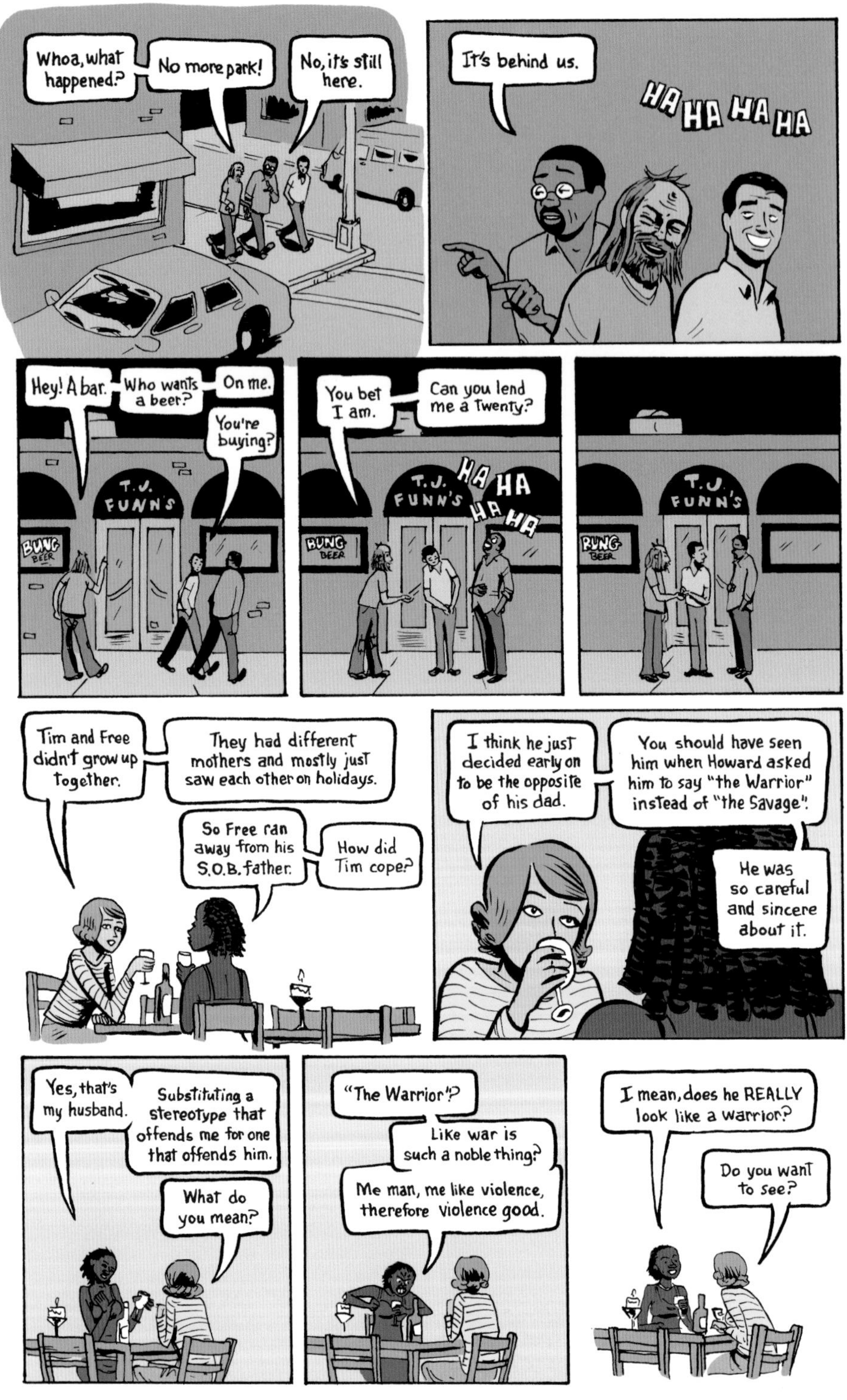

Whoa, what happened?
No more park!
No, it's still here.
It's behind us.
HA HA HA HA
Hey! A bar.
Who wants a beer?
On me.
You're buying?
You bet I am.
Can you lend me a Twenty?
T.J. FUNN'S
HA HA HA HA
BUNG BEER
Tim and Free didn't grow up together.
They had different mothers and mostly just saw each other on holidays.
So Free ran away from his S.O.B. father.
How did Tim cope?
I think he just decided early on to be the opposite of his dad.
You should have seen him when Howard asked him to say "the Warrior" instead of "the Savage".
He was so careful and sincere about it.
Yes, that's my husband.
Substituting a stereotype that offends me for one that offends him.
What do you mean?
"The Warrior"?
Like war is such a noble thing?
Me man, me like violence, therefore violence good.
I mean, does he REALLY look like a warrior?
Do you want to see?

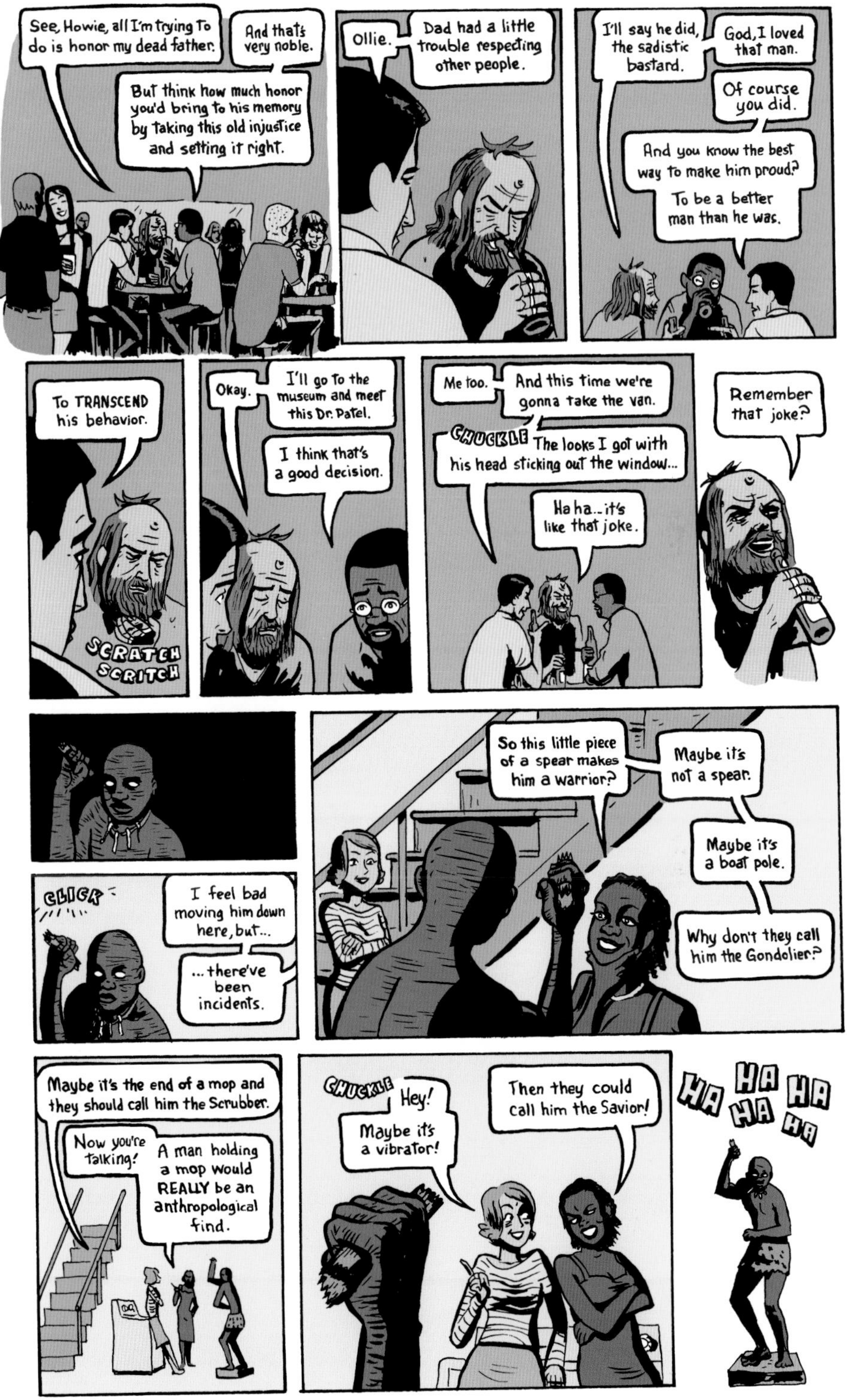
See, Howie, all I'm trying to do is honor my dead father.
And that's very noble.
But think how much honor you'd bring to his memory by taking this old injustice and setting it right.
Ollie.
Dad had a little trouble respecting other people.
I'll say he did, the sadistic bastard.
God, I loved that man.
Of course you did.
And you know the best way to make him proud?
To be a better man than he was.
To TRANSCEND his behavior.
SCRATCH SCRITCH
Okay.
I'll go to the museum and meet this Dr. Patel.
I think that's a good decision.
Me too.
And this time we're gonna take the van.
CHUCKLE
The looks I got with his head sticking out the window...
Ha ha... it's like that joke.
Remember that joke?
CLICK
I feel bad moving him down here, but...
...there've been incidents.
So this little piece of a spear makes him a warrior?
Maybe it's not a spear.
Maybe it's a boat pole.
Why don't they call him the Gondolier?
Maybe it's the end of a mop and they should call him the Scrubber.
Now you're talking!
A man holding a mop would REALLY be an anthropological find.
CHUCKLE
Hey!
Maybe it's a vibrator!
Then they could call him the Savior!
HA HA HA HA HA

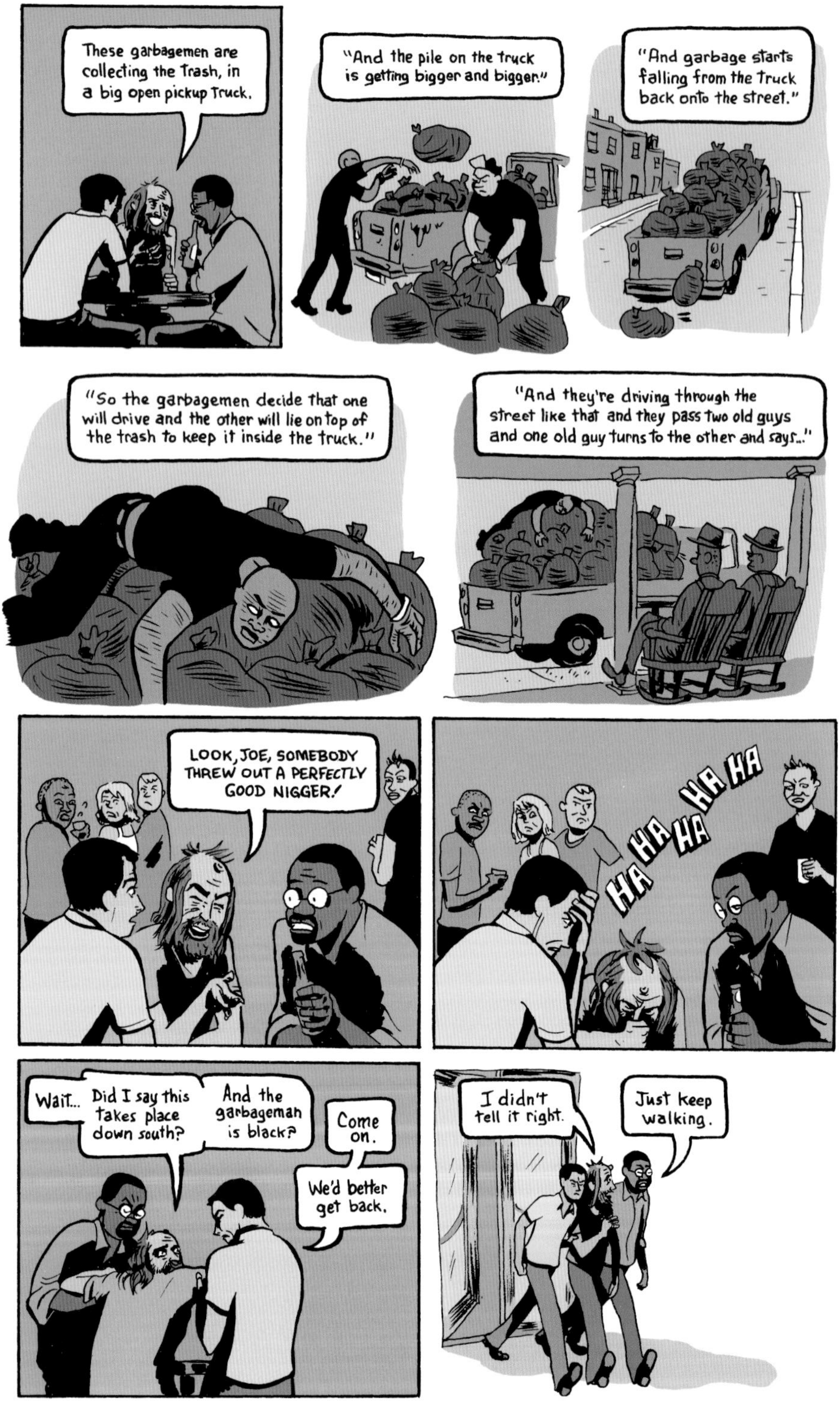
These garbagemen are collecting the trash, in a big open pickup truck.
"And the pile on the truck is getting bigger and bigger."
"And garbage starts falling from the truck back onto the street."
"So the garbagemen decide that one will drive and the other will lie on top of the trash to keep it inside the truck."
"And they're driving through the street like that and they pass two old guys and one old guy turns to the other and says..."
LOOK, JOE, SOMEBODY THREW OUT A PERFECTLY GOOD NIGGER!
HA HA HA HA HA
Wait...
Did I say this takes place down south?
And the garbageman is black?
Come on.
We'd better get back.
I didn't tell it right.
Just keep walking.

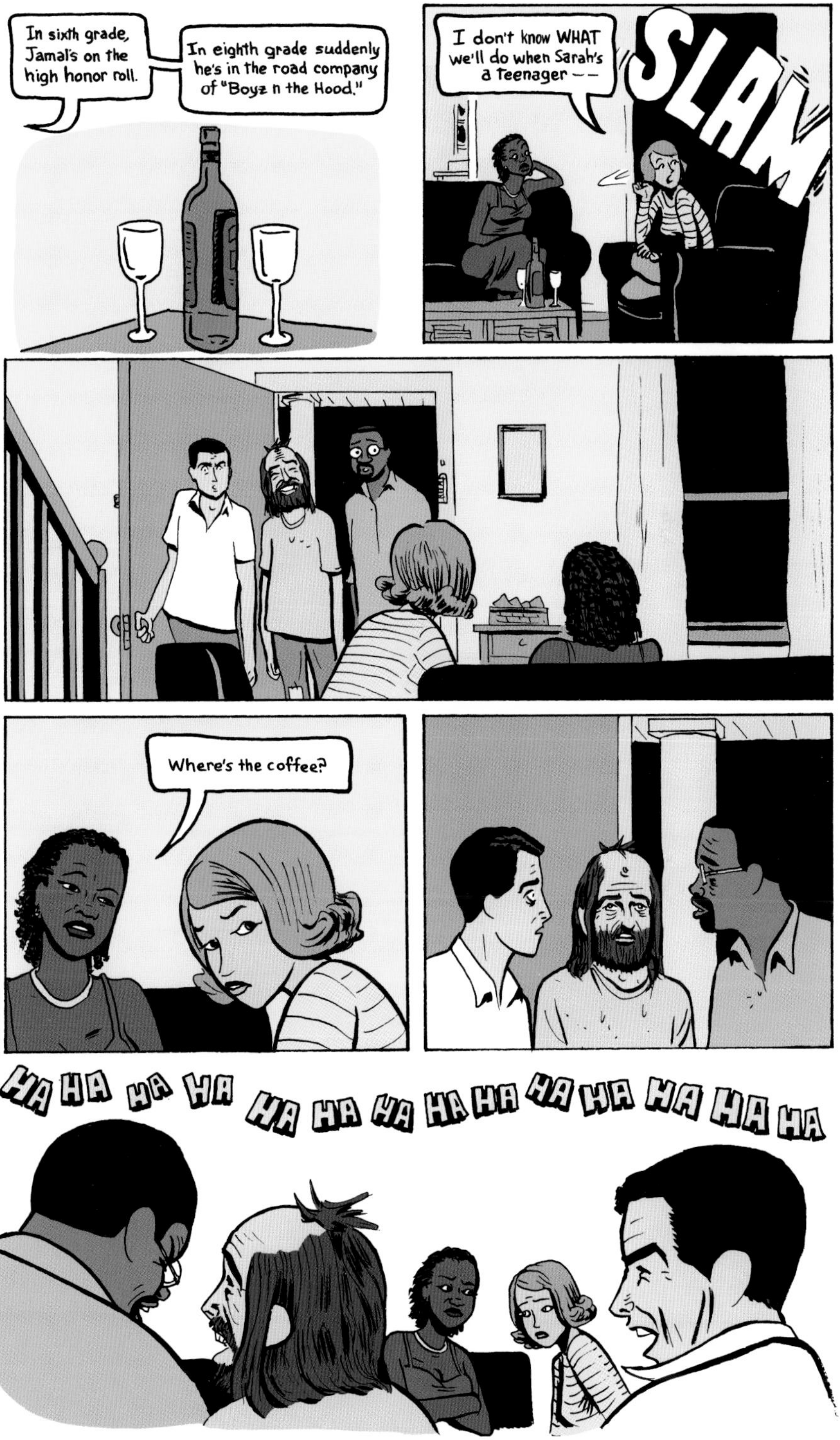

In sixth grade, Jamal's on the high honor roll.
In eighth grade suddenly he's in the road company of "Boyz n the Hood."
I don't know WHAT we'll do when Sarah's a teenager --
SLAM
Where's the coffee?
HA HA HA HA HA HA HA HA HA HA HA HA HA HA HA

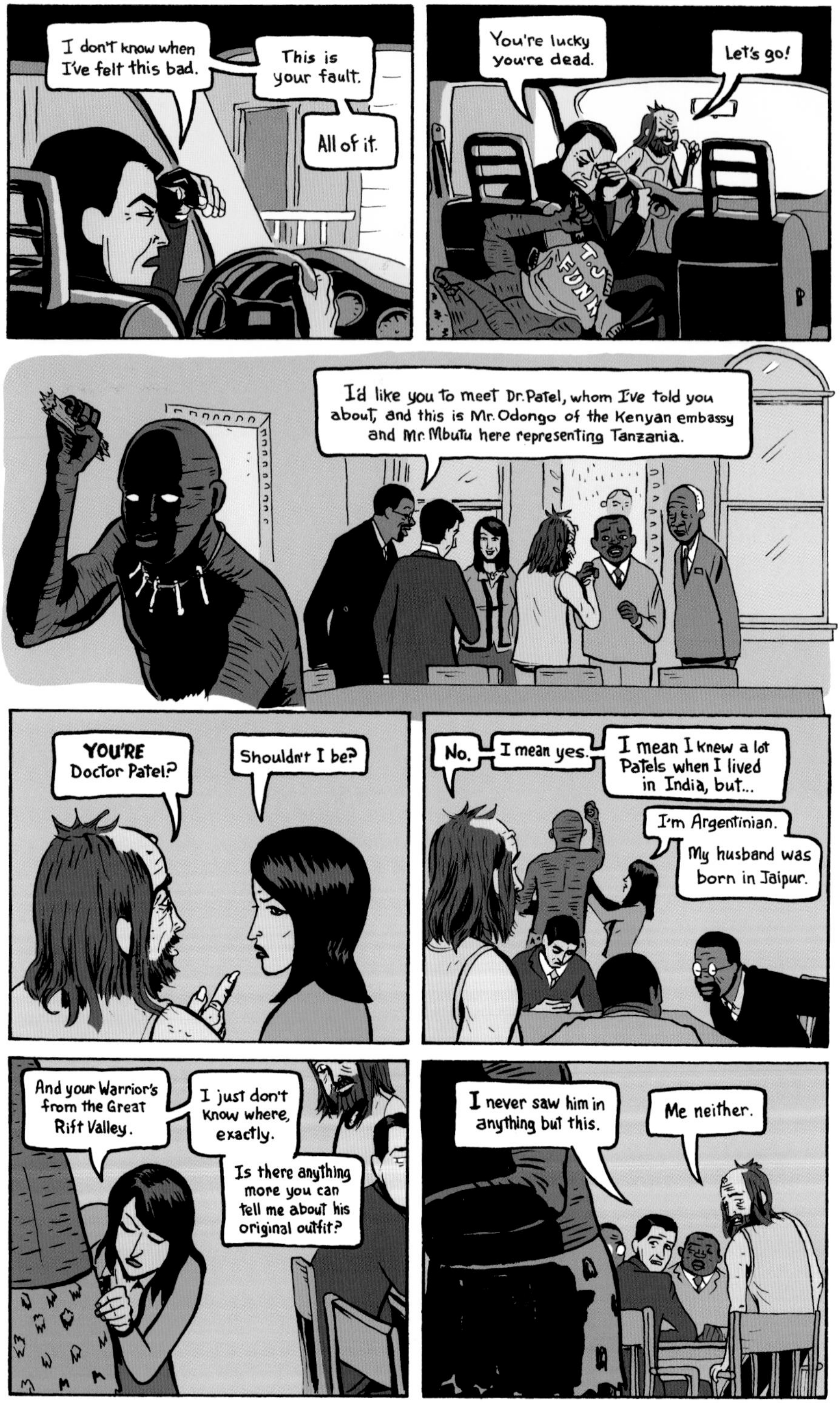
I don't know when I've felt this bad.
This is your fault.
All of it.
You're lucky you're dead.
Let's go!
T.J. FUNK
I'd like you to meet Dr. Patel, whom I've told you about, and this is Mr. Odongo of the Kenyan embassy and Mr. Mbutu here representing Tanzania.
YOU'RE Doctor Patel?
Shouldn't I be?
No.
I mean yes.
I mean I knew a lot Patels when I lived in India, but...
I'm Argentinian.
My husband was born in Jaipur.
And your Warrior's from the Great Rift Valley.
I just don't know where, exactly.
Is there anything more you can tell me about his original outfit?
I never saw him in anything but this.
Me neither.

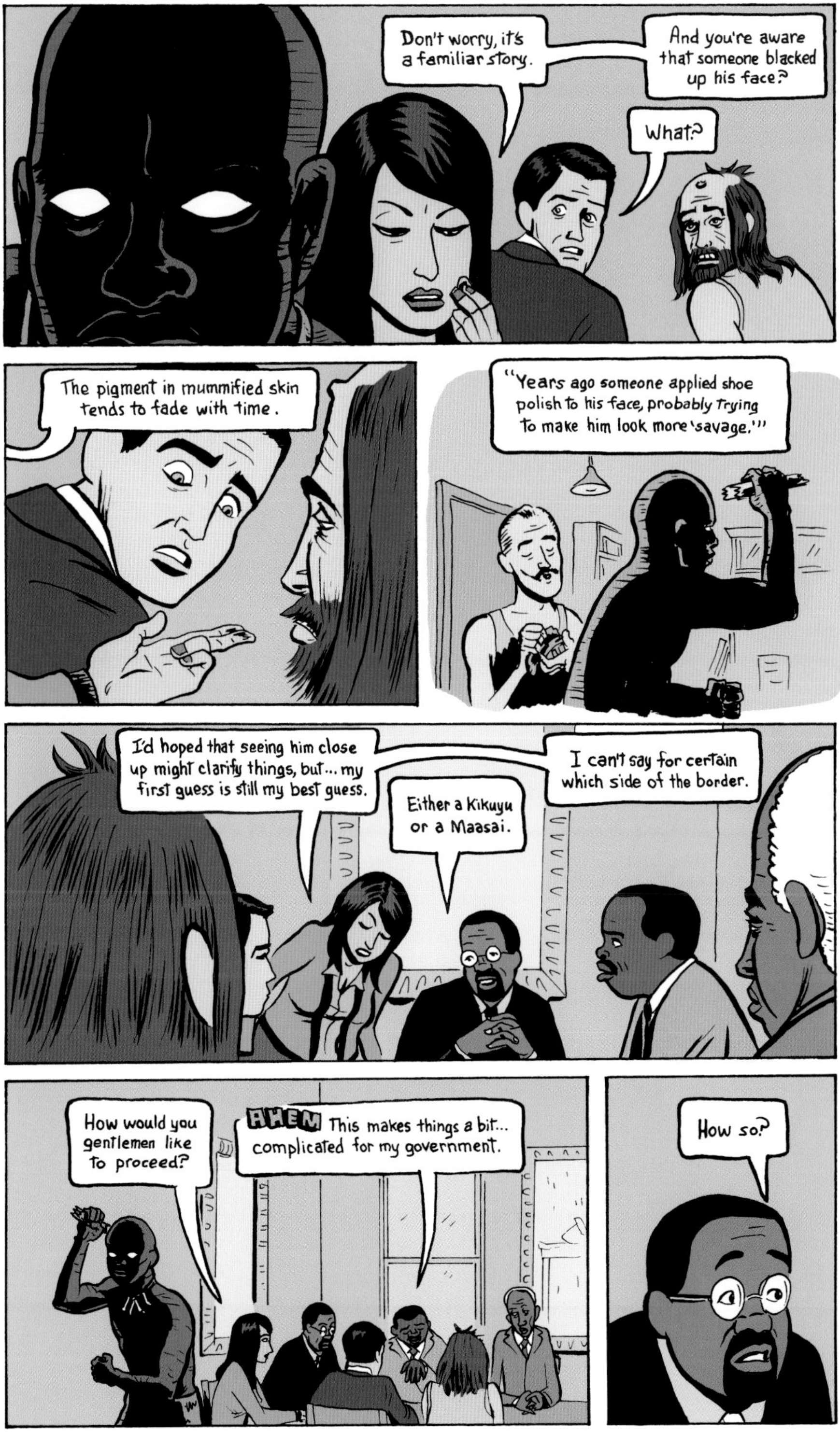
Don't worry, it's a familiar story.
And you're aware that someone blacked up his face?
What?
The pigment in mummified skin tends to fade with time.
"Years ago someone applied shoe polish to his face, probably trying to make him look more 'savage.'"
I'd hoped that seeing him close up might clarify things, but... my first guess is still my best guess.
I can't say for certain which side of the border.
Either a Kikuyu or a Maasai.
How would you gentlemen like to proceed?
AHEM This makes things a bit... complicated for my government.
How so?

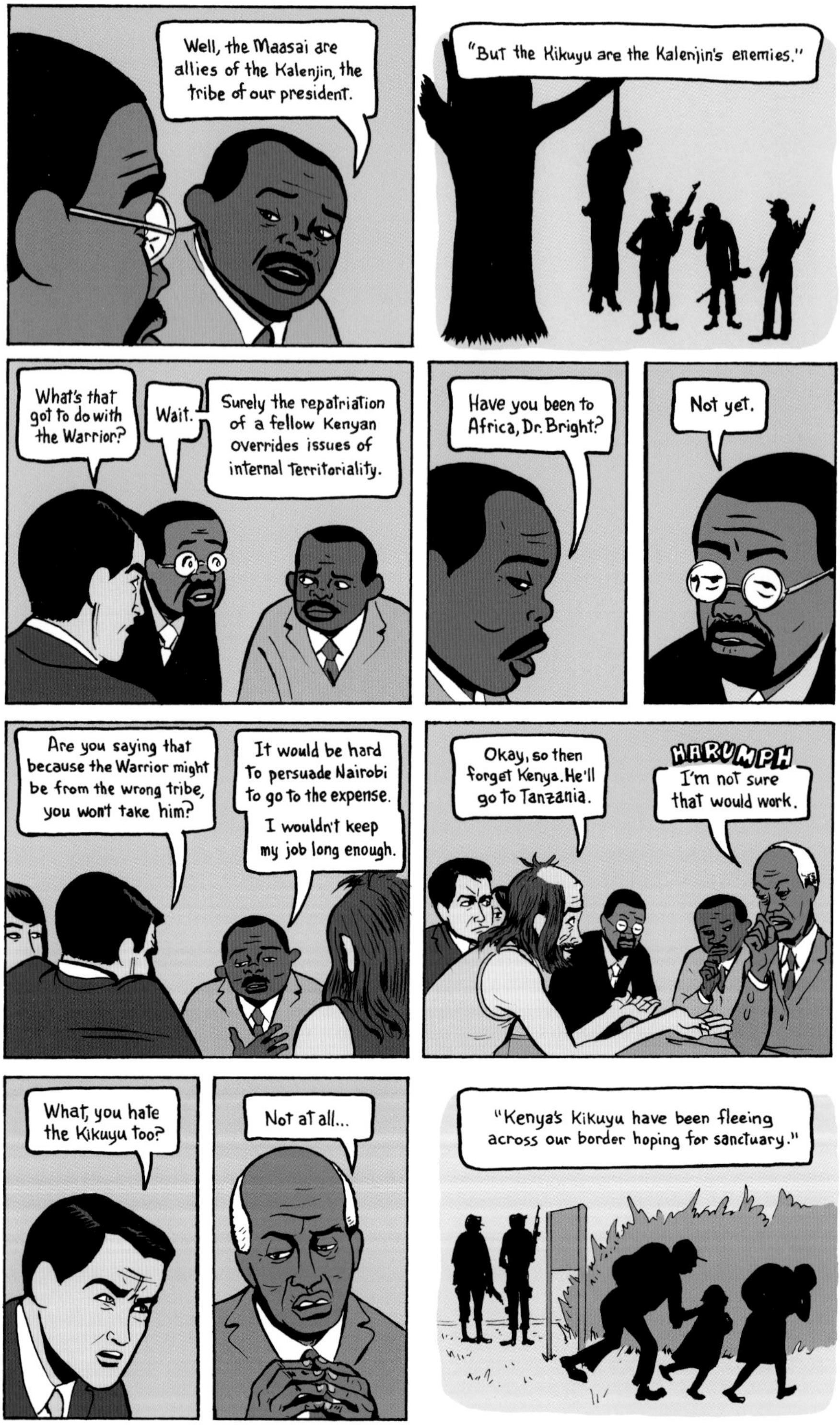
Well, the Maasai are allies of the Kalenjin, the tribe of our president.
"But the Kikuyu are the Kalenjin's enemies."
What's that got to do with the Warrior?
Wait.
Surely the repatriation of a fellow Kenyan overrides issues of internal territoriality.
Have you been to Africa, Dr. Bright?
Not yet.
Are you saying that because the Warrior might be from the wrong tribe, you won't take him?
It would be hard to persuade Nairobi to go to the expense.
I wouldn't keep my job long enough.
Okay, so then forget Kenya. He'll go to Tanzania.
HARUMPH
I'm not sure that would work.
What, you hate the Kikuyu too?
Not at all...
"Kenya's Kikuyu have been fleeing across our border hoping for sanctuary."

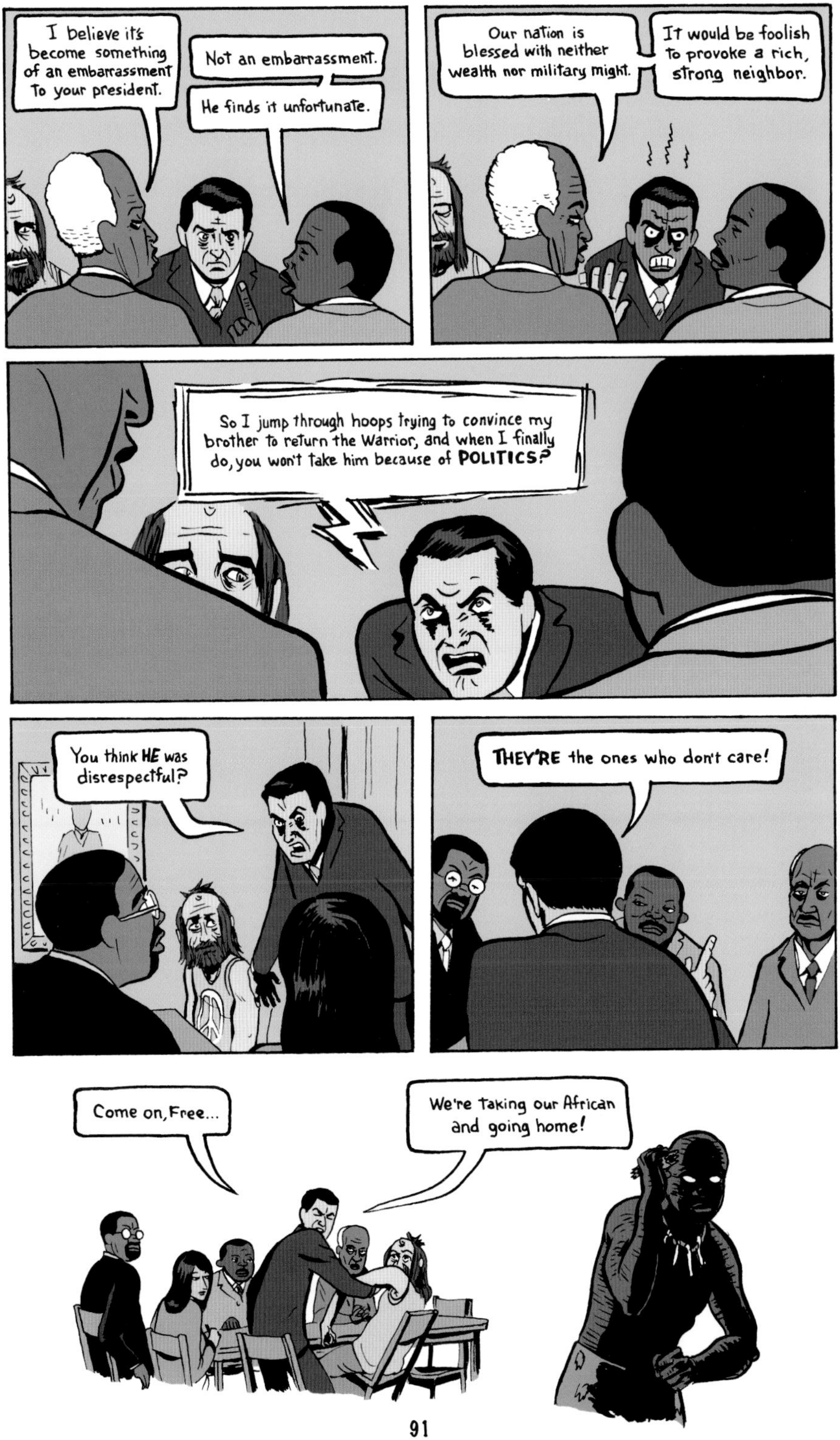

I believe it's become something of an embarrassment to your president.
Not an embarrassment.
He finds it unfortunate.
Our nation is blessed with neither wealth nor military might.
It would be foolish to provoke a rich, strong neighbor.
So I jump through hoops trying to convince my brother to return the Warrior, and when I finally do, you won't take him because of POLITICS?
You think HE was disrespectful?
THEY'RE the ones who don't care!
Come on, Free...
We're taking our African and going home!

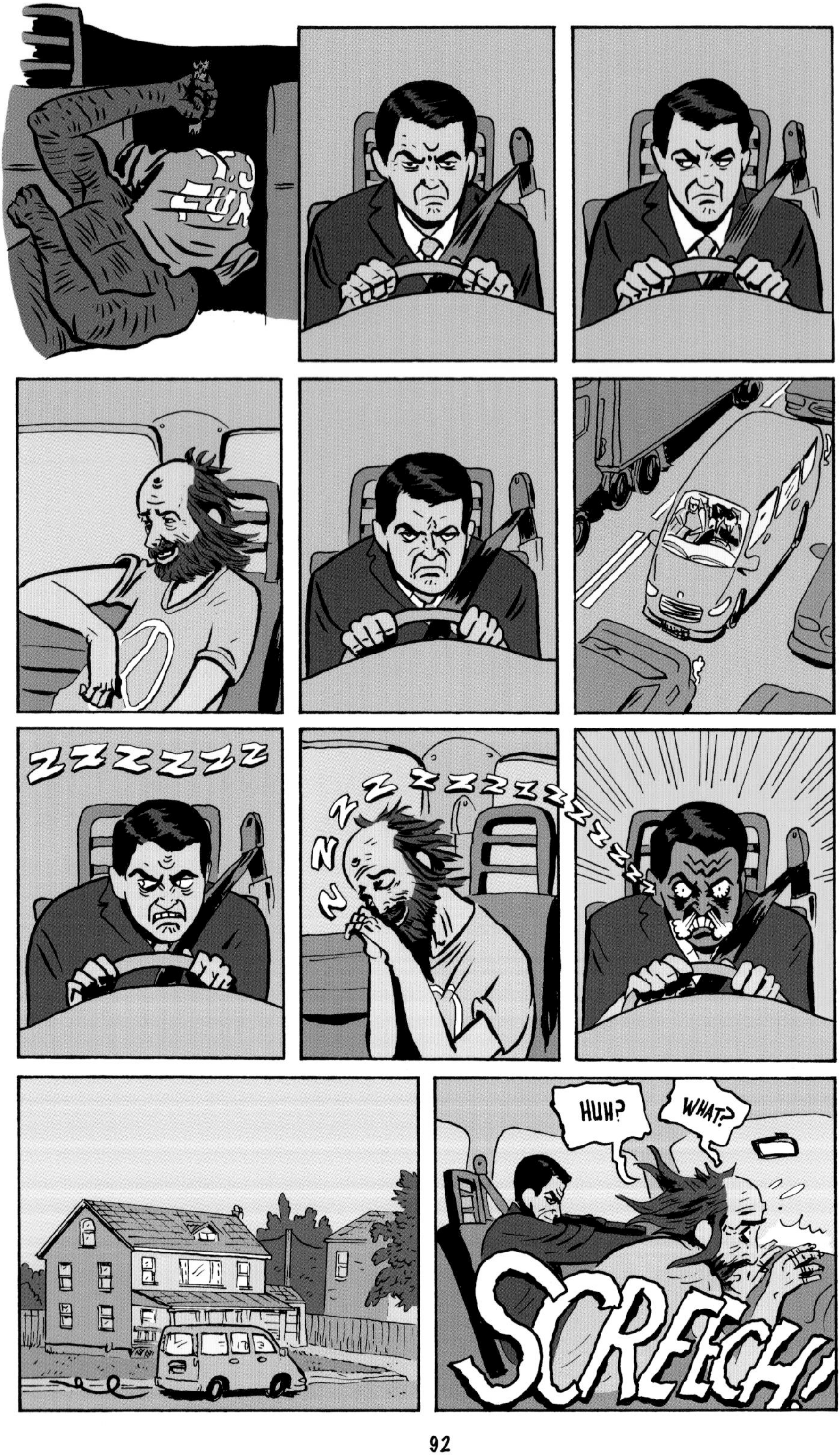
FUN
ZZZZZZZ
ZZZZZZZZZZZZZZZZ
HUH?
WHAT?
SCREECH!

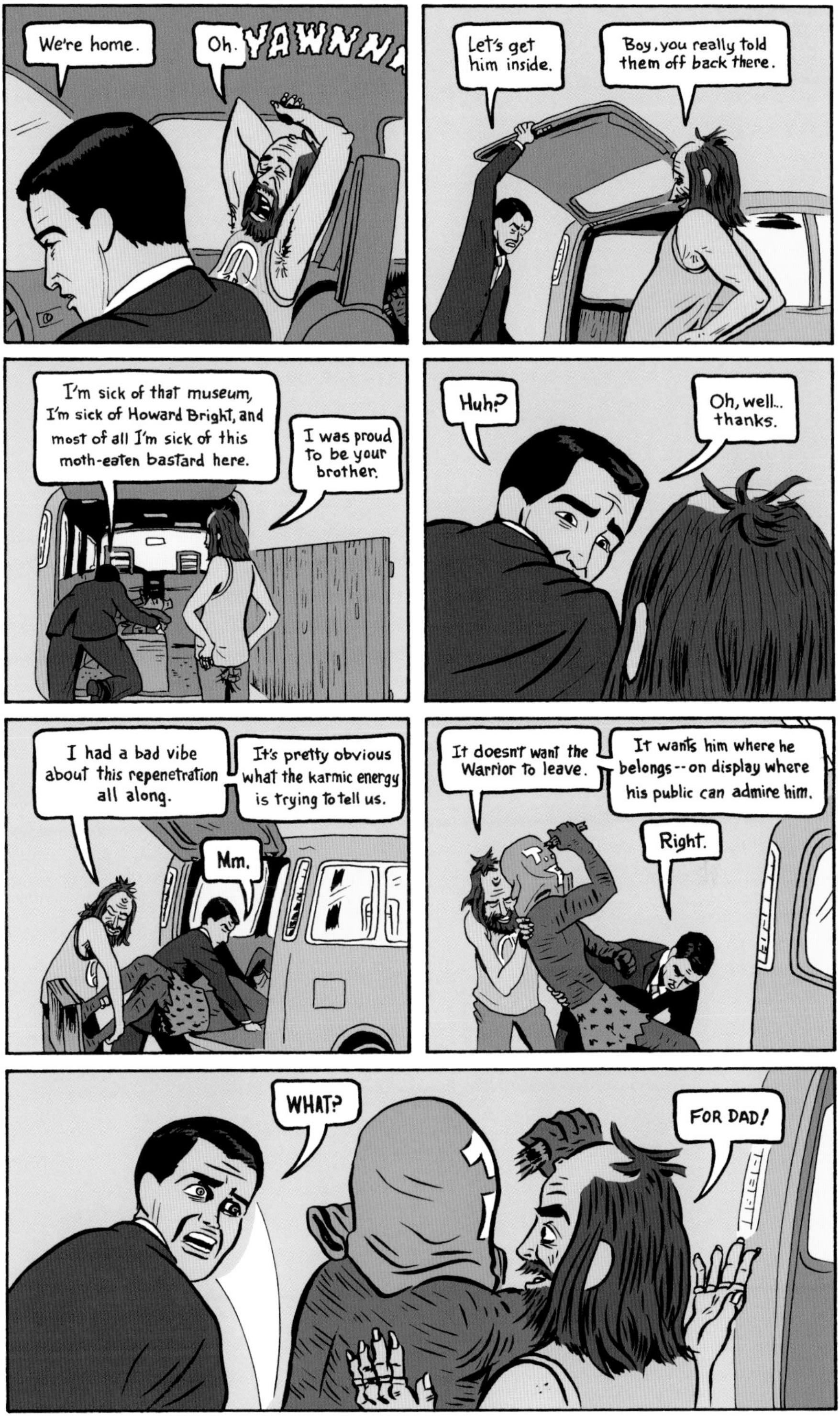
We're home.
Oh. YAWNNN
Let's get him inside.
Boy, you really told them off back there.
I'm sick of that museum, I'm sick of Howard Bright, and most of all I'm sick of this moth-eaten bastard here.
I was proud to be your brother.
Huh?
Oh, well... thanks.
I had a bad vibe about this repenetration all along.
It's pretty obvious what the karmic energy is trying to tell us.
Mm.
It doesn't want the Warrior to leave.
It wants him where he belongs -- on display where his public can admire him.
Right.
WHAT?
FOR DAD!

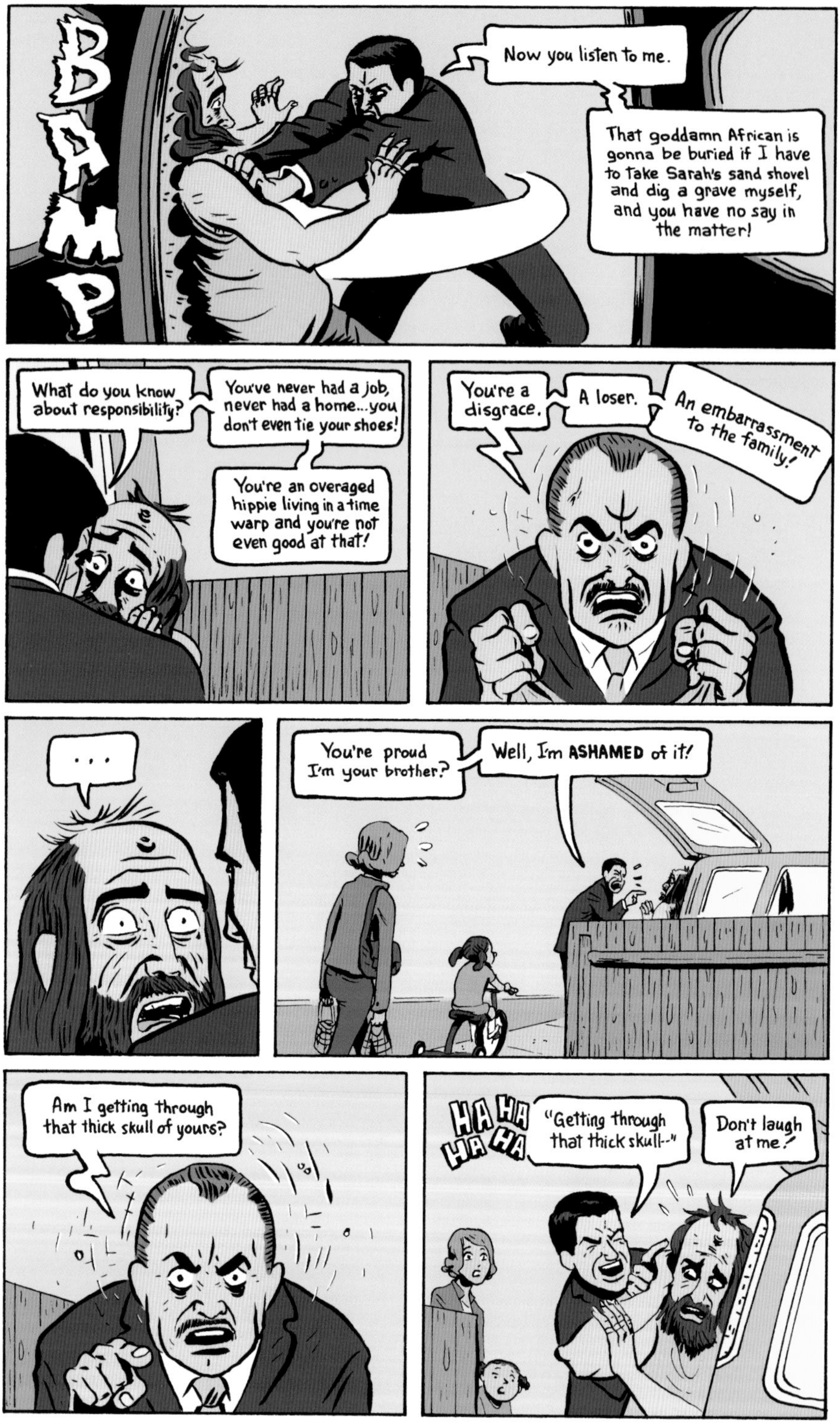
BAMP
Now you listen to me.
That goddamn African is gonna be buried if I have to take Sarah's sand shovel and dig a grave myself, and you have no say in the matter!
What do you know about responsibility?
You've never had a job, never had a home...you don't even tie your shoes!
You're an overaged hippie living in a time warp and you're not even good at that!
You're a disgrace.
A loser.
An embarrassment to the family!
. . .
You're proud I'm your brother?
Well, I'm ASHAMED of it!
Am I getting through that thick skull of yours?
HA HA HA HA
"Getting through that thick skull--"
Don't laugh at me.

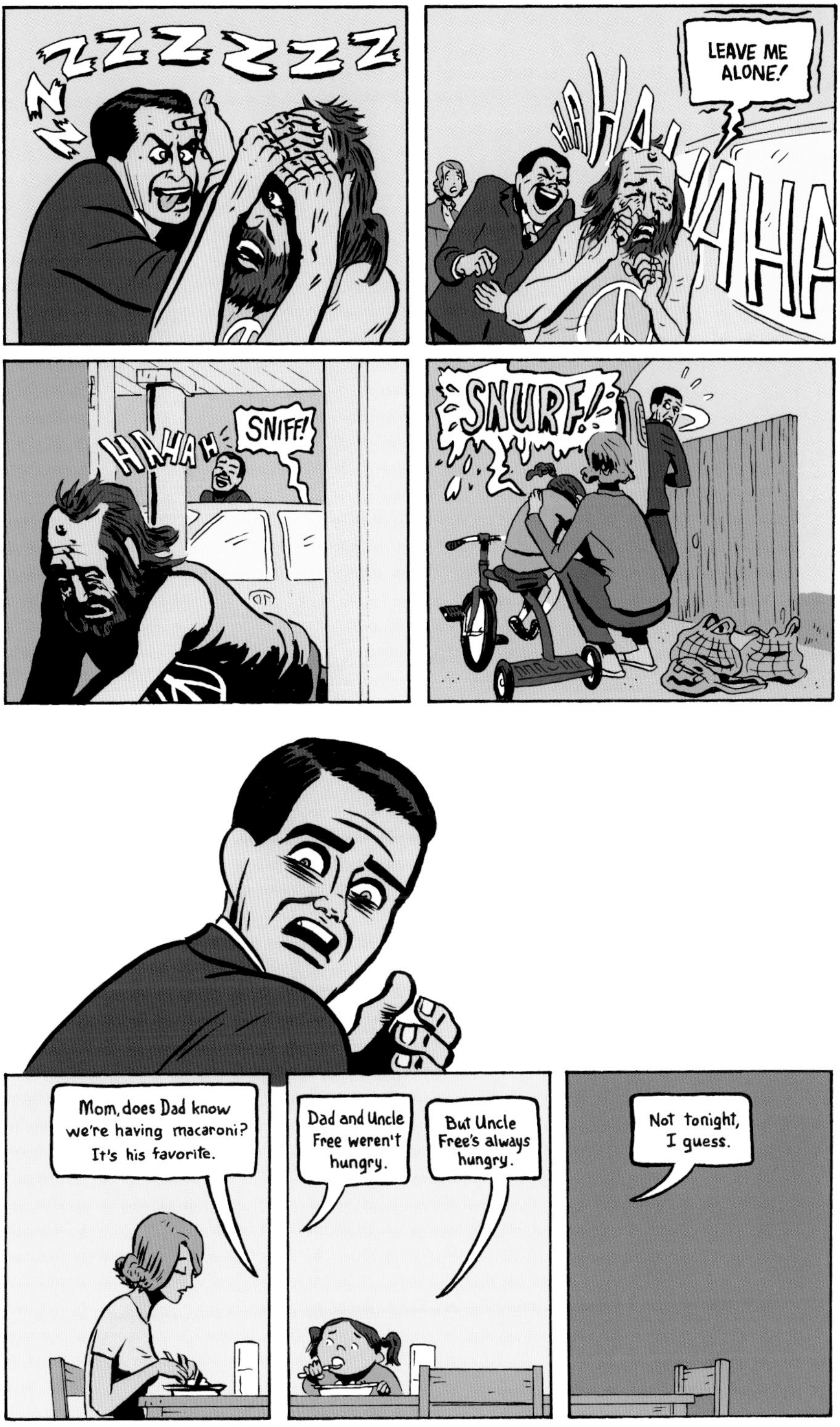
ZZZZZZZZ
LEAVE ME ALONE!
HA HA HA
HAHA
HAHAH
SNIFF!
SNURF!
Mom, does Dad know we're having macaroni? It's his favorite.
Dad and Uncle Free weren't hungry.
But Uncle Free's always hungry.
Not tonight, I guess.

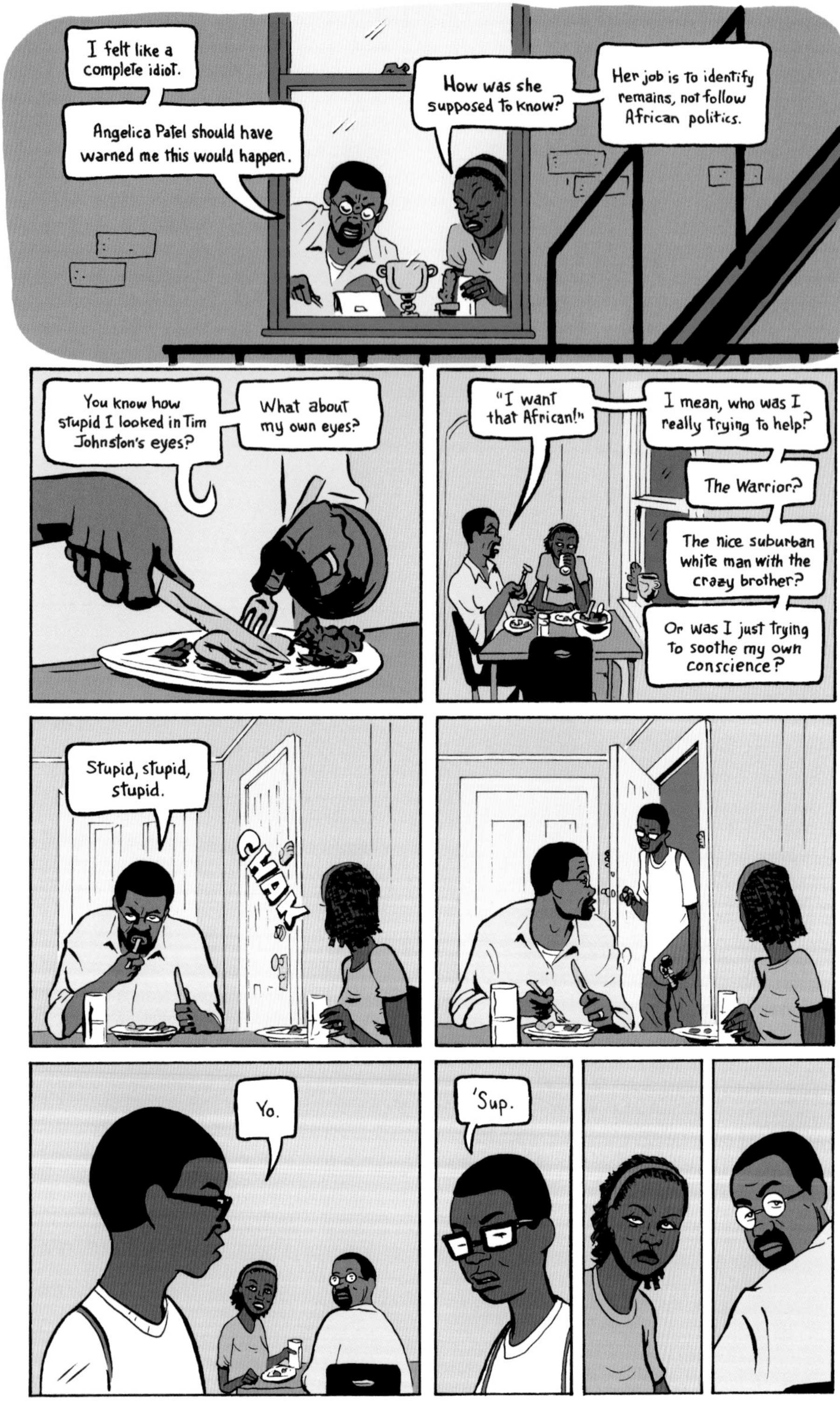
I felt like a complete idiot.
Angelica Patel should have warned me this would happen.
How was she supposed to know?
Her job is to identify remains, not follow African politics.
You know how stupid I looked in Tim Johnston's eyes?
What about my own eyes?
"I want that African!"
I mean, who was I really trying to help?
The Warrior?
The nice suburban white man with the crazy brother?
Or was I just trying to soothe my own conscience?
Stupid, stupid, stupid.
CHAK
Yo.
'Sup.

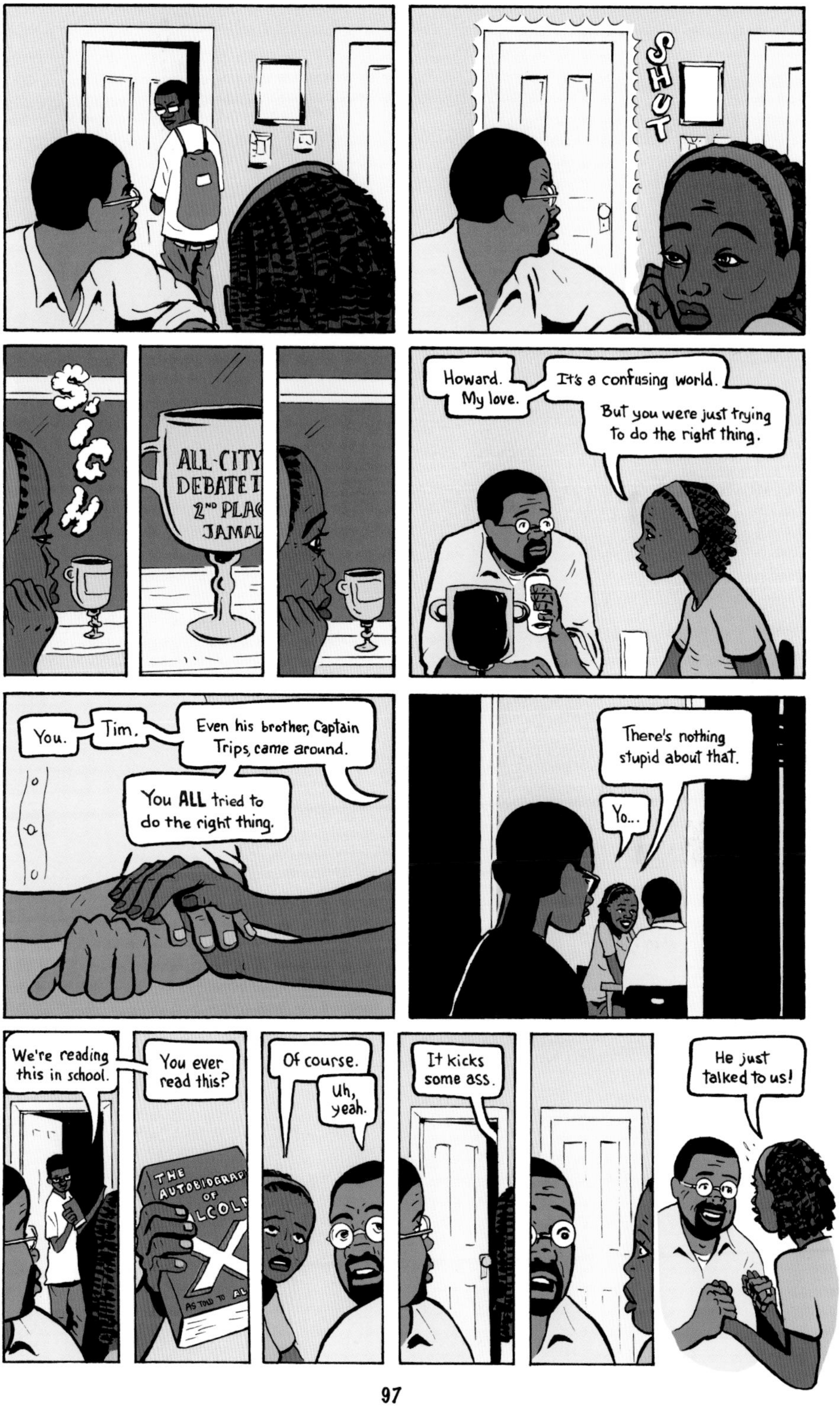
SHUT
SIGH
ALL-CITY DEBATE T
2ND PLAC
JAMAL
Howard. My love.
It's a confusing world.
But you were just trying to do the right thing.
You.
Tim.
Even his brother, Captain Trips, came around.
You ALL tried to do the right thing.
There's nothing stupid about that.
Yo...
We're reading this in school.
You ever read this?
THE AUTOBIOGRAP OF LCOL X
AS TOLD TO AL
Of course.
Uh, yeah.
It kicks some ass.
He just talked to us!

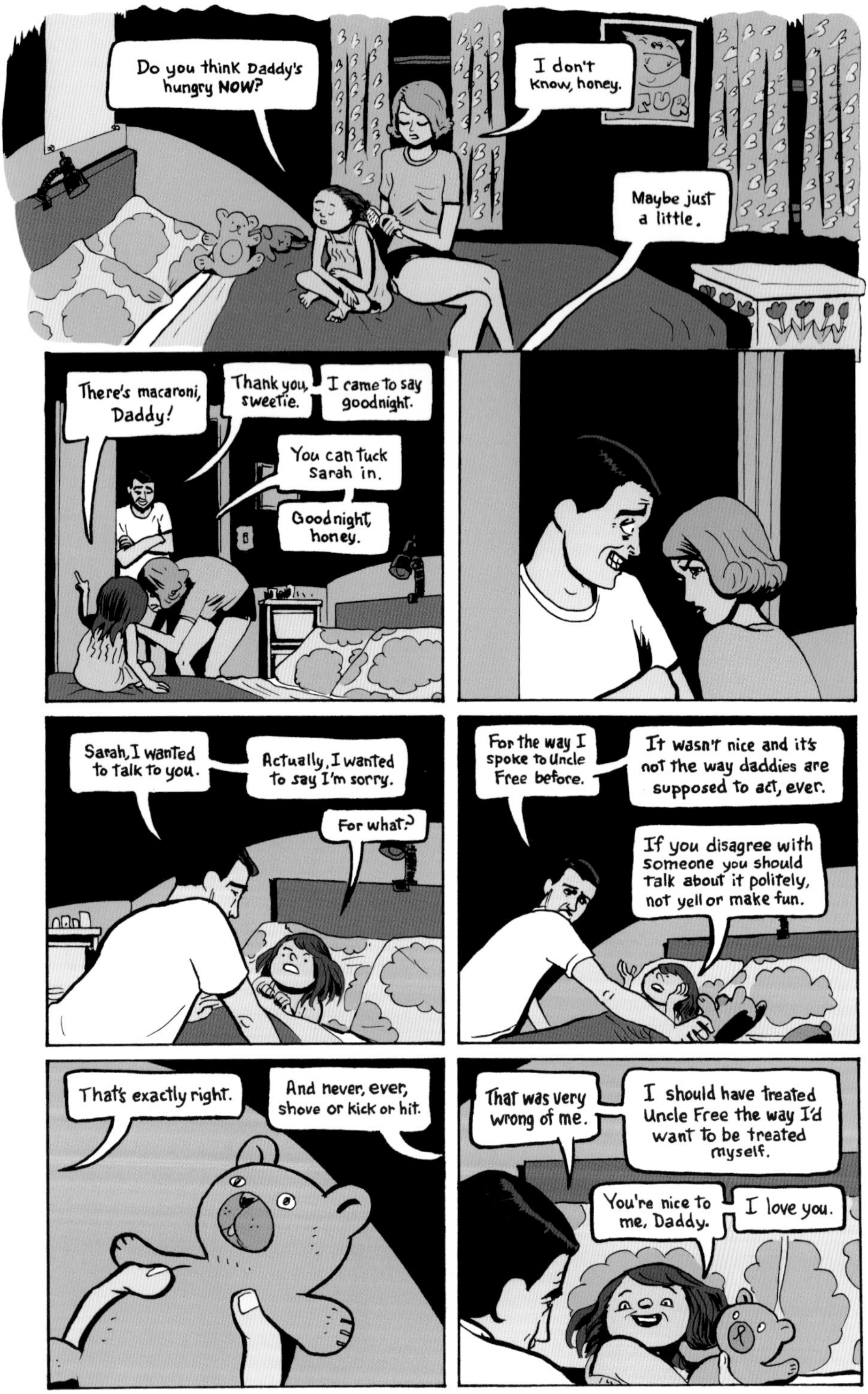
Do you think Daddy's hungry NOW?
I don't know, honey.
Maybe just a little.
There's macaroni, Daddy!
Thank you, sweetie.
I came to say goodnight.
You can tuck Sarah in.
Goodnight, honey.
Sarah, I wanted to talk to you.
Actually, I wanted to say I'm sorry.
For what?
For the way I spoke to Uncle Free before.
It wasn't nice and it's not the way daddies are supposed to act, ever.
If you disagree with someone you should talk about it politely, not yell or make fun.
That's exactly right.
And never, ever, shove or kick or hit.
That was very wrong of me.
I should have treated Uncle Free the way I'd want to be treated myself.
You're nice to me, Daddy.
I love you.

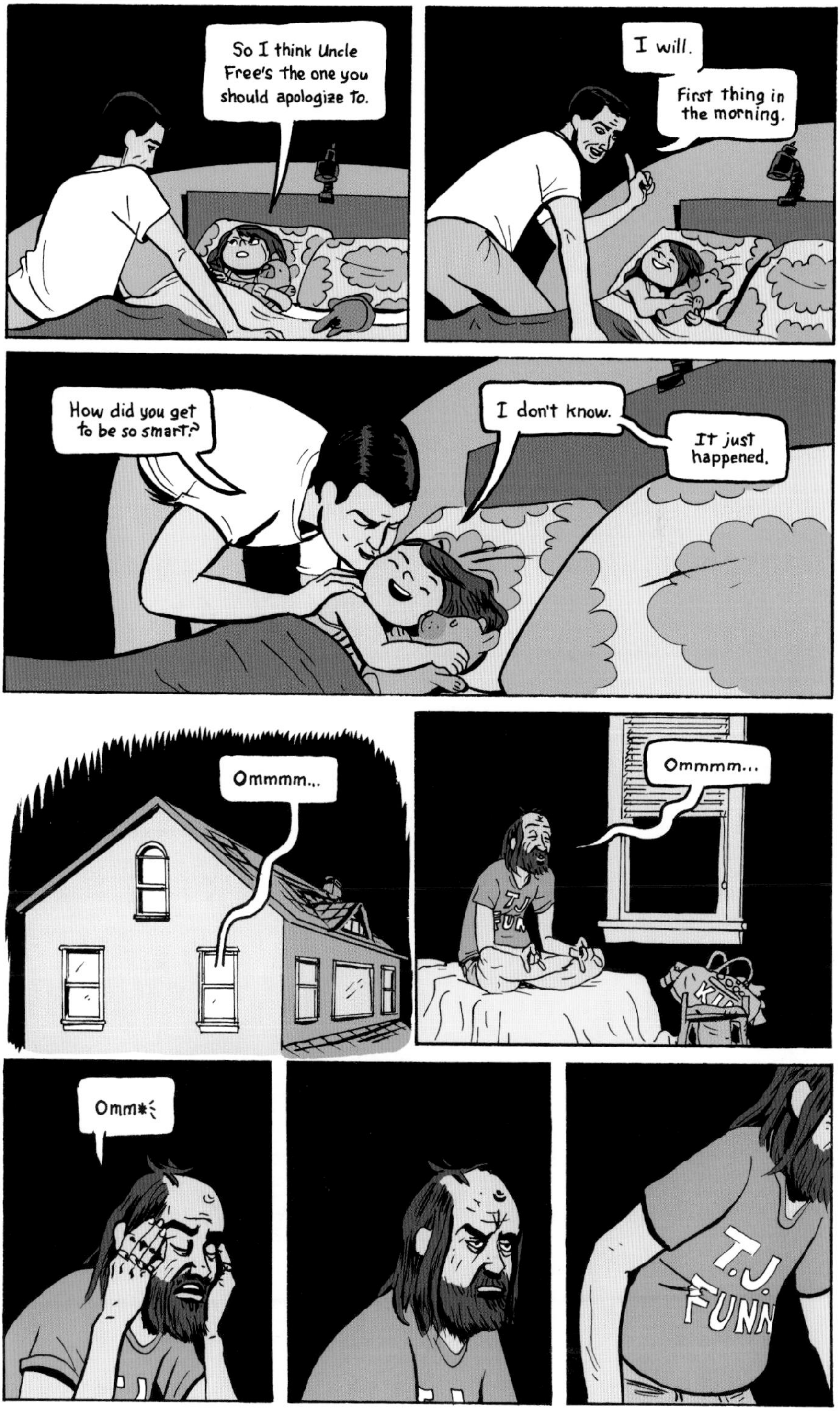
So I think Uncle Free's the one you should apologize to.
I will.
First thing in the morning.
How did you get to be so smart?
I don't know.
It just happened.
Ommmm...
Ommmm...
Omm*!
T.J. FUNN

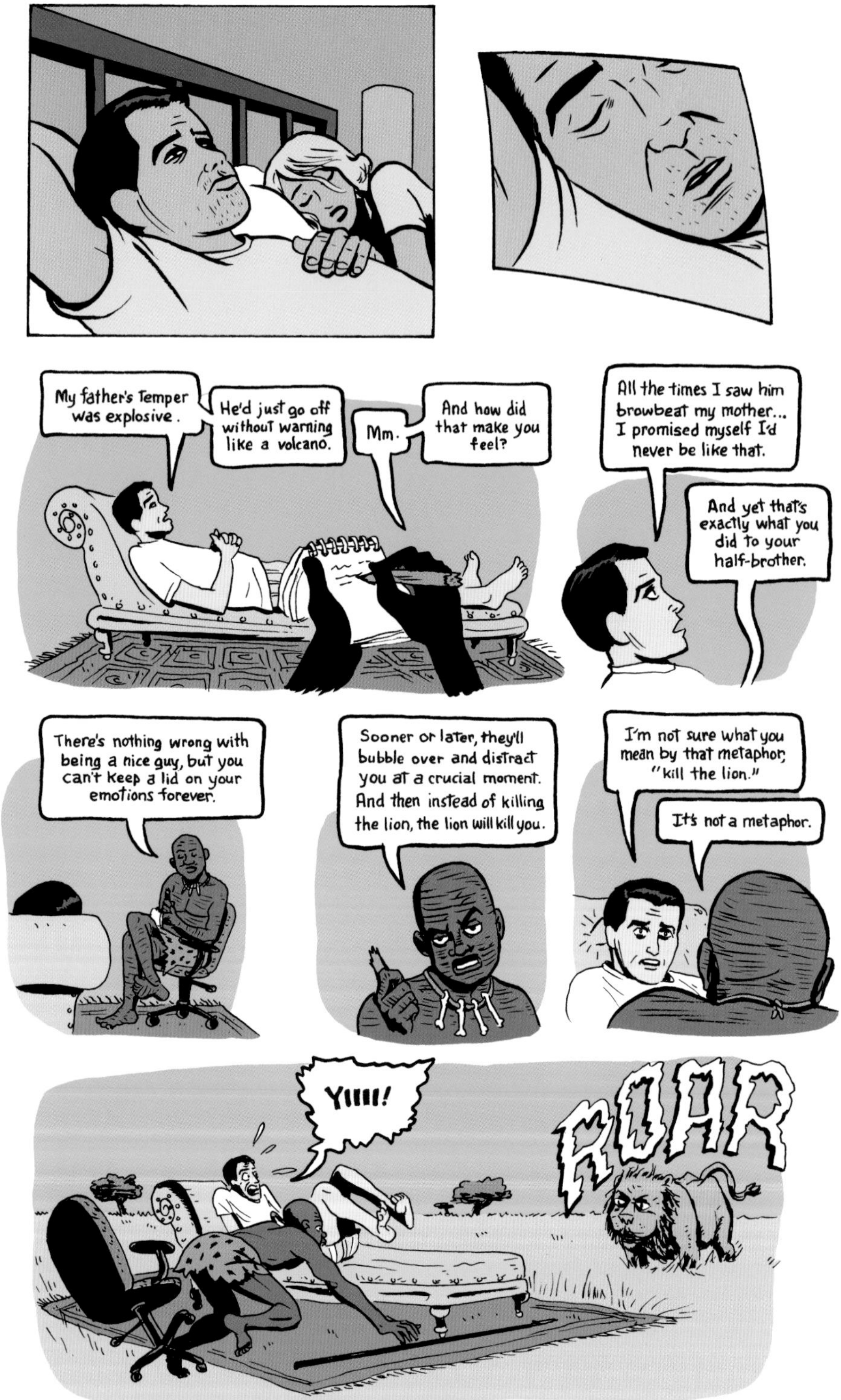
My father's temper was explosive.
He'd just go off without warning like a volcano.
Mm.
And how did that make you feel?
All the times I saw him browbeat my mother... I promised myself I'd never be like that.
And yet that's exactly what you did to your half-brother.
There's nothing wrong with being a nice guy, but you can't keep a lid on your emotions forever.
Sooner or later, they'll bubble over and distract you at a crucial moment. And then instead of killing the lion, the lion will kill you.
I'm not sure what you mean by that metaphor, "kill the lion."
It's not a metaphor.
YIIII!
ROAR

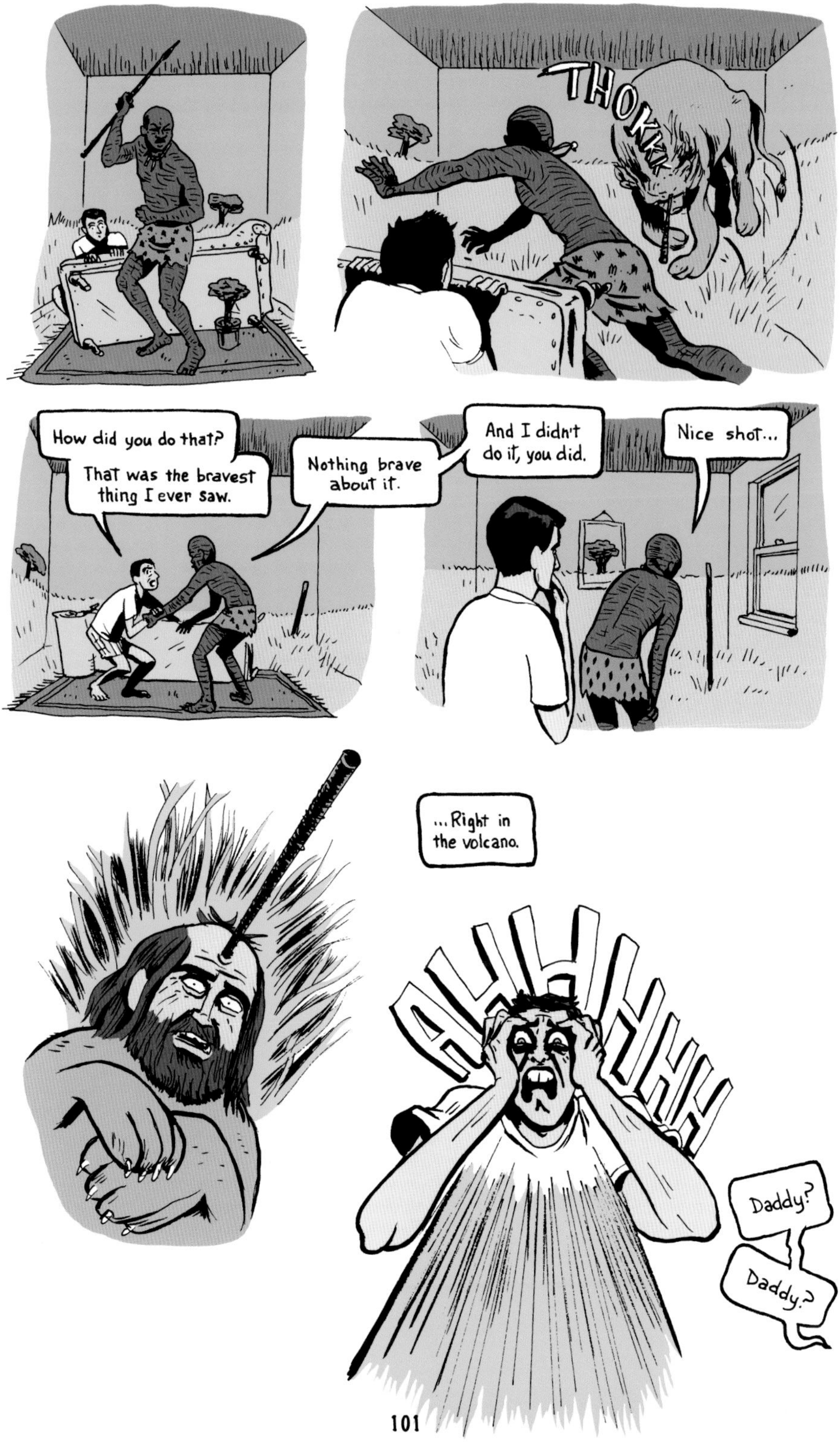
THOKK
How did you do that?
That was the bravest thing I ever saw.
Nothing brave about it.
And I didn't do it, you did.
Nice shot...
...Right in the volcano.
AHHHHHH
Daddy?
Daddy?

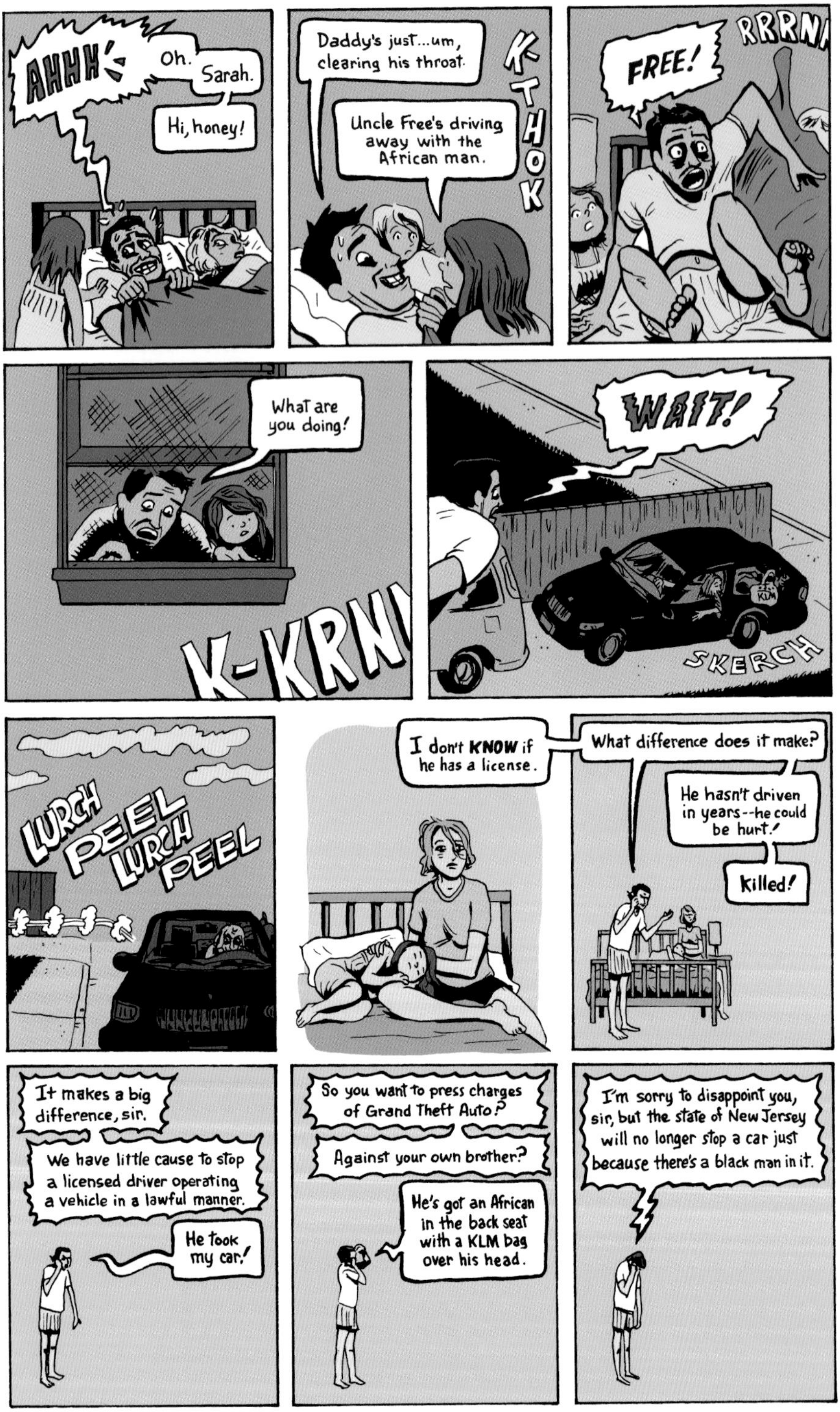
AHHH
Oh.
Sarah.
Hi, honey!
Daddy's just...um, clearing his throat.
KTHOK
Uncle Free's driving away with the African man.
RRRN
FREE!
What are you doing!
K-KRN
WAIT!
KLM
SKERCH
LURCH PEEL LURCH PEEL
I don't **KNOW** if he has a license.
What difference does it make?
He hasn't driven in years--he could be hurt!
Killed!
It makes a big difference, sir.
We have little cause to stop a licensed driver operating a vehicle in a lawful manner.
He took my car!
So you want to press charges of Grand Theft Auto?
Against your own brother?
He's got an African in the back seat with a KLM bag over his head.
I'm sorry to disappoint you, sir, but the state of New Jersey will no longer stop a car just because there's a black man in it.

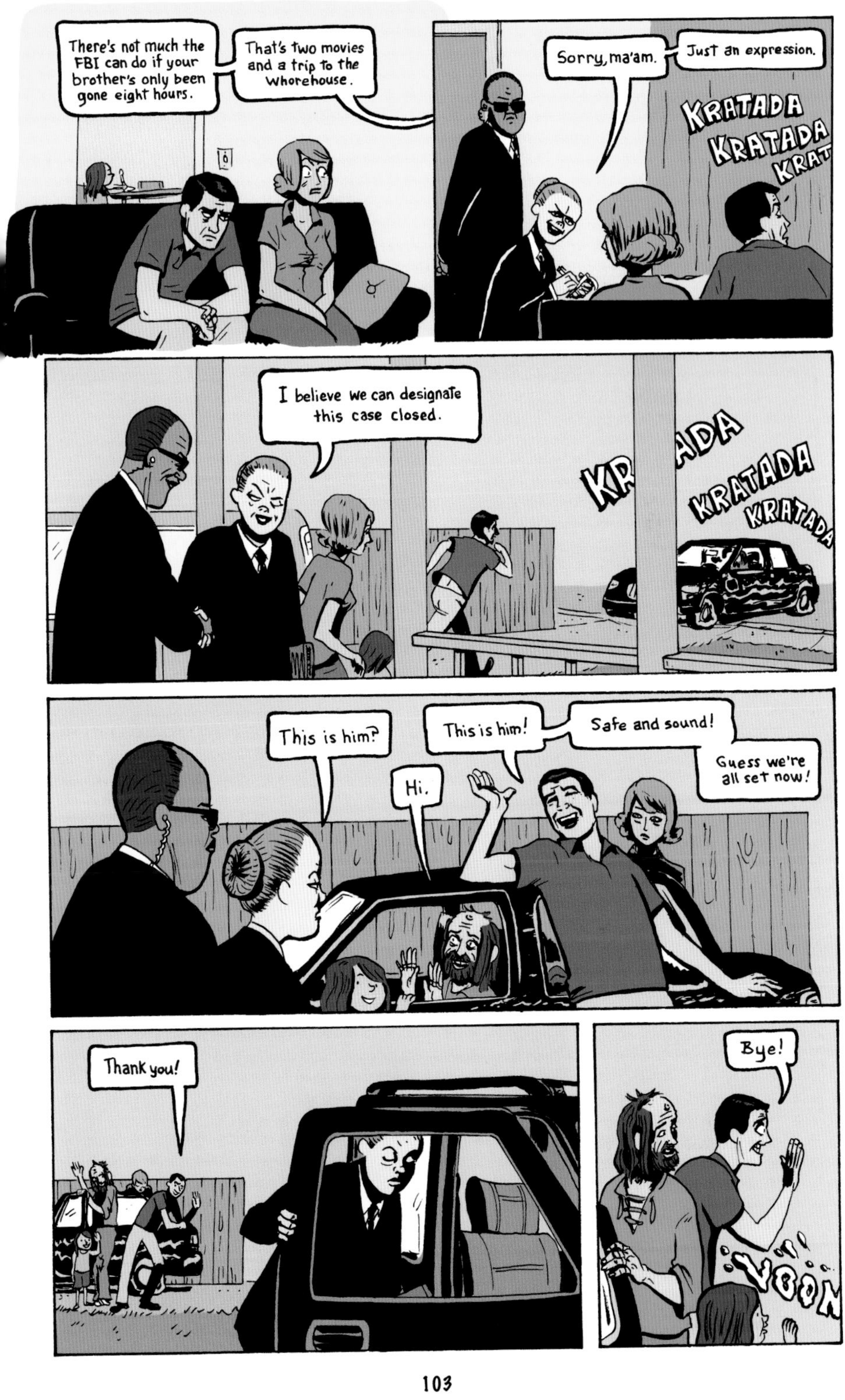

There's not much the FBI can do if your brother's only been gone eight hours.
That's two movies and a trip to the whorehouse.
Sorry, ma'am.
Just an expression.
KRATADA
KRATADA
KRAT
I believe we can designate this case closed.
KR ADA
KRATADA
KRATADA
This is him?
This is him!
Safe and sound!
Guess we're all set now!
Hi.
Thank you!
Bye!
VOOM

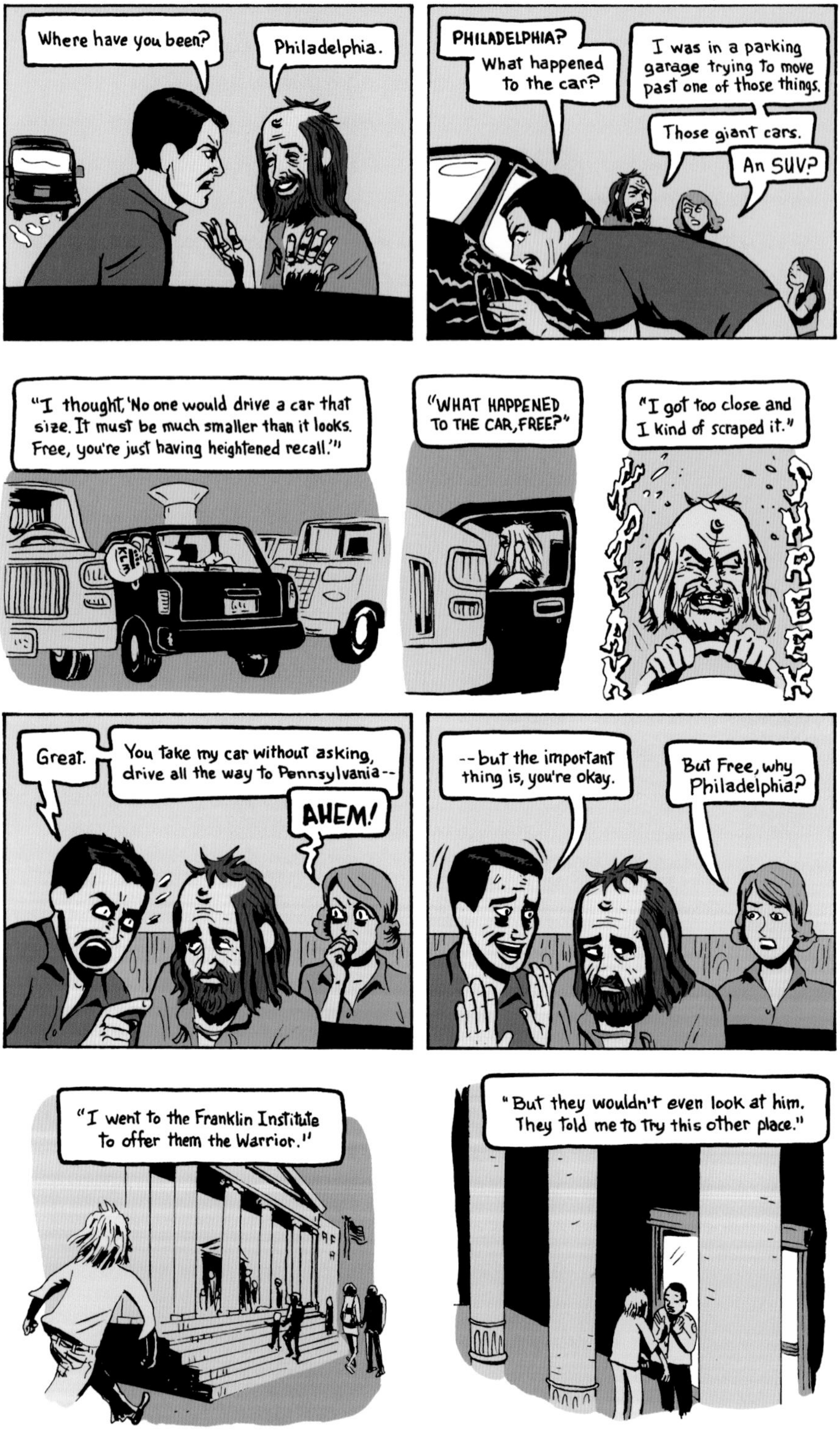
Where have you been?
Philadelphia.
PHILADELPHIA? What happened to the car?
I was in a parking garage trying to move past one of those things.
Those giant cars.
An SUV?
"I thought, 'No one would drive a car that size. It must be much smaller than it looks. Free, you're just having heightened recall.'"
"WHAT HAPPENED TO THE CAR, FREE?"
"I got too close and I kind of scraped it."
KREAK
SHREEK
Great.
You take my car without asking, drive all the way to Pennsylvania--
AHEM!
--but the important thing is, you're okay.
But Free, why Philadelphia?
"I went to the Franklin Institute to offer them the Warrior."
"But they wouldn't even look at him. They told me to try this other place."

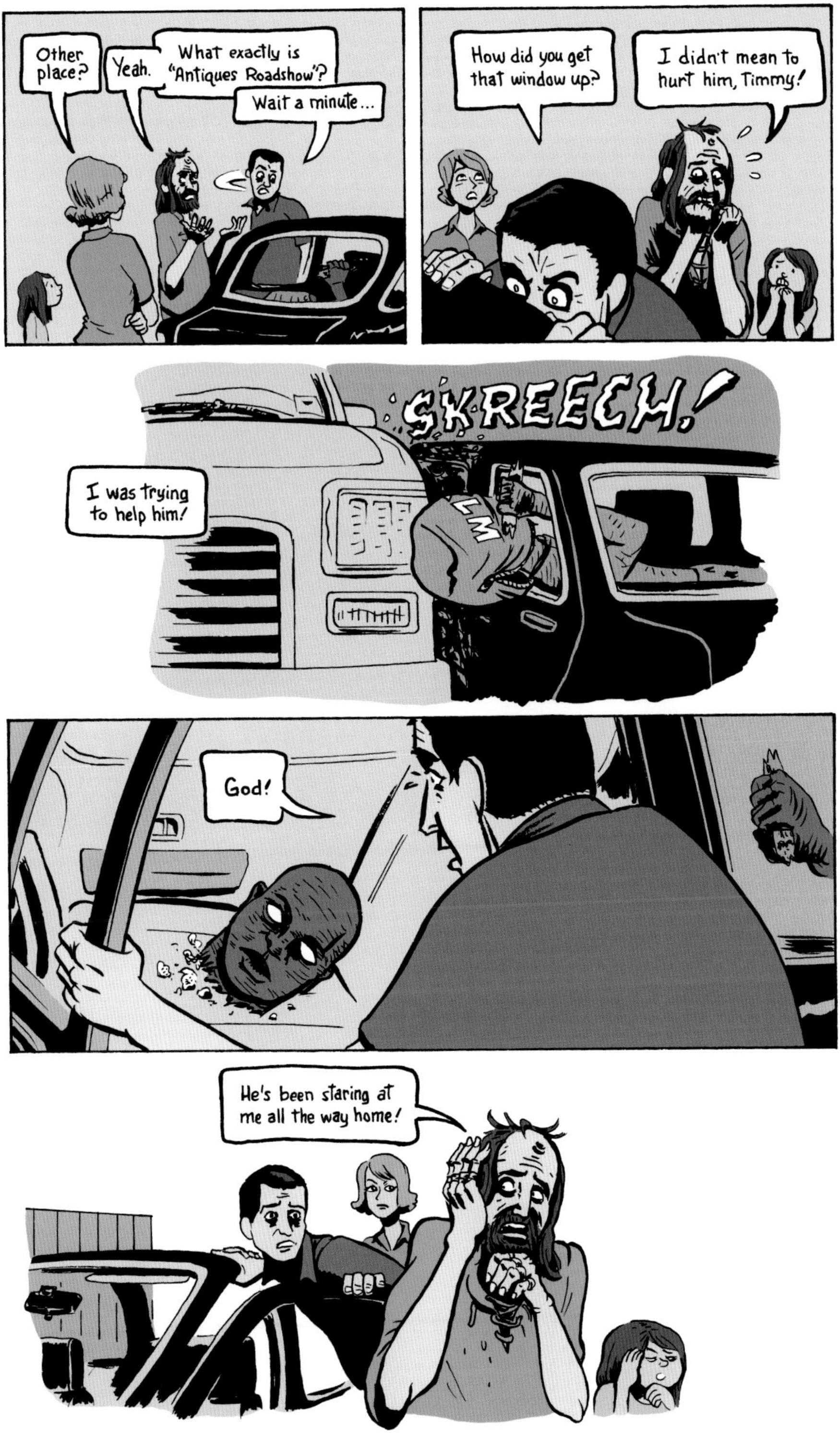

Other place?
Yeah.
What exactly is "Antiques Roadshow"?
Wait a minute...
How did you get that window up?
I didn't mean to hurt him, Timmy!
SKREECH!
I was trying to help him!
LM
God!
He's been staring at me all the way home!

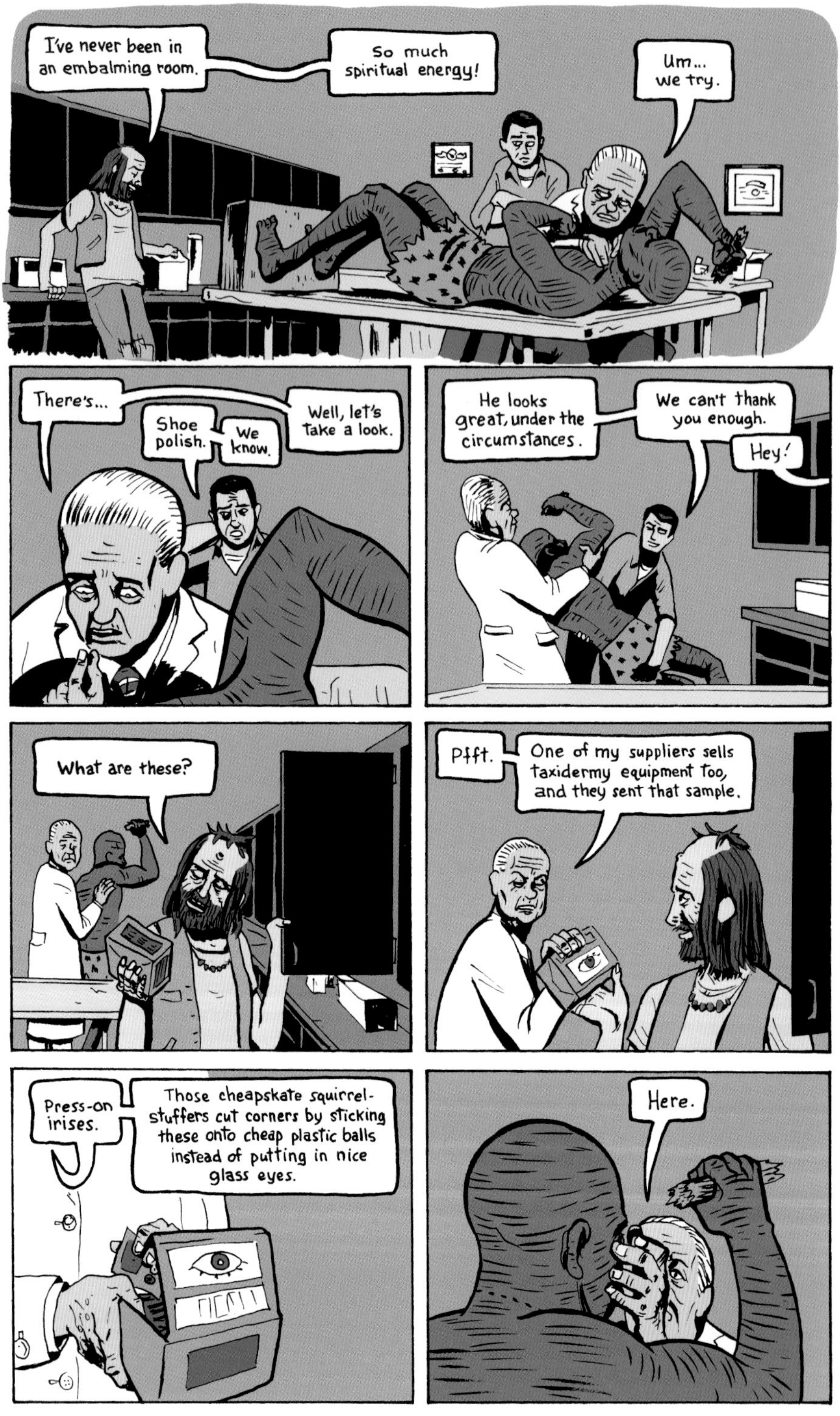
I've never been in an embalming room.
So much spiritual energy!
Um... we try.
There's...
Well, let's take a look.
Shoe polish.
We know.
He looks great, under the circumstances.
We can't thank you enough.
Hey!
What are these?
Pfft.
One of my suppliers sells taxidermy equipment too, and they sent that sample.
Press-on irises.
Those cheapskate squirrel-stuffers cut corners by sticking these onto cheap plastic balls instead of putting in nice glass eyes.
Here.

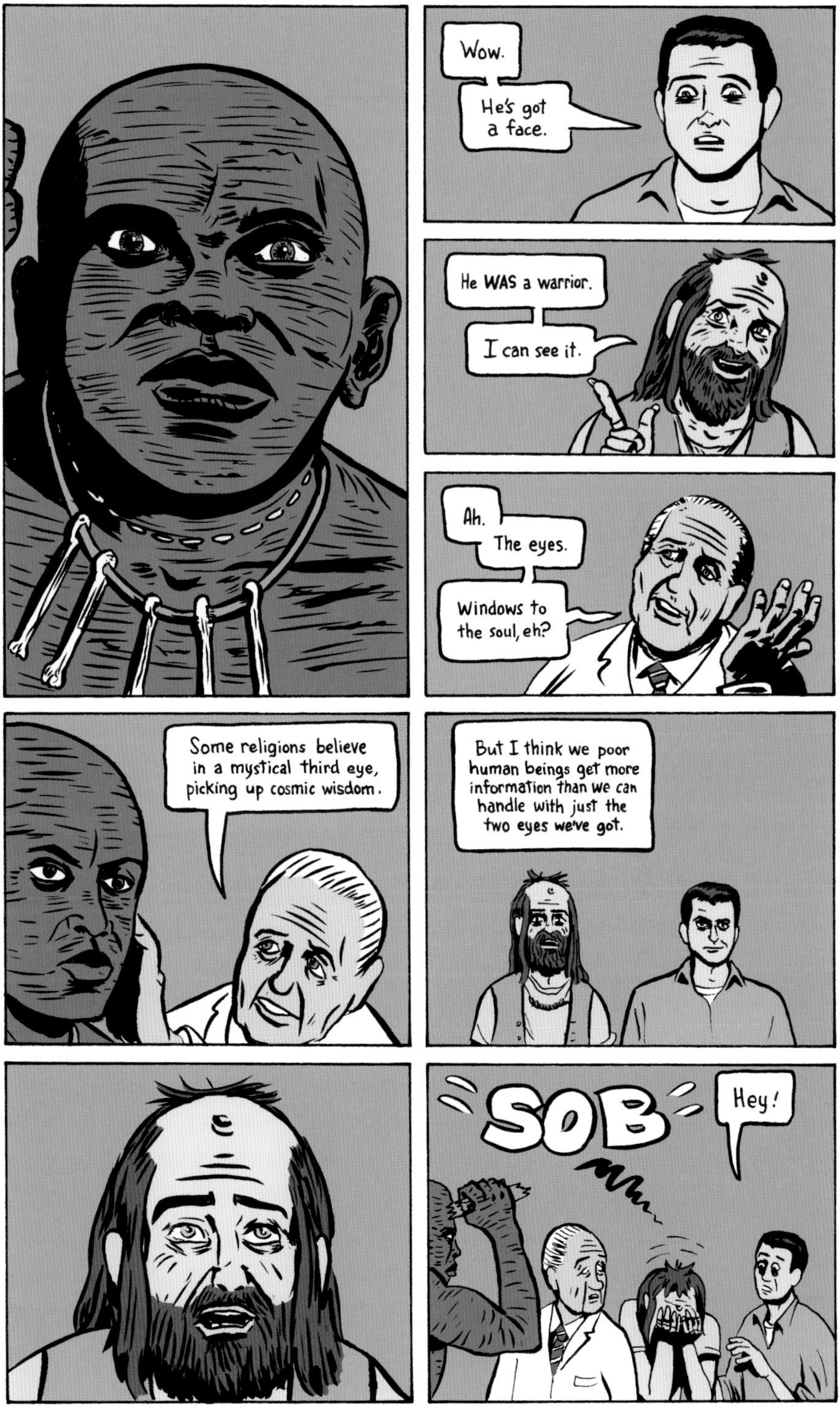
Wow.
He's got a face.
He WAS a warrior.
I can see it.
Ah.
The eyes.
Windows to the soul, eh?
Some religions believe in a mystical third eye, picking up cosmic wisdom.
But I think we poor human beings get more information than we can handle with just the two eyes we've got.
SOB
Hey!

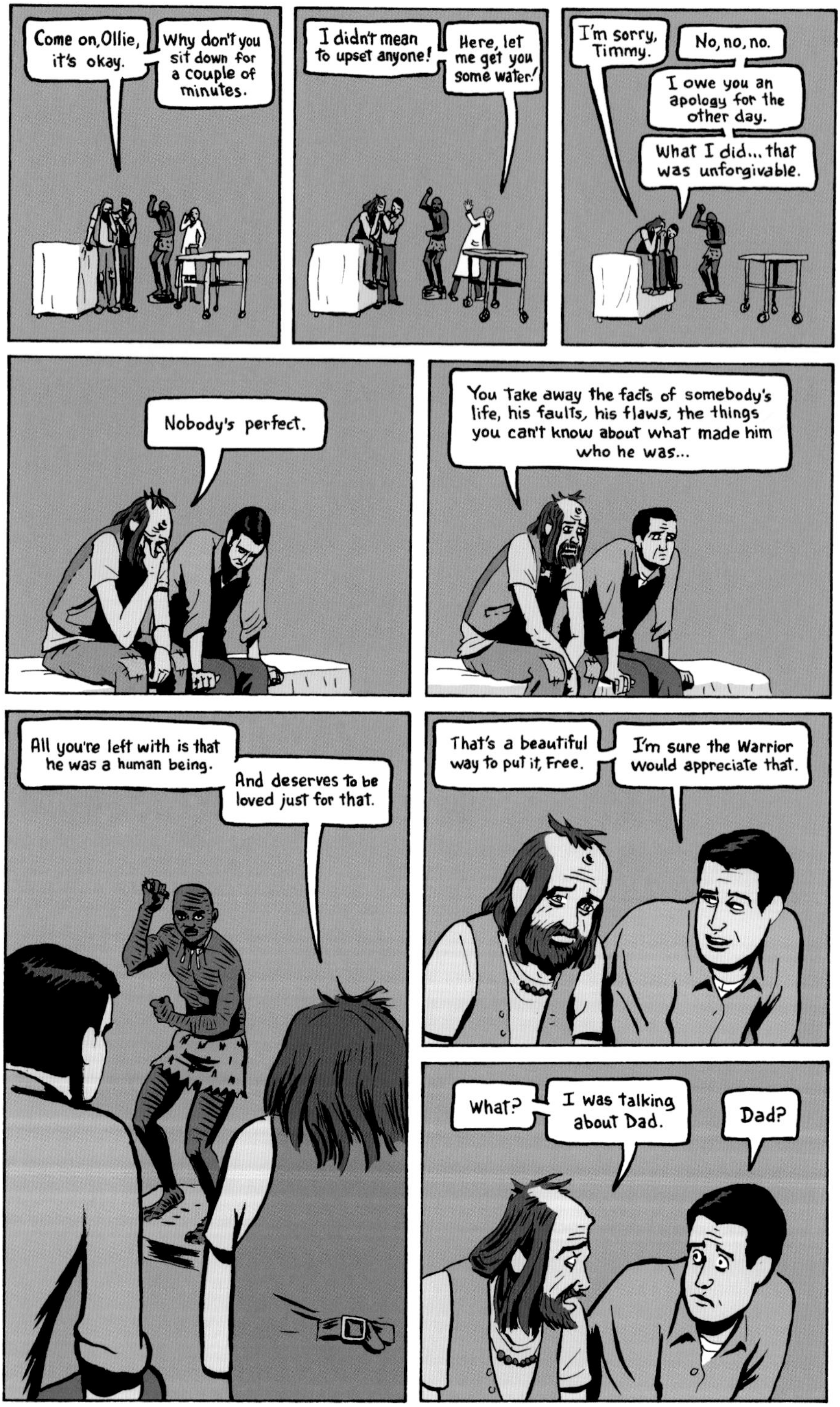
Come on, Ollie, it's okay.
Why don't you sit down for a couple of minutes.
I didn't mean to upset anyone!
Here, let me get you some water!
I'm sorry, Timmy.
No, no, no.
I owe you an apology for the other day.
What I did... that was unforgivable.
Nobody's perfect.
You take away the facts of somebody's life, his faults, his flaws, the things you can't know about what made him who he was...
All you're left with is that he was a human being.
And deserves to be loved just for that.
That's a beautiful way to put it, Free.
I'm sure the Warrior would appreciate that.
What?
I was talking about Dad.
Dad?

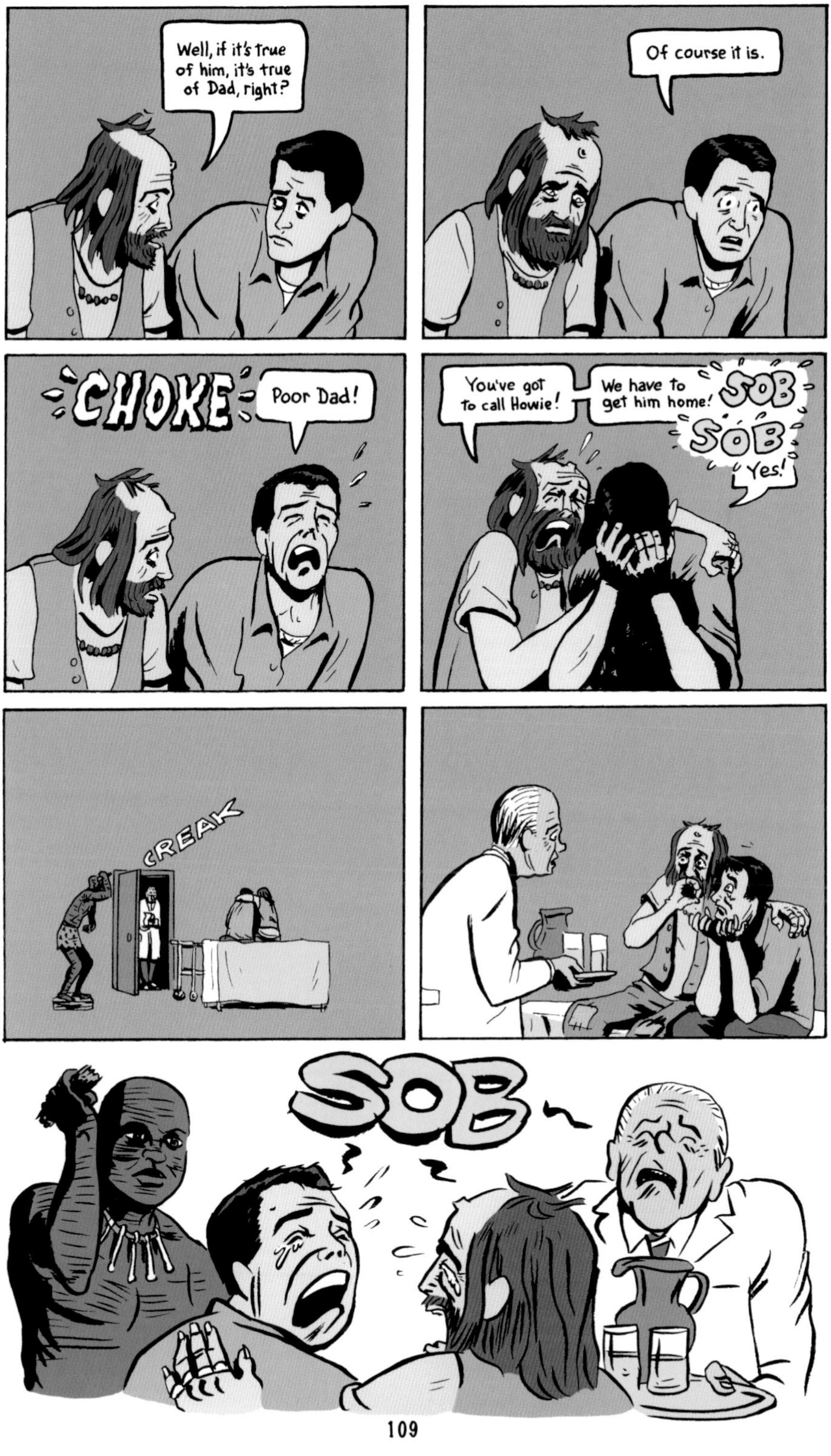
Well, if it's true of him, it's true of Dad, right?
Of course it is.
CHOKE
Poor Dad!
You've got to call Howie!
We have to get him home!
SOB
SOB
Yes!
CREAK
SOB

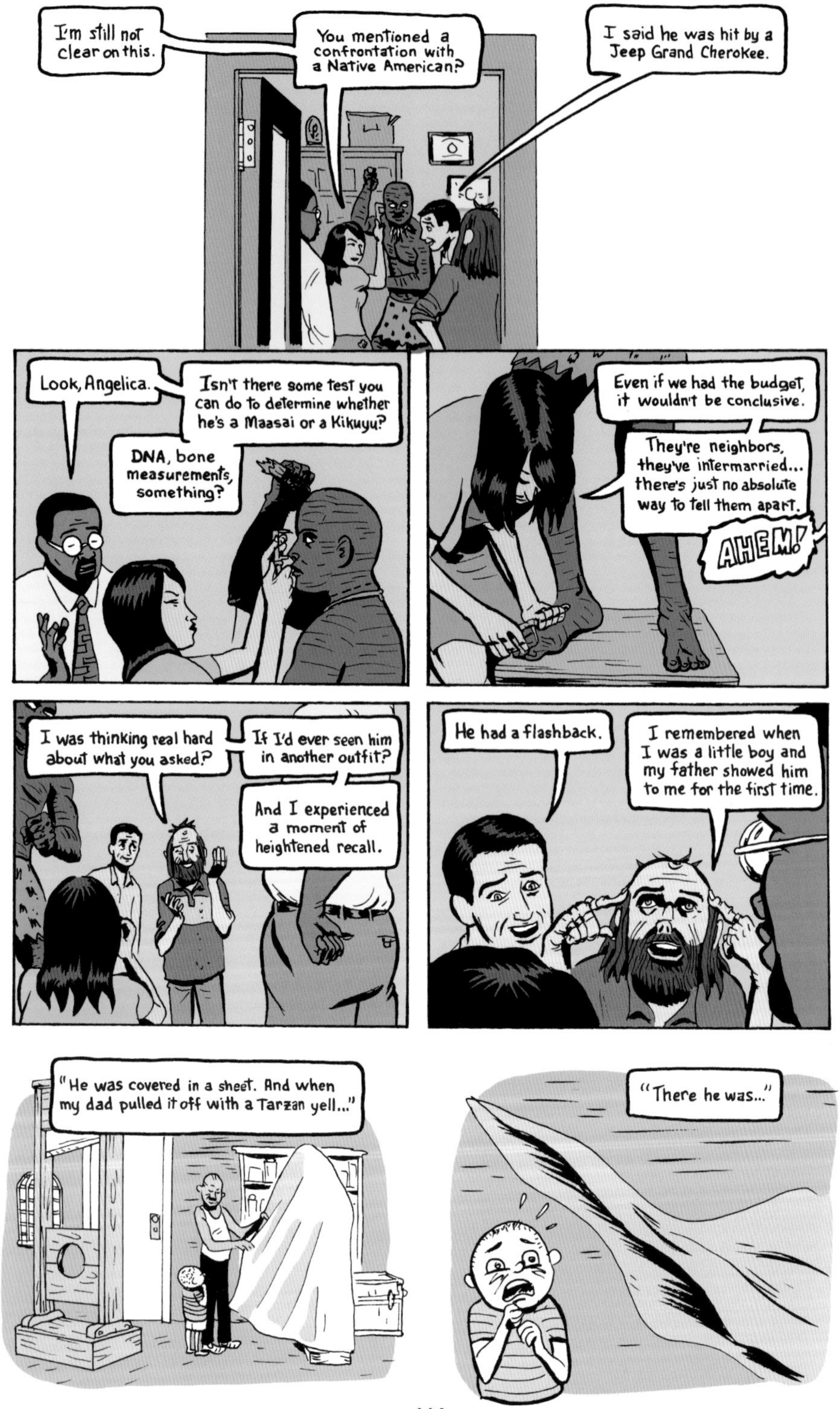
I'm still not clear on this.
You mentioned a confrontation with a Native American?
I said he was hit by a Jeep Grand Cherokee.
Look, Angelica.
Isn't there some test you can do to determine whether he's a Maasai or a Kikuyu?
DNA, bone measurements, something?
Even if we had the budget, it wouldn't be conclusive.
They're neighbors, they've intermarried... there's just no absolute way to tell them apart.
AHEM!
I was thinking real hard about what you asked?
If I'd ever seen him in another outfit?
And I experienced a moment of heightened recall.
He had a flashback.
I remembered when I was a little boy and my father showed him to me for the first time.
"He was covered in a sheet. And when my dad pulled it off with a Tarzan yell..."
"There he was..."

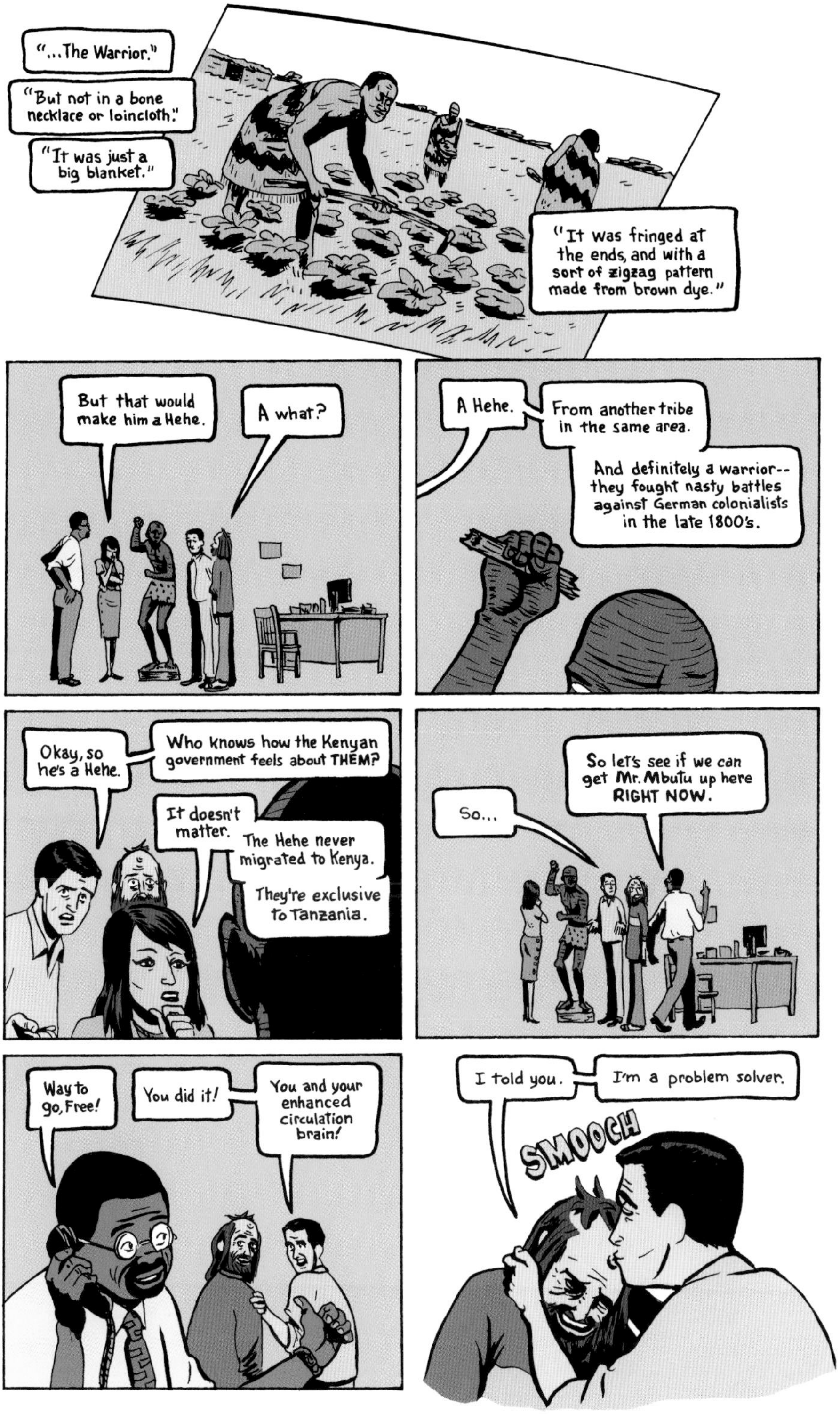
"...The Warrior."
"But not in a bone necklace or loincloth."
"It was just a big blanket."
"It was fringed at the ends, and with a sort of zigzag pattern made from brown dye."
But that would make him a Hehe.
A what?
A Hehe.
From another tribe in the same area.
And definitely a warrior--they fought nasty battles against German colonialists in the late 1800's.
Okay, so he's a Hehe.
Who knows how the Kenyan government feels about THEM?
It doesn't matter.
The Hehe never migrated to Kenya.
They're exclusive to Tanzania.
So...
So let's see if we can get Mr. Mbutu up here RIGHT NOW.
Way to go, Free!
You did it!
You and your enhanced circulation brain!
I told you.
I'm a problem solver.
SMOOCH

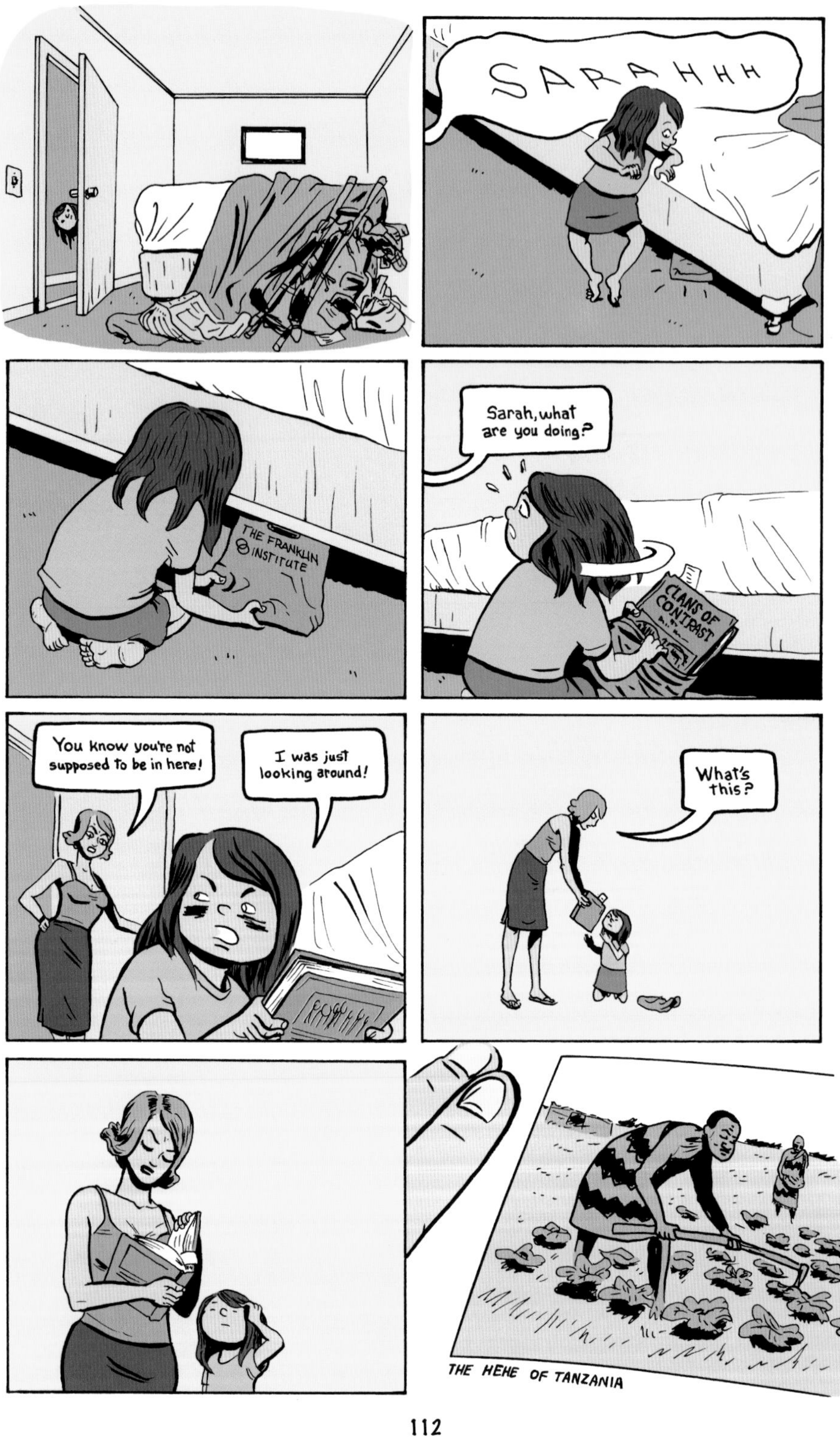
SARAHHH
THE FRANKLIN INSTITUTE
Sarah, what are you doing?
CLANS OF CONTRAST
You know you're not supposed to be in here!
I was just looking around!
What's this?
THE HEHE OF TANZANIA

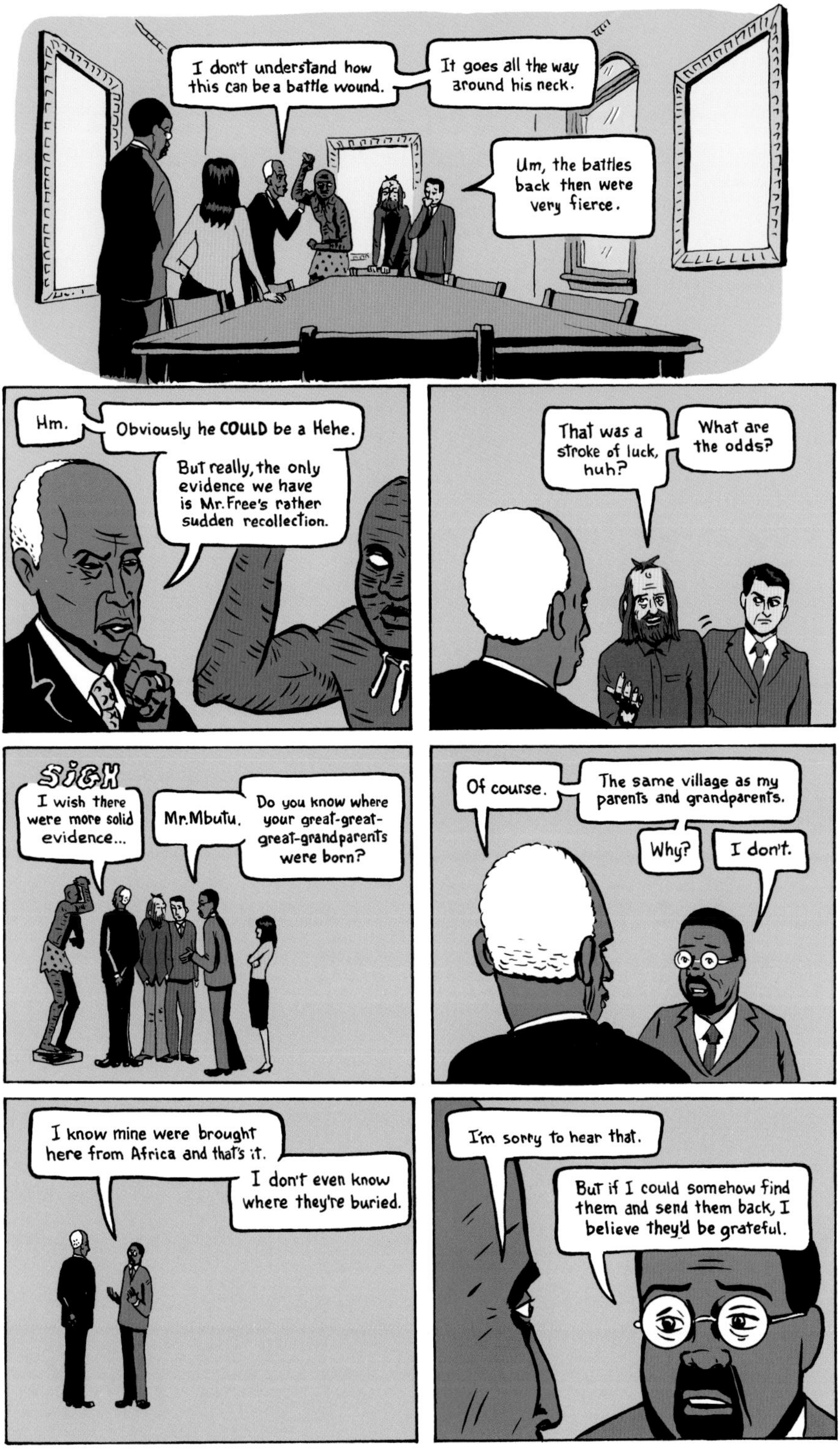
I don't understand how this can be a battle wound.
It goes all the way around his neck.
Um, the battles back then were very fierce.
Hm.
Obviously he COULD be a Hehe.
But really, the only evidence we have is Mr. Free's rather sudden recollection.
That was a stroke of luck, huh?
What are the odds?
SIGH
I wish there were more solid evidence...
Mr. Mbutu.
Do you know where your great-great-great-grandparents were born?
Of course.
The same village as my parents and grandparents.
Why?
I don't.
I know mine were brought here from Africa and that's it.
I don't even know where they're buried.
I'm sorry to hear that.
But if I could somehow find them and send them back, I believe they'd be grateful.

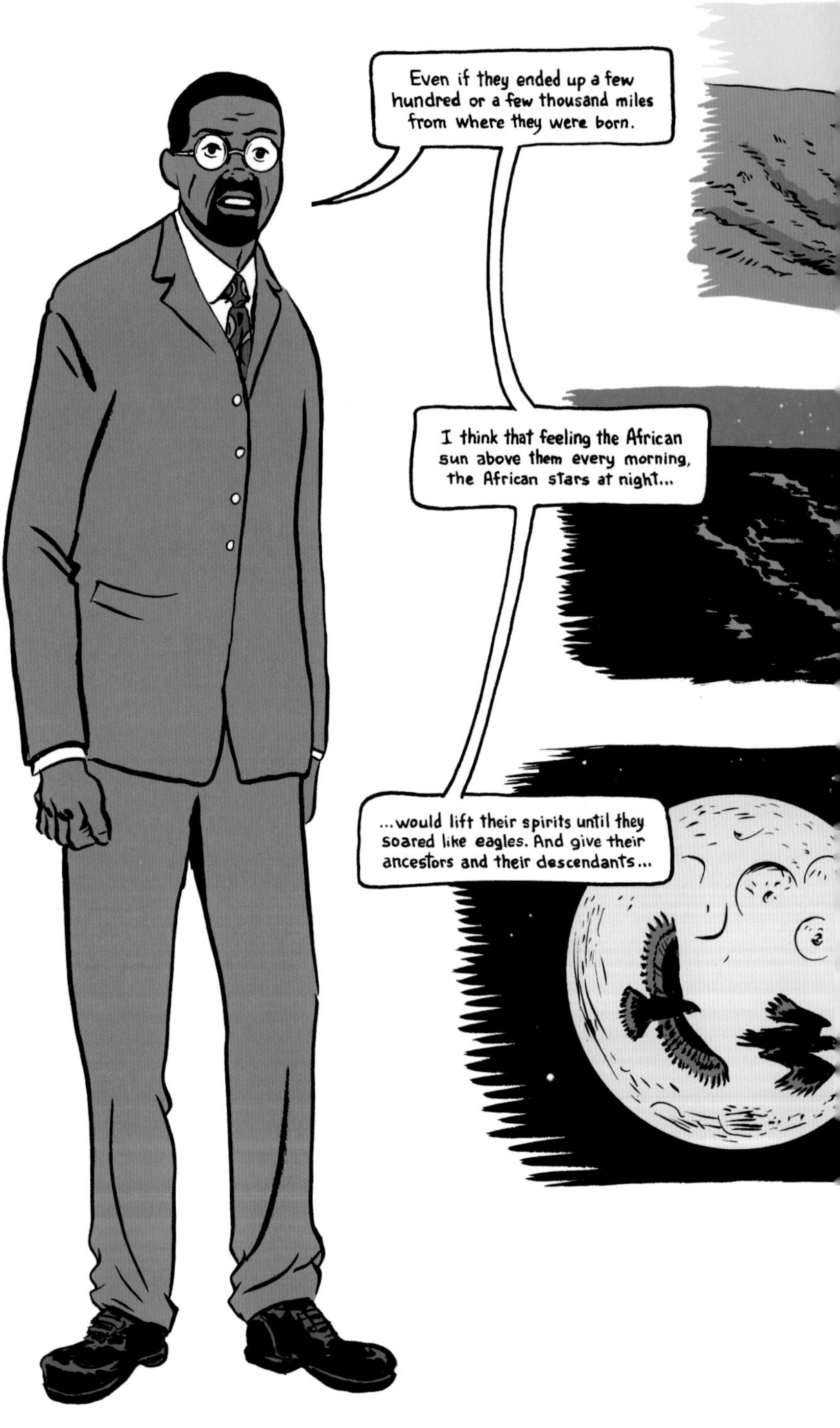
Even if they ended up a few hundred or a few thousand miles from where they were born.
I think that feeling the African sun above them every morning, the African stars at night...
...would lift their spirits until they soared like eagles. And give their ancestors and their descendants...

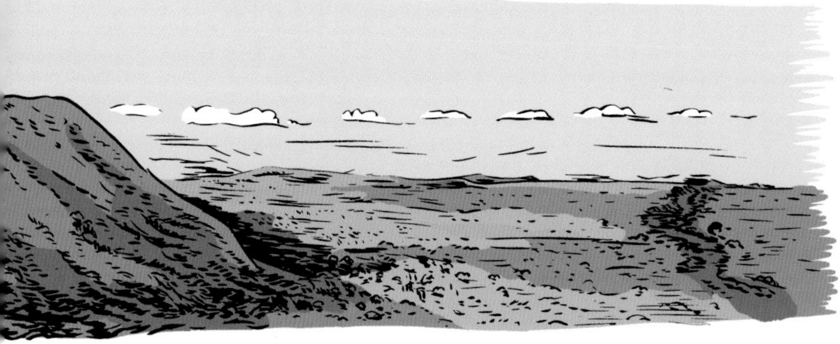

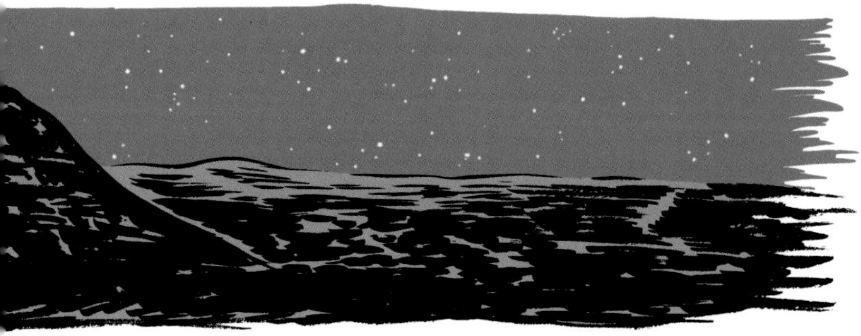

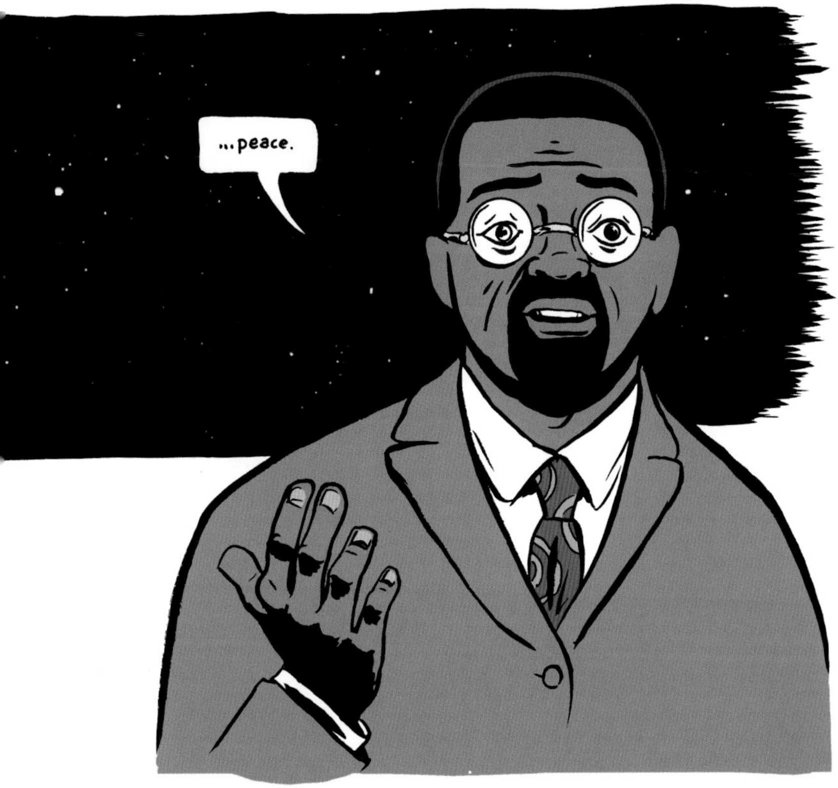
...peace.

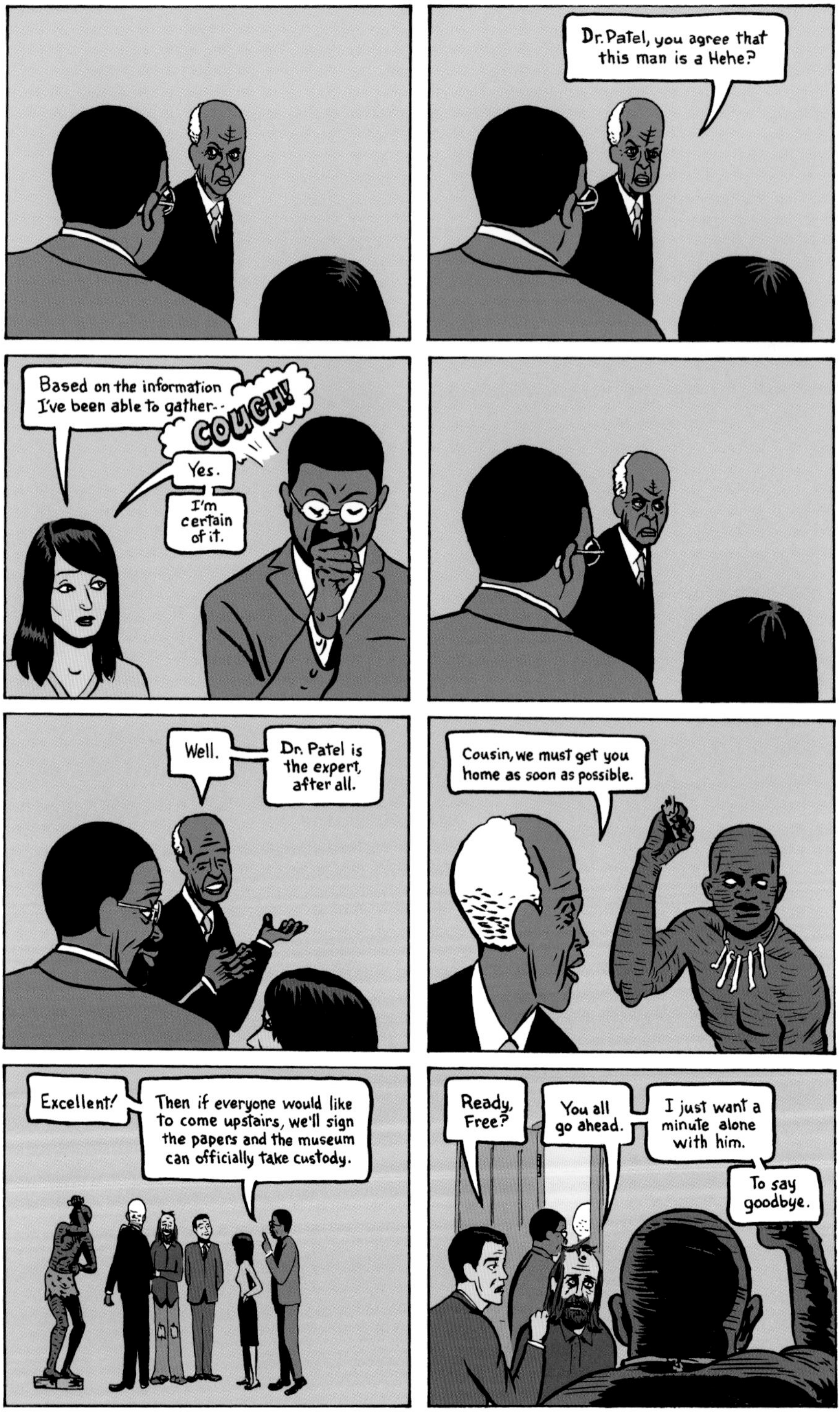
Dr. Patel, you agree that this man is a Hehe?
Based on the information I've been able to gather- -
COUGH!
Yes.
I'm certain of it.
Well.
Dr. Patel is the expert, after all.
Cousin, we must get you home as soon as possible.
Excellent!
Then if everyone would like to come upstairs, we'll sign the papers and the museum can officially take custody.
Ready, Free?
You all go ahead.
I just want a minute alone with him.
To say goodbye.

Well.

I guess that's it.

If Howie's right about all those spirits... and you happen to see my father... will you tell him I did the right thing?

But, uh, try not to sneak up on him...

He's scared of black people.

Yes.

You're going home.

Where am I going?

Hey.

You ready to sign some autographs?

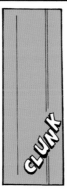

CLUNK

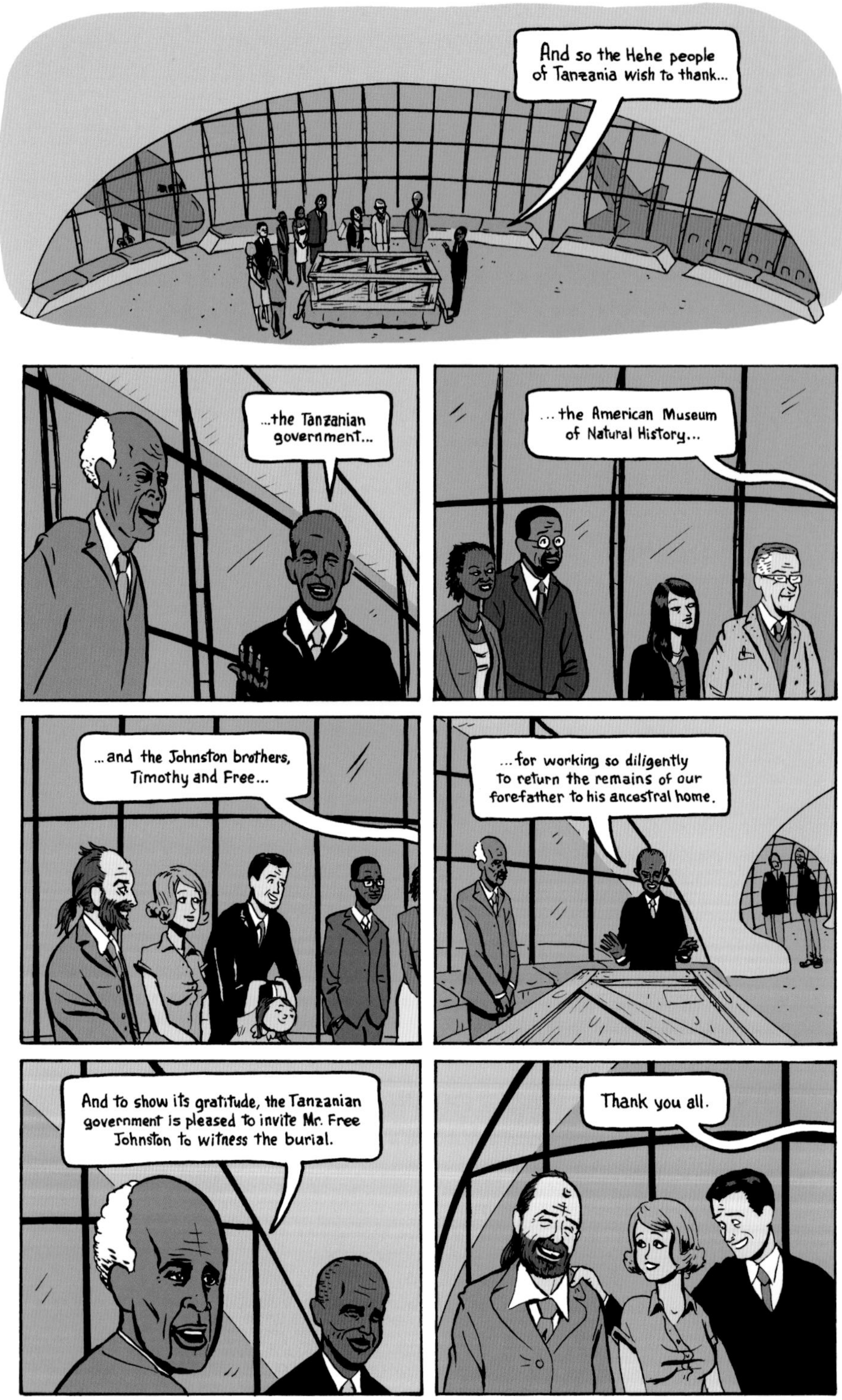
And so the Hehe people of Tanzania wish to thank...
...the Tanzanian government...
...the American Museum of Natural History...
...and the Johnston brothers, Timothy and Free...
...for working so diligently to return the remains of our forefather to his ancestral home.
And to show its gratitude, the Tanzanian government is pleased to invite Mr. Free Johnston to witness the burial.
Thank you all.

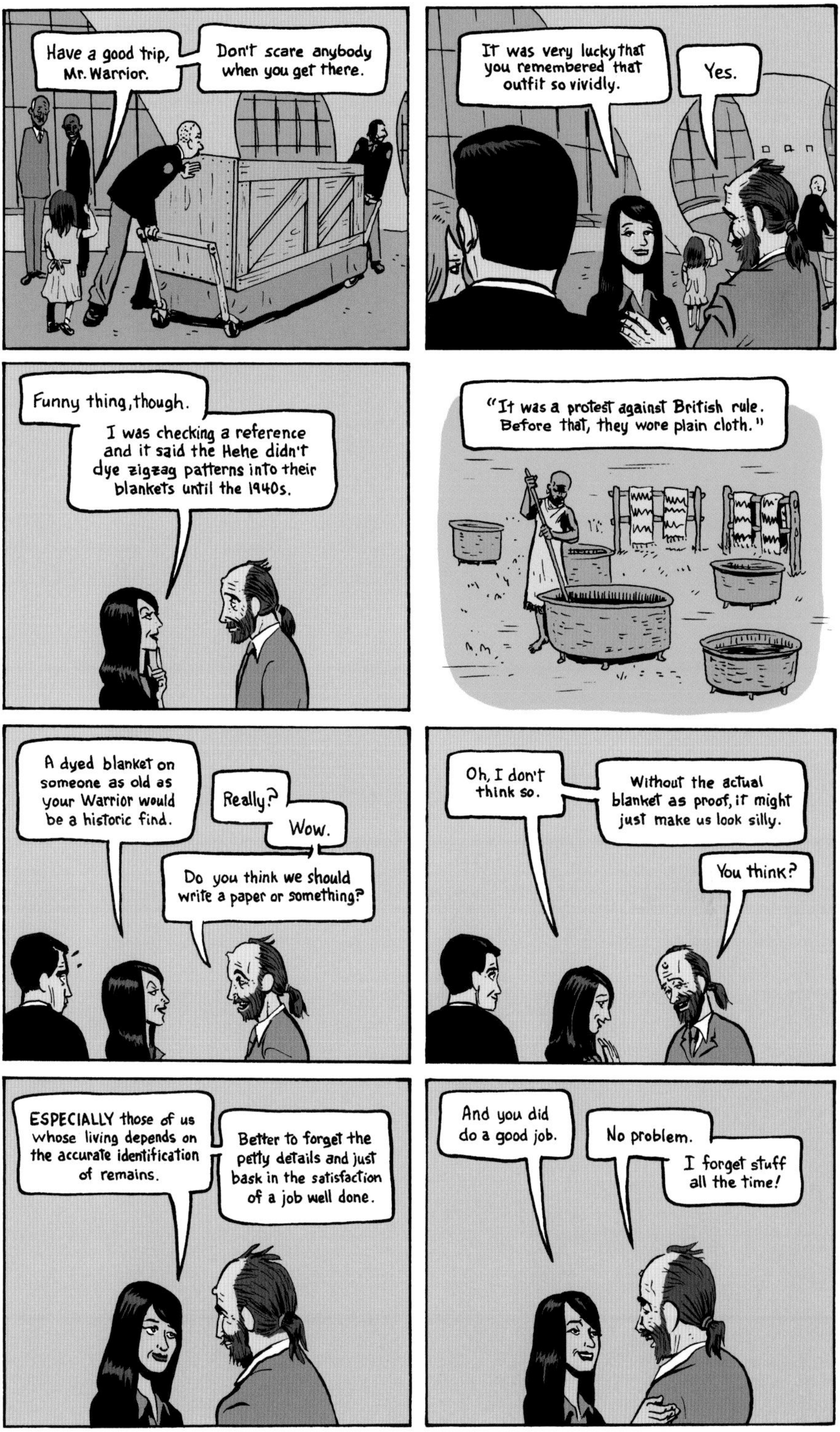
Have a good trip, Mr. Warrior.
Don't scare anybody when you get there.
It was very lucky that you remembered that outfit so vividly.
Yes.
Funny thing, though.
I was checking a reference and it said the Hehe didn't dye zigzag patterns into their blankets until the 1940s.
"It was a protest against British rule. Before that, they wore plain cloth."
A dyed blanket on someone as old as your Warrior would be a historic find.
Really?
Wow.
Do you think we should write a paper or something?
Oh, I don't think so.
Without the actual blanket as proof, it might just make us look silly.
You think?
ESPECIALLY those of us whose living depends on the accurate identification of remains.
Better to forget the petty details and just bask in the satisfaction of a job well done.
And you did do a good job.
No problem.
I forget stuff all the time!

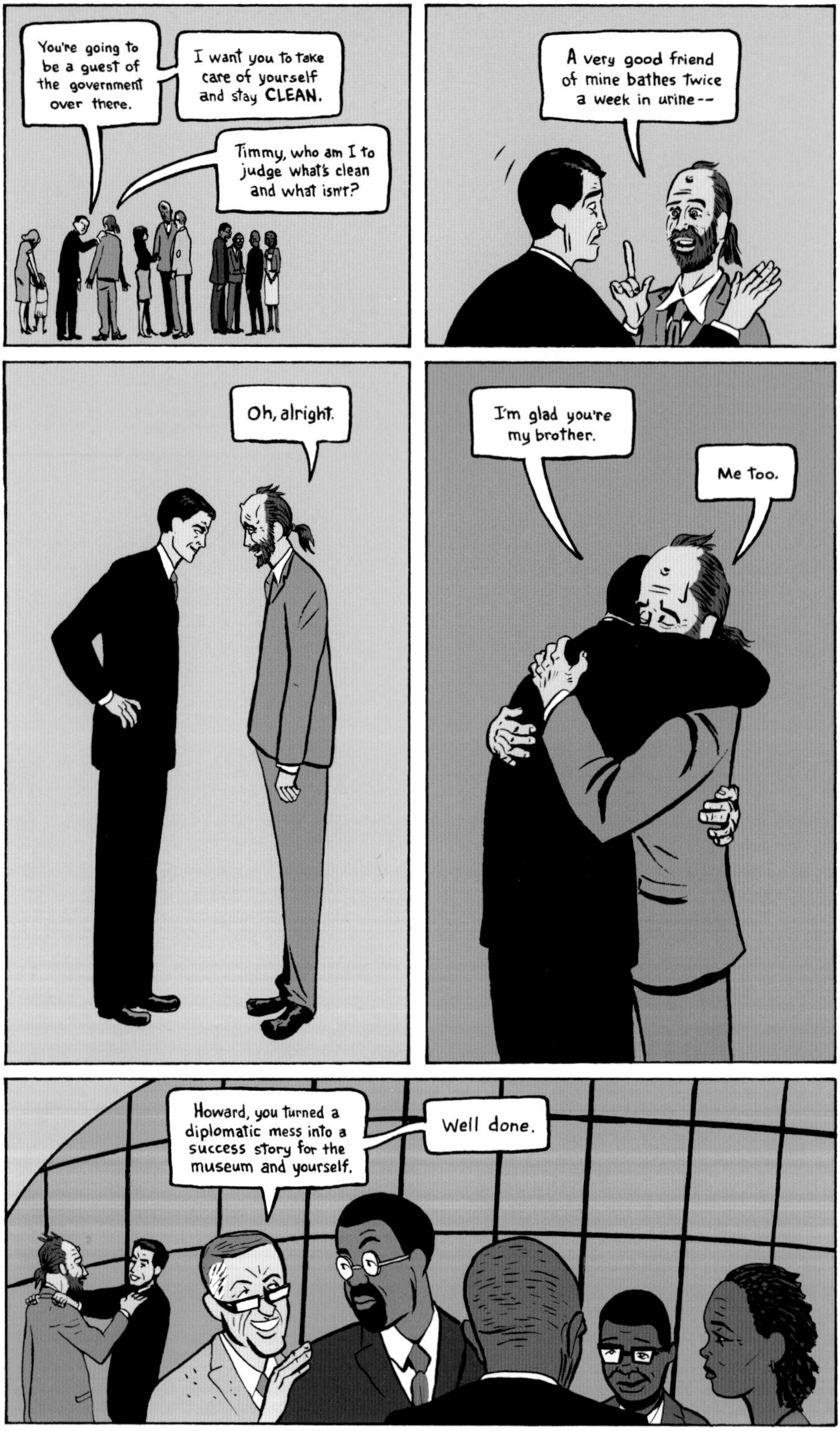
You're going to be a guest of the government over there.
I want you to take care of yourself and stay CLEAN.
Timmy, who am I to judge what's clean and what isn't?
A very good friend of mine bathes twice a week in urine--
Oh, alright.
I'm glad you're my brother.
Me too.
Howard, you turned a diplomatic mess into a success story for the museum and yourself.
Well done.

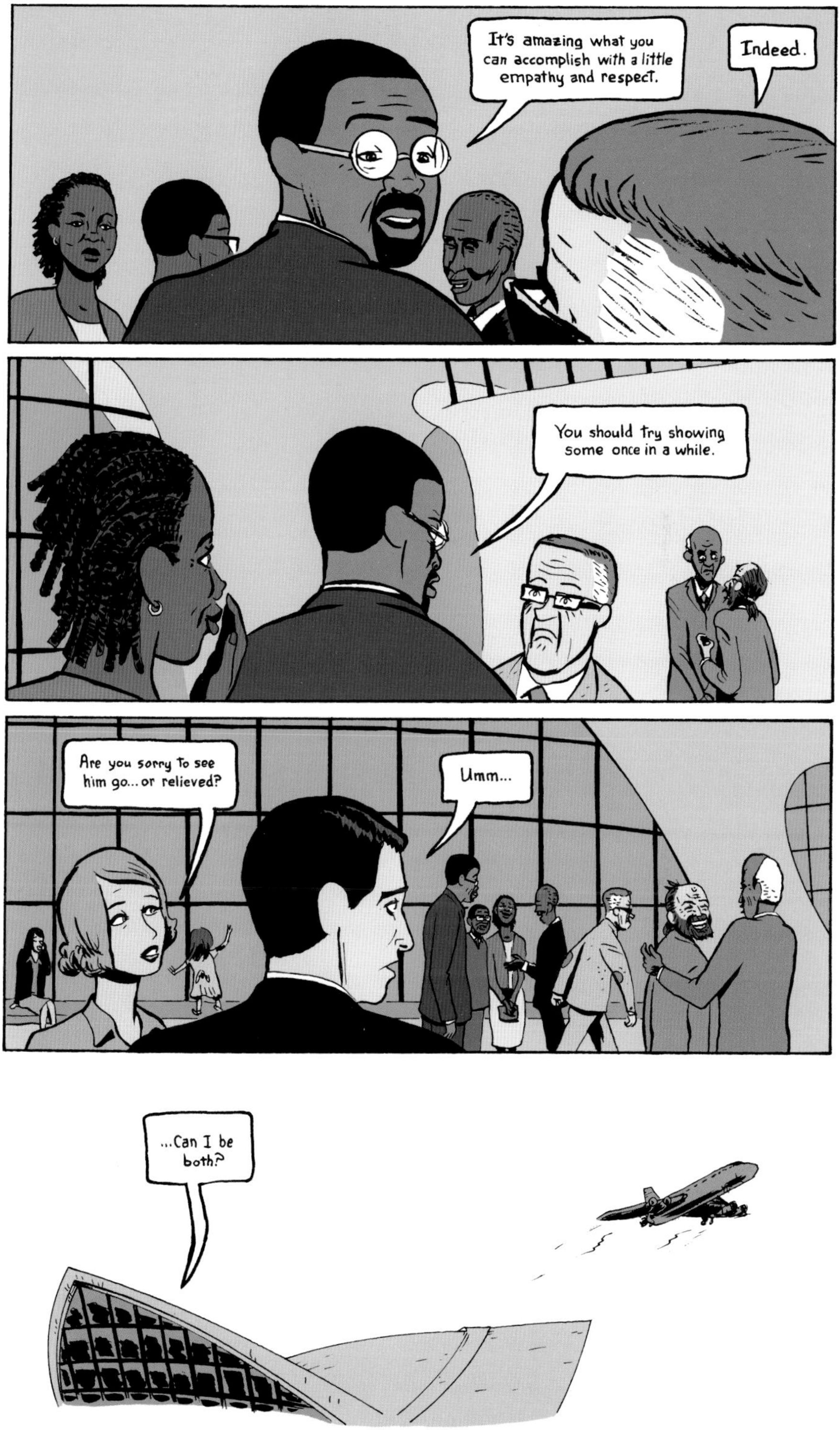
It's amazing what you can accomplish with a little empathy and respect.
Indeed.
You should try showing some once in a while.
Are you sorry to see him go... or relieved?
Umm...
...Can I be both?

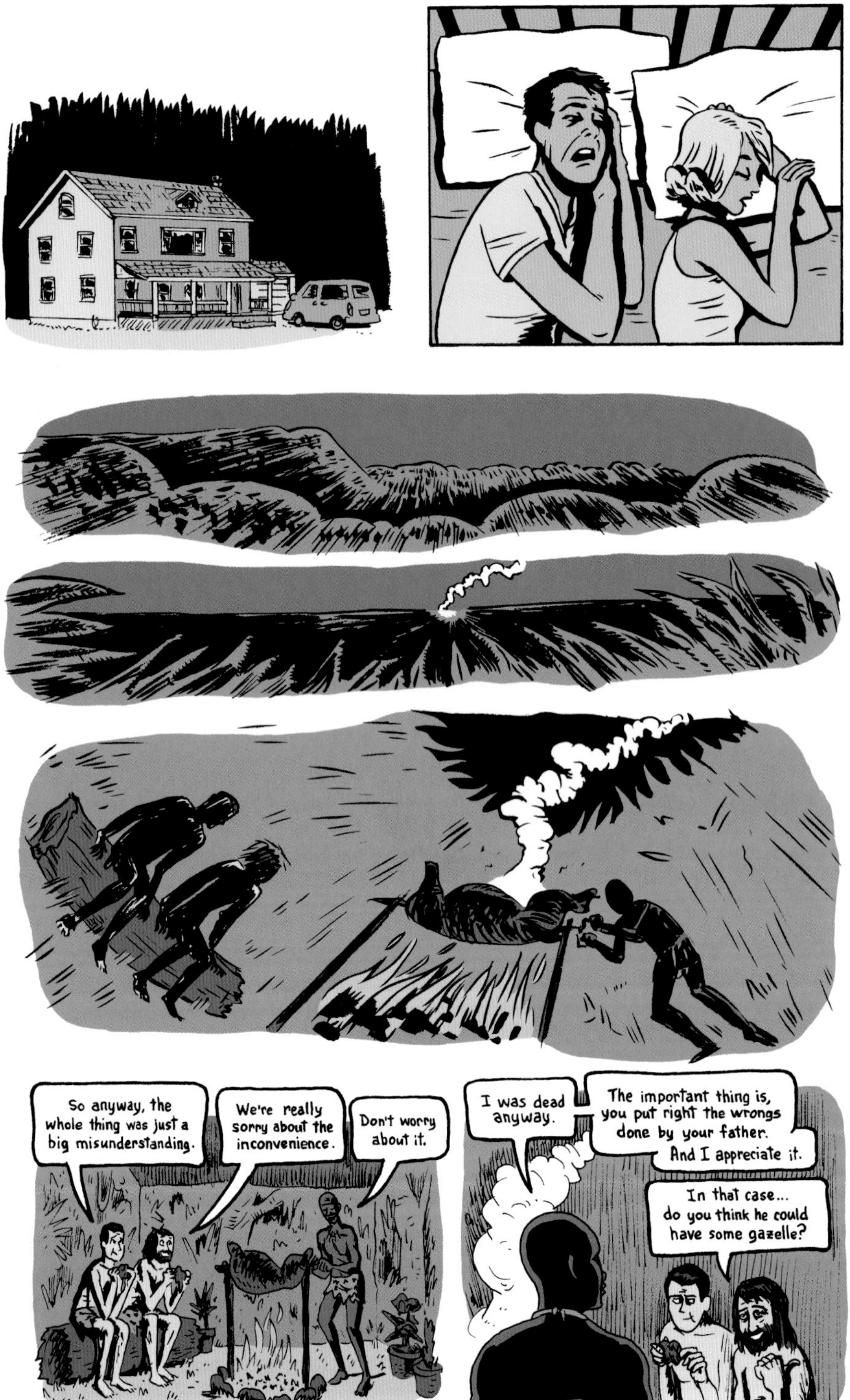
So anyway, the whole thing was just a big misunderstanding.
We're really sorry about the inconvenience.
Don't worry about it.
I was dead anyway.
The important thing is, you put right the wrongs done by your father.
And I appreciate it.
In that case... do you think he could have some gazelle?

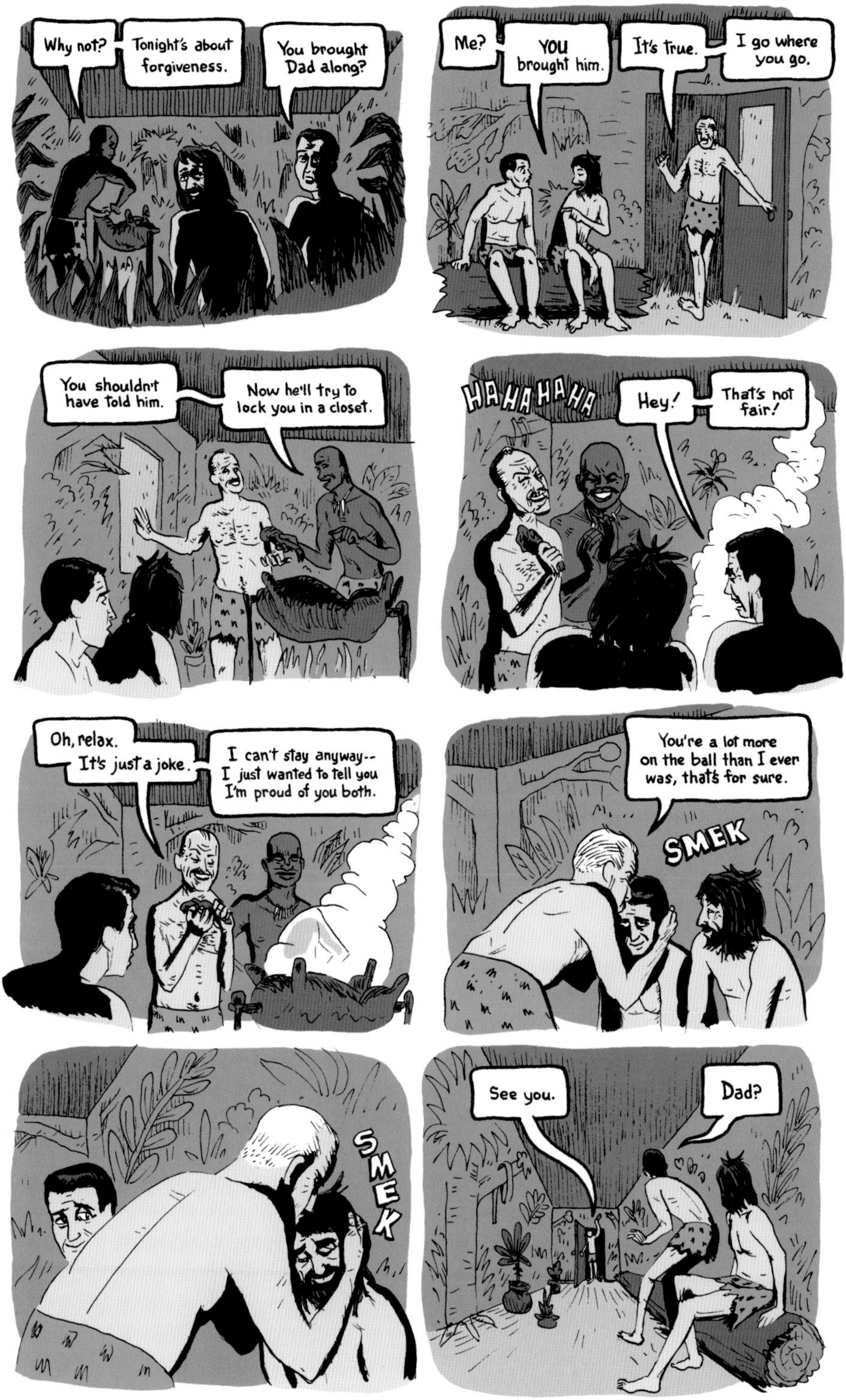

Why not?
Tonight's about forgiveness.
You brought Dad along?
Me?
YOU brought him.
It's true.
I go where you go.
You shouldn't have told him.
Now he'll try to lock you in a closet.
HAHAHAHA
Hey!
That's not fair!
Oh, relax. It's just a joke.
I can't stay anyway-- I just wanted to tell you I'm proud of you both.
You're a lot more on the ball than I ever was, that's for sure.
SMEK
SMEK
See you.
Dad?

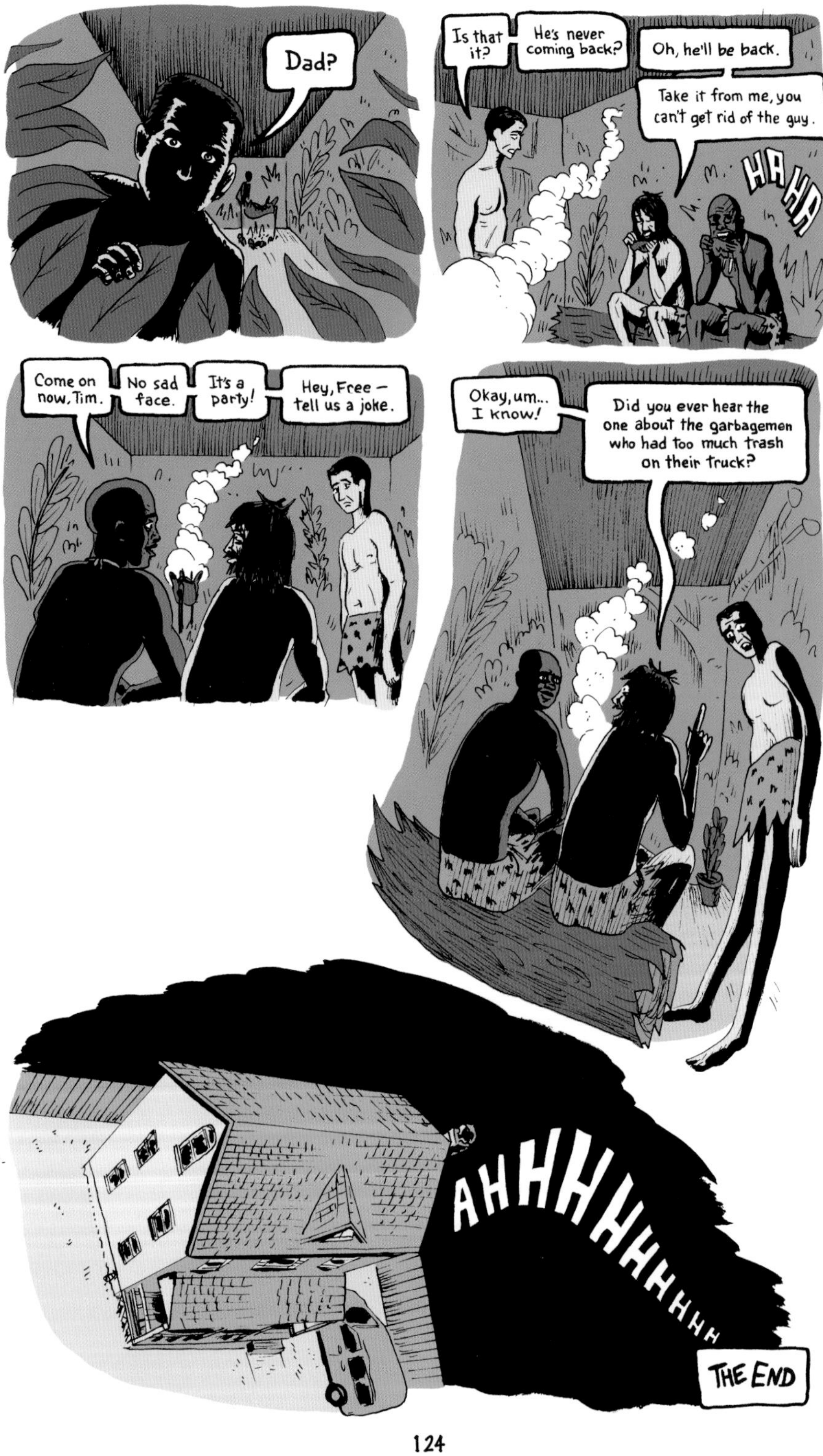
Dad?
Is that it?
He's never coming back?
Oh, he'll be back.
Take it from me, you can't get rid of the guy.
HAHA
Come on now, Tim.
No sad face.
It's a party!
Hey, Free — tell us a joke.
Okay, um... I know!
Did you ever hear the one about the garbagemen who had too much trash on their truck?
AHHHHHHHhhhh
THE END

The :01 Collection

EMMANUEL GUIBERT
ALAN'S WAR
THE MEMORIES OF G.I. ALAN COPE

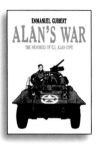

ALAN'S WAR by Emmanuel Guibert
"This epic graphic memoir spans oceans and generations, with a narrative as engrossing as the artistry that illustrates it." – *Kirkus*, starred review

LAIKA
NICK ABADZIS

LAIKA by Nick Abadzis
Winner of the 2008 Eisner Award
"A luminous masterpiece filled with pathos and poignancy."
– *Kirkus*, starred review

SFAR & GUIBERT
The Professor's Daughter

THE PROFESSOR'S DAUGHTER by Joann Sfar and Emmanuel G
"Proof that the perfect man may stil under wraps." – *O Magazine*

Notes for a War Story
Gipi

NOTES FOR A WAR STORY by Gipi
"Gipi reveals the susceptible nature of teenagers during wartime. . . . an inevitable story about a boy becoming a man under the most extreme conditions."
– *School Library Journal*

Three Shadows
Cyril Pedrosa

THREE SHADOWS by Cyril Pedrosa
"Pedrosa's intriguing, poignant fable unfolds beautifully in both words and pictures." – *Booklist*

MISSOURI BOY
by Leland Myrick

MISSOURI BOY by Leland Myr
"The tenderness and intimacy of the words and pictures set the book ap
– *Booklist*, starred review

EDDIE CAMPBELL
THE FATE of THE ARTIST

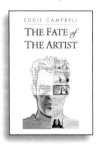

THE FATE OF THE ARTIST by Eddie Campbell
"Playful and wise."
– *Booklist*, starred review

JOANN SFAR
KLEZMER

KLEZMER by Joann Sfar
"Profane, messy, jagged and wildly enthusiastic, much like klezmer itself." – *Publisher's Weekly*

STASSEN
DEOGRATIAS
A TALE OF RWANDA

DEOGRATIAS by J.P. Stassen
"Heartbreaking power."
– *Publisher's Weekly*, starred review

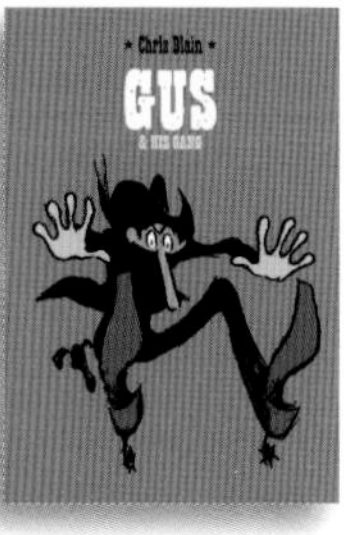
Chris Blain
GUS

GUS by Chris Blain
"[Blain] never fails to be dazzlingly original in his riffs on life and lust in the ol' West." – *The Oregonian*

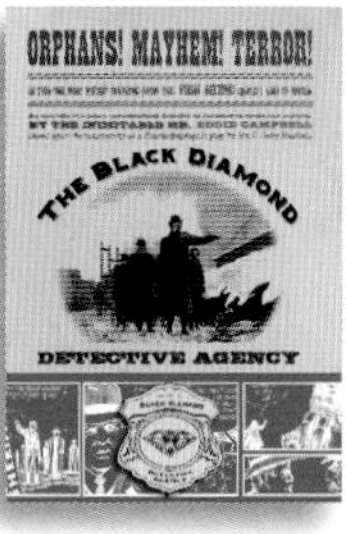
ORPHANS! MAYHEM! TERROR!
THE BLACK DIAMOND
DETECTIVE AGENCY

THE BLACK DIAMOND DETECTIVE AGENCY by Eddie Campbell
"A visually stunning graphic narrative with all sorts of complicated plot twists." – *Kirkus*

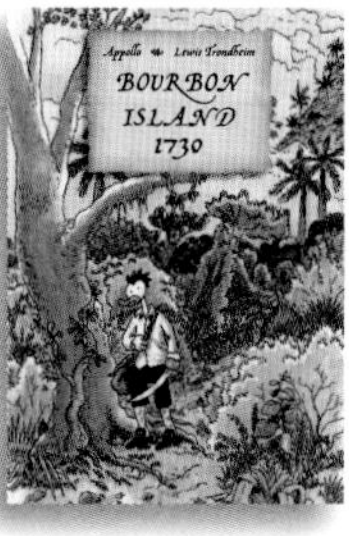
BOURBON ISLAND 1730

BOURBON ISLAND 1730 by Appollo & Lewis Trondheim
"[A] swashbuckling tale of 18th-century piracy and colonial tension." – *Kirkus*

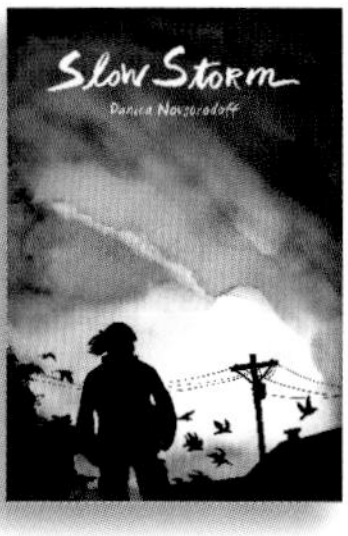
Slow Storm
Danica Novgorodoff

SLOW STORM by Danica Novgorodoff
"A very literate and rich graphic novel." – *VOYA*

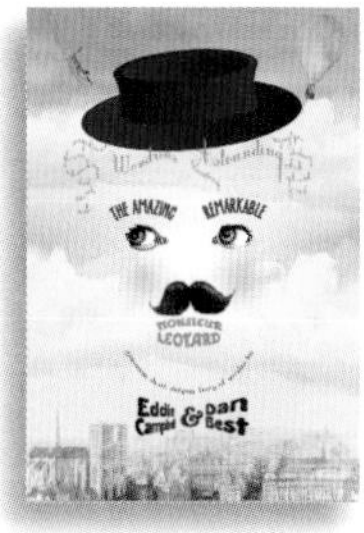
THE AMAZING
REMARKABLE
MONSIEUR LEOTARD
Eddie Campbell & Dan Best

THE AMAZING REMARKABLE MONSIEUR LEOTARD by Eddie Campbell & Dan Best
"Campbell's deftly casual watercolors are as delightful as the freewheeling story." – *Booklist*

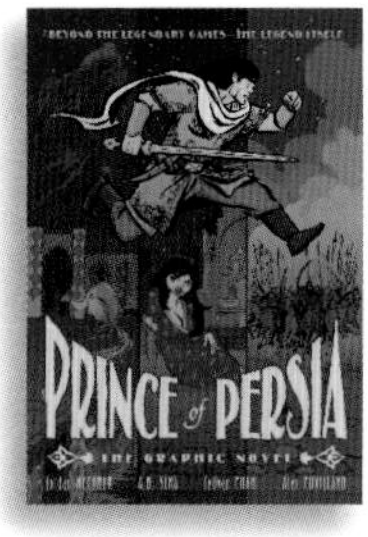
PRINCE of PERSIA
THE GRAPHIC NOVEL

PRINCE OF PERSIA by Jordan Mechner, A.B. Sina, LeUyen Pham, & Alex Puvilland
"A story defined by layers instead of linearity, with drama, adventure, and revelation all unfolding in equal measure." – *Booklist*, starred review

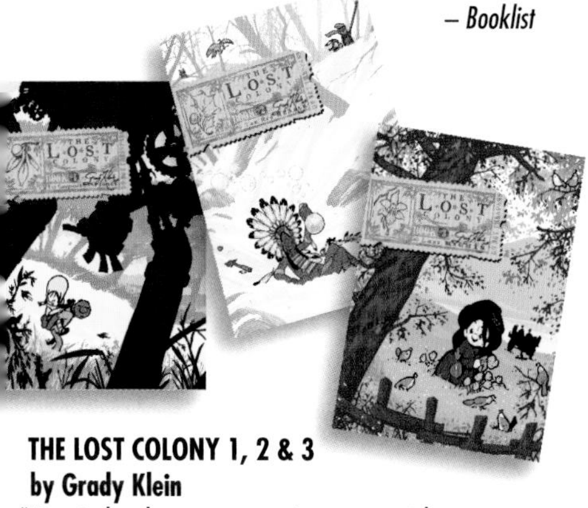
THE LOST COLONY

THE LOST COLONY 1, 2 & 3 by Grady Klein
"Historical and contemporary American racial, economic, and social issues lie at the heart of this witty, sophisticated, candy-colored adventure." – *Booklist*

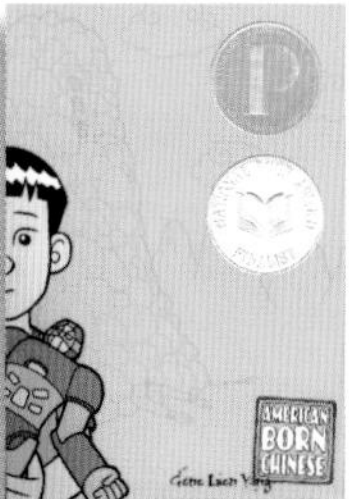
AMERICAN BORN CHINESE
Gene Luen Yang

AMERICAN BORN CHINESE by Gene Luen Yang
Winner of the Printz Award
"Like Toni Morrison's *The Bluest Eye* and Laurence Yep's *Dragonwings*, this novel explores the impact of the American dream on those outside the dominant culture in a finely wrought story that is an effective combination of humor and drama."
– *School Library Journal*, starred review

First Second

New York & London

Copyright © 2009 by Glenn Eichler and Nick Bertozzi

Published by First Second
First Second is an imprint of Roaring Brook Press,
a division of Holtzbrinck Publishing Holdings Limited Partnership
175 Fifth Avenue, New York, NY 10010

Distributed in Canada by H. B. Fenn and Company Ltd.
Distributed in the United Kingdom by Macmillan Children's Books,
a division of Pan Macmillan.

Design by Danica Novgorodoff

Colored by Nick Bertozzi and Chris Sinderson

Cataloging-in-Publication Data
is on file at the Library of Congress.

ISBN-13: 978-1-59643-308-3
ISBN-10: 1-59643-308-6

First Second books are available for special promotions and premiums.
For details, contact: Director of Special Markets, Holtzbrinck Publishers.

First Edition October 2009
Printed in China
10 9 8 7 6 5 4 3 2 1